FROM MONTAIGNE TO MOLIÈRE

FROM MONTAIGNE
TO MOLIÈRE

OR

THE PREPARATION FOR THE CLASSICAL AGE
OF FRENCH LITERATURE

BY

ARTHUR TILLEY
FELLOW OF KING'S COLLEGE, CAMBRIDGE

SECOND EDITION, REVISED

CAMBRIDGE
AT THE UNIVERSITY PRESS
1923

CAMBRIDGE
UNIVERSITY PRESS

University Printing House, Cambridge CB2 8BS, United Kingdom

Cambridge University Press is part of the University of Cambridge.

It furthers the University's mission by disseminating knowledge in the pursuit of education, learning and research at the highest international levels of excellence.

www.cambridge.org
Information on this title: www.cambridge.org/9781107544680

© Cambridge University Press 1923

First published 1923
First paperback edition 2015

A catalogue record for this publication is available from the British Library

ISBN 978-1-107-54468-0 Paperback

Fig. 27. Moses submitted to the ordeal of fire and gold.

Fig. 28. Moses directs the making of his tomb.

For EU product safety concerns, contact us at Calle de José Abascal, 56–1°, 28003 Madrid, Spain or eugpsr@cambridge.org.

PREFACE TO THE FIRST EDITION

THE change which came over English poetry between
the death of Shakespeare and the appearance of Pope
has been traced by Mr Gosse in his well-known volume
From Shakespeare to Pope. The similar change from a
literature of imagination to a literature of reason which
took place in France between the death of Montaigne
and the production of Molière's *Les Précieuses Ridicules*,
or, in other words, the transition from the Renaissance
to the Classical Age, is the subject of the following pages.
I have not attempted to write a complete history of
French literature during this period, but rather to give
an account of the various forces, political, religious,
social, and literary, which helped to bring about this
change. Even in those chapters which deal exclusively
with the literary forces, such as those on Malherbe and
Corneille, there will be found nothing like a complete
critical estimate of the writers. The chapter on the
Catholic revival is a sketch, necessarily brief and imperfect, of a large and important subject, which still
awaits its historian. The chapter entitled "The Reign
of Bad Taste" deals with matters which are still the
subject of considerable controversy—namely, the origin
of *préciosité* and the influence of Italy and Spain. I have
tried to show that true *préciosité*, though it had its germ
in the Hôtel de Rambouillet, did not develop into a real

malady till the days of Mlle de Scudéry, and that it was
in no way due, as is often stated by English writers, to
an influx of Marinism and Gongorism.

Of the authorities on which I have principally relied,
a certain number, more especially those of recent date,
will be found mentioned either in the text or in the notes.
But for the benefit of students, and as a further acknow-
ledgment of my debts, I will mention some others here.
The first place is naturally due to vol. IV of the *Histoire
de la langue et de la littérature française*, edited by the
late L. Petit de Julleville, a volume of high and singularly
even excellence. On all historical matters, including the
history of the Catholic revival, I have consulted the
Histoire de France, edited by M. Lavisse, vol. VI, part ii
(by M. Mariéjol), and vol. VII, part i, pp. 1–117 (by M.
Lavisse). For ecclesiastical history the Abbé Guettée's
sound and impartial *Histoire de l'Église de France*,
12 vols., 1847–56, is valuable. The *Essai historique sur
l'influence de la religion en France pendant le XVIIᵉ
siècle*, by M.-J. Picot, 2 vols., 1824, written from the
point of view of a devout Catholic, is uncritical, but it
is the only account of the Catholic revival as a whole
with which I am acquainted. It is hardly necessary to
mention Sainte-Beuve's great work on *Port-Royal* (third
edition, 7 vols., 1867): "He who does not know the
literature of Port-Royal does not know the seventeenth
century," says M. Gazier, the greatest living authority
on Port-Royal. It may be said with equal truth that he
who does not know Sainte-Beuve's *Port-Royal* does not
know the seventeenth century.

Turning to the literary forces of the period, Malherbe, Corneille, and Pascal have all been edited in monumental editions for *Les grands écrivains de la France*; while there are excellent monographs on Corneille (by G. Lanson), Descartes (by A. Fouillée), and Pascal (by E. Boutroux) in the series of *Les grands écrivains français*. That on Malherbe in the same series by the Duc de Broglie is disappointing. Five essays, three of considerable importance, on this period will be found in vol. IV of Brunetière's *Essais critiques*. I must also mention K. Schirmacher, *Théophile de Viau*, Leipsic, 1897; P. Morillot, *Scarron et le genre burlesque*, 1888; l'Abbé Fabre, *Chapelain et nos deux premières académies*, 1890; and Ch. Livet, *Précieux et précieuses*, second edition, 1870. Cousin's brilliant volumes, of which the most important is *La société française au XVIIᵉ siècle d'après le Grand Cyrus de Mlle de Scudéry*, 2 vols., 1852, must be used with caution. The best and most trustworthy account of the Hôtel de Rambouillet and the *Précieuses* is that by E. Bourciez in the *Histoire de la langue et de la littérature française*. I am also indebted to sundry articles in the *Revue d'histoire littéraire de la France*, the *Archiv für das Studium der neueren Sprachen und Litteraturen*, and the *Zeitschrift für französische Sprache und Litteratur*.

Mr T. F. Crane's *La société française au dix-septième siècle*, New York, 1889, and his edition of Boileau's *Les héros de roman*, Boston, 1902, both with good bibliographical references, will be found very useful by students; and I would specially commend a little book by F. Vial and L. Denise, entitled, *Idées et doctrines* *littéraires du XVIIe siècle*, 1906. Recent English works are Miss Haldane's *Descartes, his Life and Times*, 1905; *Angélique of Port-Royal*, by A. K. H., 1905; and *The Story of Port-Royal*, by Mrs Romanes, 1907; while the whole period is treated with judgment and penetration by Professor Grierson in two chapters of his *First Half of the Seventeenth Century* (vol. VII of *Periods of European Literature*), 1906.

In conclusion, I have to express my warm gratitude to my friend the Rev. H. F. Stewart, Fellow and Dean of St John's College, Cambridge, who has read the whole of the proofs.

A. T.

BEMBRIDGE,
 September 4, 1908

PREFACE TO THE SECOND EDITION

I HAVE carefully revised the text and have made a few additions, but the plan and scope of this little volume remain unaltered. It still only professes to be an account of the various forces which prepared the way for the Classical Age of French Literature; it is not a complete history of the literature of the period, nor does it attempt a full critical estimate of the chief literary figures—neither of Malherbe, nor of Corneille, nor of Descartes, nor of Pascal.

Of the works which have appeared on the subject since the publication of the first edition in 1908 and which have assisted me in the task of revision, the first in importance is M. Bremond's great *Histoire littéraire du sentiment religieux en France depuis la fin des guerres de religion jusqu'à nos jours*, of which five volumes have been published. In these will be found intimate portraits of the chief figures of the Catholic revival, of St François de Sales (vol. i), of Mme Acarie and Sainte Chantal (vol. ii), of Bérulle, Condren, St Vincent de Paul, Olier, and Eudes (vol. iii), of Saint-Cyran, Antoine Arnould, Pascal, and the Mère Agnès (vol. iv). M. Bremond does not conceal his likes or dislikes, whether of persons or opinions, and he impresses his own personality upon every page. In vol. iv he makes a vigorous assault on Jansenism, which in his eyes is a "veritable monster." He is concerned chiefly with the spiritual side of the Catholic revival; the more outward aspects of the movement have been recently summarised by the Chanoine L. Prunel in *La Renaissance Catholique en France au XVIIe siècle*, 1921, and by M. Georges Goyau in vol. VI (*Histoire religieuse*) pp. 378–444 of the *Histoire de la Nation Française* (1922), now being published under the direction of M. Gabriel Hanotaux. Both sketches are accurate and helpful, but that of M. Goyau shows a larger measure of tolerance and charity. In this country Miss E. K. Sanders, the biographer of Bossuet and Fénelon, has made interesting contributions to the subject in *Vincent de Paul* (1913) and *Sainte Chantal* (1918).

To the indefatigable M. Émile Magne, on whom has descended the mantle of Tallemant des Réaux, we owe numerous books on the social history of the age, the most important being *Voiture and les origines de l'Hôtel de Rambouillet*, 1911, and *Voiture et les années de gloire de l'Hôtel de Rambouillet*, 1912. The latest fruit of his researches is *La fin troublée de Tallemant des Réaux*, 1922, and he has written on Boisrobert and Scarron. The relation of the Hôtel de Rambouillet to *préciosité* is discussed by M. J.-E. Fidaõ-Justiniani in *L'esprit classique et la préciosité au XVII*ᵉ* siècle*, 1914, and Chapelain is the subject of a monograph by M. G. Collas—*Jean Chapelain, étude historique et littéraire*, 1912. The same writer has edited the *Sentiments de l'Académie sur le Cid* from a manuscript in the Bibliothèque Nationale.

The third volume (1908) of M. E. Lintilhac's *Histoire générale du théâtre en France*, which deals with *La Comédie* (17ᵐᵉ siècle), has led me to make one or two additions to the chapter on "Comedy before Molière." It is due to Signor Croce's eminence as a critic to mention his *Ariosto, Shakespeare, e Corneille*, 1920, but his curious insensibility to form renders his appreciation of Corneille—that master of dramatic construction—of little value. Few will agree with him that "the four great tragedies should, like the later ones, be read by the lover of poetry only in an anthological fashion."

M. F. Lachèvre's numerous volumes relating to the *Libertins* of the 17th century, especially the one entitled *Disciples et successeurs de Théophile de Viau, Des Barreaux, Saint-Pavin* (1911), are of great importance for the study of Pascal's *Pensées*. The edition of Pascal's collected works in the series of *Les grands écrivains de la France*, edited by MM. Brunschvicg, P. Boutroux and F. Gazier, has been completed in 14 volumes, and the Manchester University Press has recently published (1920) a scholarly edition of *Les Lettres Provinciales*, by Dr H. F. Stewart, whose penetrating and sympathetic study, *The Holiness of Pascal* (Cambridge University Press, 1915), had appeared five years earlier. In both volumes he acknowledges his debt to M. E. Jovy's *Pascal inédit* (5 vols., 1908–1912), "whose researches may be said to have revolutionized the study o Pascal." Mention should also be made of Paquier's *Le Jansénisme* (1908), Viscount Saint Cyres's *Pascal* (1909), and V. Giraud's *Blaise Pascal, études d'histoire morale* (1910), in which he has collected his previously published essays on the subject.

Lastly, I may perhaps be permitted to refer to a forthcoming book on *The Classical Movement in French Literature*, which Dr Stewart and I have completed for the Cambridge University Press, on the lines of *The Romantic Movement in French Literature*. Here will be found several of the *pièces justificatives* of the present volume—texts from Deimier and Racan, from Tallemant des Réaux and Pellisson, from Ogier and Mairet and Corneille, from Descartes and Pascal, and also reproductions of three pages of Malherbe's famous copy of Desportes.

A. T.

November, 1922

CONTENTS

FROM MONTAIGNE TO MOLIÈRE

CHAPTER I

INTRODUCTORY

THE period of French literature that separates Molière from Montaigne was not particularly productive either in great names or in great works. It is true that two of its names, Corneille and Pascal, stand among the first dozen on the whole roll of French letters, and that a third, Descartes, is that of France's greatest philosopher; but Pascal's work did not appear till the very close of the period, three years before Molière's return to Paris from the provinces, and Pascal himself was a year younger than Molière. As for Descartes, his place as a man of letters is at the highest estimate far below his place as a philosopher, and his influence on literature, important though it undoubtedly is, has been the subject of much controversy. Five or six plays of Corneille, the *Discours de la Méthode*, the *Lettres Provinciales*—these are the masterpieces of the period. Together they fill but three small volumes.

But though the period is not among the greatest, it is of signal importance and interest for the student of literary history. It is important, because it prepared the way for what still remains the greatest age of French literature, the full years from 1659 to 1687. It is interesting, because it is a period of transition between two great literary ages of definitely marked but widely different character. Therefore, like all periods of transition, it is an age of conflicting aims and antagonistic ideals, of rudiments and survivals, of experiments and failures. Yet through it all we can detect a continuous movement—a movement interrupted at times by adverse forces, but still always advancing towards the classical ideal.

It is the course of this movement that I shall endeavour to trace in the following pages, dwelling more on the forces which helped it than on the forces which hindered it. In other words, I propose to consider this period chiefly as one of preparation for the Classical Age.

The Classical Age of French Literature is a term of somewhat elastic meaning. It may be used, as Brunetière uses it in the title of his unfinished *Histoire de la Littérature française classique*, for the whole period, from 1515 to 1830, during which French literature was dominated more or less by the classical ideal. Or, as in M. Lanson's well-known *Histoire de la Littérature française*, it may be confined to that portion of it which falls between the production of the *Cid* (1636) and the close of the reign of Louis XIV (1715). Thirdly, it may be still further limited to that comparatively brief period of maturity when the classical ideal was realised in its fullest perfection. Thus Brunetière, in the introduction to his history, designates the years from 1660 to 1695 as the Classical Age *par excellence*. It is in this sense that I intend to use the term in these pages. But I prefer to date it in the more precise fashion of Brunetière in his earlier *Manuel*—namely, from the production of *Les Précieuses Ridicules* (1659) to the outbreak of the Quarrel between the Ancients and the Moderns (1687). The latter event may be regarded as marking the turning-point of the Classical period of French literature, just as the War of the League of Augsburg (1688) marks the turning-point in the fortunes of Louis XIV. From this time the classical ideal begins to deteriorate. While the adherence to the rules of classicism becomes more and more slavish and unintelligent, the true spirit of classicism gradually fades away.

Now, the literature of this period of maturity, the masterpieces of which followed one another in such rapid succession that the great majority were produced during the first fifteen years, is remarkably homogeneous in character.

Underlying the various forms in which it manifested itself we find certain well-defined characteristics. In the first place, it is a social literature. With the exception, perhaps, of Racine, who treats of passions as they affect the individual, rather than as they affect society, the chief theme of all the writers is man as a social animal; and, being social, the literature is necessarily objective and impersonal; it is a literature of observation. It is only La Fontaine, the most original and independent member of the school, whose charming personality occasionally intrudes into his theoretically impersonal form of art.

Secondly, it is a rational literature, a literature in which the reason exercises a more potent sway than the imagination. Though it is untrue that Molière creates types rather than characters, and that Racine's "personages are abstractions rather than real men and women" (Taine), it is not on the creative side that this literature is the strongest. Further, both its prose and its poetry prefer a language which makes a sparing use of images, which is abstract rather than concrete, and which, in fine, is the expression of thought rather than of vision. And it is especially noticeable that the older writers—Molière, La Fontaine, Bossuet, Mme de Sévigné, all of whom were over thirty at the beginning of the period—write in a more concrete and imaginative style than Boileau or even Racine, who were not much past twenty. The poetical quality of Racine's style rests rather on harmonious versification than on imaginative expression. "C'est la versification la plus souple, et du rhythme le plus varié....Et c'est le style le plus beau de clarté, d'exactitude, de justesse, de propriété.... Souvent, nu et familier, il rase la prose, mais avec des ailes" (Lemaître). Molière's verse, from the nature of his art, is more often unadorned and familiar than Racine's; it more often approaches prose; but it is to the comic poet that concrete images suggest themselves most readily. Of all the great writers of the period the one whose style is the most habitually imaginative is Bossuet. Yet it is significant that, after his arrival at Paris, where he first began to preach in 1659, his style became more logical and less imaginative. It is no less significant that Bourdaloue, who succeeded him as a preacher ten years later, and whose cold and austere oratory captivated his hearers solely through their reason, drew uninterruptedly for thirty years even larger crowds than his great predecessor.

A third feature of this literature is its devotion to form, and its recognition that perfect form can only be attained by patient workmanship and rigorous self-criticism.

> Polissez-le sans cesse et le repolissez.
> Soyez-vous à vous-même un sévère critique,

preached Boileau, and he was only preaching what Pascal, the great forerunner of the school, had practised when he rewrote passages of his *Provincial Letters* six or even ten times. La Rochefoucauld was for ever remodelling his *Maxims*. La Fontaine, in other respects the most indolent of men, spared no pains to work up his *Fables* to that height of perfection at which art seems like nature. Bossuet touched and retouched with artistic care the manuscript which was to serve only as a foundation for the actual sermon. The only great writer of the period whose work at times falls short of this perfection of form is Molière, and that for a similar reason to that given by Pascal when he apologised for the length of his sixteenth Provincial Letter, "because," as he said, "he had not had time to make it shorter." "Time to make it shorter"—that is one of the great secrets of the school of 1660. They realised that classical art demands selection, renunciation, sacrifice; the elimination of all that is vulgar and commonplace; the pruning away of superfluous ornament; and, above all, the subordination of the writer to his subject. Molière was certainly not deficient in wit, yet there is hardly a line in the whole of his plays which is written merely for the sake of the wit, and not as an expression of character or as part of the action of the play.

The result of this devotion to form and workmanship, of this scrupulous self-restraint and self-criticism, is that the total output of the school is comparatively small in quantity, and that it reaches a uniformly high level of excellence. Now, this implies not only a vigorous spirit of self-criticism, but a high standard of taste. Hence, a fourth characteristic of this literature is that it is a central literature. The material centre is Paris. Molière and Boileau were born there; all the writers lived there. Moreover, while in the sixteenth century the standard of taste, so far as there was one at all, was that of the Court, it is now determined by what Vaugelas calls "la plus saine partie de la cour et des écrivains du temps"—or, in other words, by the *élite* of the educated society of Paris. Thus the literature is not only central in the sense that it is all produced in one place, that place being the national capital; but it is also central in the sense of Matthew Arnold's well-known essay on *The Literary Influence of Academies*—in the sense that its ideas are "of the centre," that it rejects local and temporary topics and confines itself to those which are of universal and permanent interest. And this great characteristic is due, not to the sole influence of the nascent French Academy, as Matthew Arnold contends, but to a variety of influences which worked together in Paris, and of which not the least important was the criticism of Boileau.

These, then, are some of the characteristics of the literature of the French Classical Age. It is social, rational, careful of form, central. In other words, it is the complete antithesis of the literature of the sixteenth century, which is individualistic, imaginative, careless of form, provincial. Take as an example the illustrious writer, whose *Essays* in the posthumous edition published in 1595 by the pious care of Mlle de Gournay may be said, in a sense, to mark the close of French Renaissance literature. Thinking habitually in images, Montaigne is, with Victor Hugo, the most imaginative writer of France. Artist though he was, his *Essays* are a model of delightful disorder. In spite of his eloquent apostrophe to Paris—"the glory of France, and one of the most noble ornaments of the world"—he passed the greater part of his life in the quiet seclusion of his château in Périgord; and so little did he care for a central standard of language that he turned to Gascon when French "did not serve." Lastly, he was so thorough an individualist that he said of his book, with perfect truth, that he himself was the subject of it.

On the other hand, though in all these ways (three of which affect only the literary fashion of his work) Montaigne is a perfect representative of the Renaissance, yet in his thought and in the whole subject-matter of his book he is a herald of the Classical Age. In the first place, he represents a certain reaction against the thought and the ideals of the Renaissance. He is a humanist, like nearly all the writers of the sixteenth century, but he wears his humanism with a difference. Though his *Essays* are interwoven with passages culled from ancient literature, though he regards the ancient world as on the whole far superior to the modern, though no story told by an ancient historian is too absurd for his credulity, yet his attitude towards antiquity is not the open-mouthed admiration and superstitious reverence of the earlier Renaissance. He can admire modern writers as well as ancient, and he can criticise ancient writers as well as admire them. He dares to say of Cicero, the literary god of the Renaissance, that he found his manner of writing in his moral treatises tedious. Nor does he accept the opinions of the ancients unchallenged. They must first be brought to the bar of reason and common sense. He values the great Greek and Roman writers as admirable observers of life at first hand, but their interpretation of it is not for him infallible. Each age must have its own views of the problems of life, and each writer must observe life for himself.

His favourite authors—historians, biographers, moral philosophers—were to him quarries rather than models. He studied in them "the science which treats of the knowledge of myself, and which instructs one how to die well and how to live well." It was for that reason that "Plutarch was his man." But it was in no mere spirit of self-love and self-complacency that he made himself the object of his study. It was because in his humility he thought himself an average sample of human nature. Thus his individualism was at once a complement and a corrective to the individualism of the Renaissance. If the individual is to have free play for his ideas and aspirations, if he is to follow the guidance of his own nature, he must before all things know himself, and know how to live.

It was in this spirit that Montaigne introduced into French literature that habit of "psychological and moral observation" which it has never since lost, and which Brunetière truly declares to be "one of the foundations of classicism." Alike in the pulpit and on the stage, whether in maxims, or in satires, or even in fables which deal ostensibly with the animal world, the great writers of the Classical Age are, before all things, moral observers. Each writer furnishes an apt and rich commentary on the other. Molière's plays illustrate in turn a maxim of La Rochefoucauld's, a fable of La Fontaine's, or a sermon of Bossuet's or Bourdaloue's. Racine's *Athalie* seems almost directly inspired by Bossuet. Boileau in his famous satire on women speaks of himself as "the scholar, or rather the ape, of Bourdaloue." Mme de Sévigné, with her catholic but discriminating taste, admires to ecstasy the brilliant productions of her great contemporaries; but it is perhaps Bourdaloue and Nicole whose sober and accurate analysis of the human heart draws from her the accents of liveliest admiration.

The estimate of human nature held by these great moralists is very different from that high estimate which from Petrarch downwards prevailed with the chief thinkers and writers of the Renaissance, very different from that which is expressed in Rabelais's Abbey of Thelema and the Oracle of the Bottle. In unquestionably Christian writers, like Bossuet and Bourdaloue and Racine, this is only natural, but we find the same estimate in La Rochefoucauld and Molière and La Fontaine. The fact is that this reaction against the optimism of the Renaissance was produced by

the convergence of two distinct currents of thought—the
Jansenist doctrine, based on St Augustine, of the depravity
of human nature when unassisted by Divine Grace, and the
equally pessimistic view which appears in Montaigne's
brilliant exposition of ancient sceptic philosophy known as
the *Apology for Raymond de Sebonde*. It is true that this
must not be regarded as the sober expression of Montaigne's
reasoned judgment, and that in his later years, when he
had left behind him this extravagantly sceptical phase, his
estimate of human nature was rather one of tempered
optimism; but it is equally true that it was the sceptical
portions of the *Essays* which, during the first half of the
seventeenth century, had peculiar attraction for a large
class of readers. Among those who came under the spell of
the *Apology*, the most illustrious, as we know, was Pascal,
and it was in Pascal, the friend of Arnauld and the sojourner
at Port Royal, that the two currents of thought met, and
henceforth flowed in one stream. If the opinion of laymen
like La Rochefoucauld and Molière and La Fontaine was
influenced by the sceptical tone which prevailed in society
at least up till the close of the Fronde, the thought of
Churchmen, even of the Jesuit Bourdaloue, was certainly
coloured by the Jansenist movement, which was in the
main, like Puritanism, an ascetic reaction against the
æstheticism of the Renaissance.

Montaigne was very widely read during the first half of
the seventeenth century, witness the numerous editions of
the *Essays* which appeared between his death and 1660.
Moreover, he was not only widely read, but, what is not
quite the same thing, he had a very considerable influence.
During the whole of the second quarter of the century he
was the Bible of the free-thinkers, and the favourite
author of a large section of fashionable society; but when
Faguet says, as he does in *The Cambridge Modern History*,
that "every seventeenth-century man of letters read his
works incessantly and was deeply imbued with their spirit,"
he not only greatly exaggerates his influence, but he ob-
scures a marked characteristic of the literature of the

Classical Age—namely, its predominantly Christian tone. The bibliographical record makes this pretty clear. In 1659 two editions were published of the *Essays*, one at Paris and the other at Brussels; but there were no more editions till 1669, in which year both the 1659 editions were reprinted, and this was Montaigne's last appearance until Pierre Coste published a new edition in London in 1724. This decline of his popularity and influence appears also in the literature of the Classical Age. It is true that Mme de Sévigné, who loved all good literature, speaks of him as "an old friend"; that La Fontaine refers to his want of method; that Bossuet preached against him in 1669; and that Malebranche criticised him severely five years later. But in none of these nor in any of the great writers of the period is there much trace of his direct influence.

In any case, he was only one of the many forces which prepared the way for the realisation of the classical ideal. It is these forces—political, religious, social, intellectual— which I shall discuss in the following pages. First to be noticed will be the force which underlay and conditioned all the rest, the restoration of peace and order to the kingdom by Henry IV. At the same time we shall see how, by promoting national unity and by making Paris in the fullest sense a great capital, he created a new spirit of centralisation. The same feeling for order and unity is shown in the literary dictatorship of Malherbe, who at once introduced the critical spirit into literature and inaugurated the reign of reason. At this point, in order to explain that change from the pagan tone of Renaissance literature to the Christian tone of the Classical Age which I have noticed above, it will be necessary to give some account of that remarkable religious revival which began in France after the storms of the religious wars had subsided.

After this we shall see how two not dissimilar institutions, a salon with something of the spirit of an academy, and an academy with something of the spirit of a salon, took in hand the organisation of society and literature; how the one, while aiming at the refinement of society, also helped to refine and purify literature; and how the other, while having for its chief object the care of literature, and more especially of language, also tended to foster the social spirit.

So far our attention will be directed rather to political, religious, and social forces than to purely literary ones. But at this point we shall encounter a writer of real genius —the first who had appeared in France since the death of Regnier—a writer who, peculiarly sensitive to every wave of contemporary thought, created a great national drama which embodied the poetical reforms of Malherbe, the refined taste of the Hôtel de Rambouillet, and the respect for rules of the Academy; while at the same time it reflected the new spirit of the age in its glorification of the human will and the human reason.

But the first half of the seventeenth century is, as I have said, a period of transition, and, though I shall endeavour here chiefly to follow the course of the main stream, I shall also have to take note of the cross-currents and back-waters. The Renaissance ideals did not fall suddenly like the walls of Jericho before the blast of Malherbe's trumpet. The satires of Regnier and the lyrics of Théophile de Viau jut out like verdant promontories into the age of reason. Even after the death of Malherbe and the definite triumph of his principles the advance towards the classical ideal was far from uniform. Just as the old elements of political individualism and decentralisation—the great nobles, the provincial governors, the Huguenots—offered a stubborn resistance to the national policy of Richelieu, so the literary ideals of the Renaissance, though partially transformed in the process of struggle and evolution, contended fitfully with the incoming tide of the new classicism. Even Corneille was no whole-hearted worshipper at the new shrine. Classical in his sense of form and in the superb architecture of his plays, he was subject to waves of romantic feeling. He loved the romantic plots and the *panache* of his Spanish originals. He submitted to the classical rules with grumbling and under protest.

It is during the years from 1643 to 1659, a period almost coincident with the rule of Mazarin, that the conflict of aims and ideals becomes most apparent. Just as the removal of Richelieu's restraining hand let loose the forces of political disunion and anarchy which he had so ruthlessly repressed, so in literature the old elements of formlessness and provinciality and uncurbed imagination were stirred again into life by a sudden wave of bad taste. But almost at the same time there rose above the flood certain watch-towers, which at once served as barriers against the threatened submergence and as beacons of light to proclaim the new ideal of literature, that "only truth is beautiful."

Already in 1637 Descartes had asserted in his *Discours de la Méthode*, which contains the germs of almost his whole philosophy, the principle of truth in thought. In 1643 we shall find Antoine Arnauld, as ardent a Cartesian as he was a Jansenist, contending in *La Fréquente Communion* for the necessity of truth in religion. And so we shall come to Pascal, who held a closer communion with Nature than Descartes, for he approached her by way of experimental science, and who was a more effective champion of Jansenism than Arnauld, for he brought to the cause of truth in religion the weapon of a style which is as logical as Descartes's, which is as lucid as Arnauld's, but which is truer than either, for it is the expression of the whole man, of his emotions as well as of his intellect.

Finally, if we wish to find a synthesis for the various forces which ultimately united to produce the Classical Age, we cannot do better than borrow from M. Lemonnier the word "construction[1]." The construction of the nation by Henry IV and Richelieu, of its religious life by Cardinal de Bérulle and Vincent de Paul, of a standard of literary taste by Malherbe and the Académie Française, of society by Mme de Rambouillet, of the classical drama by Corneille, and of a system of philosophy by Descartes, are all described by this single word.

[1] *L'art français au temps de Richelieu et de Mazarin*, 1893.

CHAPTER II

THE RESTORATION OF PEACE AND ORDER

THE entry of Henry IV into his capital on March 22, 1594, must have been hailed by the majority of his subjects with feelings of intense satisfaction. For thirty-five years, ever since the fatal accident to Henry II in the lists of the Tournelles, France had been a prey to chronic outbreaks of disturbance, varied by long periods of actual warfare. For the last nine years this warfare had been continuous, and the whole kingdom had sunk into an abyss of anarchy and misery. Now at last there was a prospect of peace. But much still remained to be done. A considerable portion of France was still in the hands of the chiefs of the League, or of great nobles who aspired to set up independent kingdoms. The greater part of Picardy, Champagne, Burgundy, Upper Languedoc, Provence, and Brittany, all refused to acknowledge their lawful King. Moreover, the peasants of Limousin, driven to desperation by the brigandage of their lords, had broken out into open revolt. The movement spread to the neighbouring provinces of Quercy, the Agenois, Périgord, Saintonge, and La Marche, and before long the *Croquants*, as they were called, numbered 50,000. It was not till the close of 1595 that the insurrection was finally quelled.

Meanwhile other important towns had followed the example of Paris. Rouen, which came to terms five days later than the capital, brought with it Normandy; the capture of Laon and the submission of Amiens and Beauvais gave Henry nearly the whole of Picardy. Two of the principal Leaguers, the Duc de Lorraine and the young Duc de Guise, made their peace before the end of 1594. In January, 1595, Henry took the bold step of declaring war on Spain. She was already a covert enemy, helping the League with troops and money, and by this declaration of open war the League chiefs were proclaimed as the active allies of their country's foes. Their position was still further undermined by the Papal absolution, which, after much tedious diplomacy, was granted to the King on September 17, 1595. It was followed by the submission of Mayenne, Joyeuse, and Nemours. The capture of Marseilles in February, 1596, brought Épernon to terms. All France except Brittany now acknowledged Henry's authority.

But he had still Spain to face. All through the year 1596 and the greater part of 1597 the Spanish forces maintained the upper hand. The capture of Calais was followed by the still more important capture of Amiens. This last blow hit Henry hard, but he showed even more than his usual courage and resolution. He at once set to work to collect troops for the campaign, while Sully accomplished the more difficult task of finding money to pay them. At the end of six months Amiens was retaken. It was now time to finish the war, for both combatants were exhausted. After long disputes the peace of Vervins was signed on May 2, 1598. Mercœur, the last Leaguer in the field, had submitted on highly favourable conditions six weeks before, and it was from Nantes, the capital of his government of Brittany, that the famous Edict which pacified the Protestants was issued (April 13). The Wars of Religion were at last ended. Leaguer and Huguenot had laid down their arms, and France had peace within her borders as well as without.

Henry's next task was the restoration of order. The large numbers of discharged soldiers, whom peace had deprived of their only trade, led to organised brigandage in many districts. In Brittany and Poitou a cadet, it was said, of good family, who called himself "Le Capitaine Guillery," having collected a band of 400 men, carried on his practices for several years, till his stronghold was forced and his band dispersed (1604), he himself being captured and executed four years later.

The towns were little better off than the country dis-

tricts. The disorganisation of labour had thrown crowds o.
workmen out of employment, and the diarist, Pierre de
l'Estoile, writing in 1595, tells us that over 14,000 beggars
had come into Paris in a fortnight. During the first six
weeks of 1596 over 400 persons died in the Hôtel Dieu, the
greater number of hunger. Pestilence went hand in hand
with famine. In fifteen months (1596–1597) the plague
carried off 8000 persons at Abbeville; in the year 1599,
12,000.

I need not relate here how Henry IV, ably assisted by
the financial ability and probity of Sully, within the short
space of twelve years restored order and prosperity to his
kingdom; how he checked the depredations of the nobles
and gave security to life and property; how he diminished
taxation; how he promoted agriculture and the production
of silk; how he revived manufactures; and how he protected, if he did not actively encourage, commerce and
colonisation.

The most eloquent testimony to the beneficence of his
rule is the universal grief with which all France mourned
his death. Alike in Paris and in the provinces, says the
contemporary historian Pierre Matthieu, the news was
received with tears and groans. "And this regret," he
adds, "was due to the care which this prince had taken to
make his subjects live in peace[1]."

Order and peace—these were Henry's gifts to his
country. And these qualities are reflected in the literature
of his reign. In the words of M. Lanson, "La littérature,
comme la France, se repose." Reason takes the place of
imagination, licence yields to established authority, individualism is checked by the growing social spirit. The two
writers of the period who best represent these tendencies
are Pierre Charron and Jean Bertaut, both ecclesiastics.
The keynote of Charron's *La Sagesse* (1601) is order. In
form it is a highly systematised arrangement of other men's
thoughts, chiefly of Montaigne's and Du Vair's. In matter
it is a praiseworthy attempt to arrest the moral decay of

[1] Cited by Sainte-Beuve, *Causeries du Lundi*, XIII. 226.

France, due to those Wars of Religion in which latterly religion played so subordinate a part.

The same seriousness, the same regard for the moral basis of life, is shown in Bertaut's poetry—at least in his later poetry, which is comprised in a volume published in the same year as *La Sagesse*. It is composed of official poems, of which the most important are funeral panegyrics on great personages, paraphrases of Psalms, a long narrative poem, and a translation of a book of the *Æneid*. Even in the lyrical poems the Alexandrine is the prevailing metre. Bertaut's inspiration is fitful, and his uninspired passages are the flattest prose. But he is careful in the matter of language and syntax, and Malherbe spoke of him with a certain approval.

Another feature of the rule of Henry IV which had a marked influence on the development of literature was the promotion of political unity. For a hundred years after the virtual expulsion of the English from France in 1453, the unification of the kingdom made continuous progress. The great duchies—Guyenne, Maine, Anjou, Provence, Burgundy, Orleans, Brittany—which had hitherto been ruled by independent or quasi-independent dynasties, were in turn absorbed by the Crown. When, on the death of the Constable of Bourbon, fighting against his country, in 1523, his vast domains, which included the Bourbonnais, Auvergne, and La Marche, were confiscated by Francis I, the only portions of French soil which still remained more or less independent were the tiny kingdom of Navarre and the other possessions of the House of Albret.

But after the death of Henry II this centralising process was arrested by the ambition of the Guises and by the Wars of Religion, of which that ambition was in part the cause. The great families which had put themselves at the head of the two religious factions—the Condés on the Protestant side, the Guises and Montmorencys on the Catholic—began to assume the character of independent chiefs. Under Francis I the governors of the provinces had been removable at his pleasure, but now, though they still remained so in theory, they came to regard themselves in the light of hereditary rulers. On the accession of Henry IV to the throne four of the great governments were in the hands of the Guises; while their cousin, the Duc de Mercœur, whose wife, Marie de Luxembourg, was the descendant through the Penthièvres of the Dukes of Brittany, had been imprudently appointed by Henry III governor of that province. In addition to this, the two favourites of Henry III, Épernon and Joyeuse, were, as we have seen, endeavouring to set up independent kingdoms in Provence and Languedoc respectively. Moreover, especially since the Massacre of St Bartholomew, the Protestants had begun to develop republican and separatist tendencies. In the peace of Saint-Germain (1570) they had stipulated that the King should put in their hands for a term of two years four cities to serve as places of refuge. In 1573 the Protestants of the south took a further step in the direction of independence. They formed a complete system of military organisation, dividing for this purpose Languedoc into two governments. At Montauban, their chief city in Upper Languedoc, they prepared a petition to the King, dated significantly on the first anniversary of the massacre, which alike in its demands and its language assumed the tone of one armed power addressing another on equal terms. Thus the Protestants were fast taking up a position fatal to the unity of a kingdom—that of a State within a State.

These decentralising and disintegrating forces had a marked effect on literature. In the reigns of Francis I and Henry II, though there had existed an important provincial centre of thought and letters in Lyons, the Court, if not the capital, had been the chief centre of literary life; and though Francis I had too much of the restlessness characteristic of the Renaissance to remain for long together in one place, yet during the last twenty years of his life he generally resided either at Fontainebleau or in one of his palaces in the neighbourhood of Paris. Of the principal writers of his reign, Saint-Gelais, and in a less degree Marot, may be described as Court poets. Margaret of Navarre, though the Queen of an independent kingdom, was too closely bound up with the interests of her royal brother to show any sign of provincialism in her work; while Rabelais, with all his love for his native Touraine, had too large an intellect and too broad sympathies, widened, as they had been, by much experience of men and cities, to represent less than the whole of France. In the reign of Henry II we have the Pleiad, essentially a Court school of poetry, and Jacques Amyot, who brought to his great translation of Plutarch a mind cultivated by four years' travel in Italy and by intercourse with the Court as tutor to the royal Princes.

It was far otherwise during the period of the Wars of Religion. Take the greatest writer of the period—Montaigne. Though, as we have seen, he proclaims his love for Paris in one of the most eloquent passages of his *Essays*, his visits there were few and far between. He spent most of his life in his native Gascony, and the early editions of his work were published at Bordeaux. In fact, Bordeaux, with its new and flourishing College of Guyenne, served at this time as an intellectual centre for the whole south-western part of France. Here, too, were published Monluc's *Commentaires* and the earliest work of the Gascon poet, Saluste Du Bartas, whose whole poetry suffers from excessive provincialism. Further north we come to the University town of Poitiers, where from 1550 to 1560 a literary coterie flourished under the leadership of Jacques Tahureau. Other provincial towns in the west which showed considerable literary activity were Tours and Rennes, the capital of Brittany. Of greater importance were the Norman towns—Caen, the seat of a University, and Rouen, which, at the opening of the seventeenth century, was an active publishing centre, especially for dramatic literature. We must also take into account the numerous memoir-writers, who, like Brantôme and Tavannes, were writing far from the Court and the capital, without any thought of publication during their lifetime, and without any idea of conformity to a national standard of criticism or taste.

But when Henry IV, having secured peace and order, was able to turn his attention to the reorganisation of the national forces, he made it his first business to restore the lost unity of the kingdom and to set up a strong central government. In the first place, he united to the Crown his own hereditary possessions. Secondly, though he allowed the provincial governorships to remain in the hands of the great nobles, he took various measures to insure their subordination to the central authority. He transferred the government of Brittany from the Duc de Mercœur to his own son by Gabrielle d'Estrées, César de Vendôme, who received at the same time the hand of Mercœur's only daughter and heiress. He gave Provence to the young Duc de Guise in place of the capable and ambitious Épernon, who was consoled with three small governments; and he kept Mayenne under his own eye as governor of the Ile de France. Further, while he entrusted the important provinces of Guyenne and Normandy to two Princes of the blood—Condé and his brother, the Comte de Soissons—he placed by the side of each a lieutenant-general on whose fidelity he could thoroughly rely. This became the practice in most of the provinces, and the powers of the provincial governor were further curtailed by the appointment of independent governors of large towns and citadels, by the withdrawal of the departments of justice and finance from their cognizance, and by the choice of presidents for the local *parlements* who were devoted to the King's interests.

Another obstacle to the unification of the kingdom was the bad state of repair into which the roads had been allowed to fall during the Religious Wars. To remedy this evil Henry appointed Sully *Grand Voyer*, or High Commissioner of Roads, with the result that before long the existing roads were repaired and new ones were made. The next step was to organise a regular system of public carriages and relays, so as to provide a better transport for travellers and merchandise. The waterways were also utilised as means of communication. Various canals were planned, and the important Canal de Briare, which connects the Seine with the Loire, and thus serves as a waterway between Paris and the centre and west of France, was nearly completed.

Among the measures which tended to promote the unity and centralisation of the kingdom must be reckoned the improvements effected in the capital itself. The streets of the Paris of that day were narrow and ill paved, and the majority of its houses were built of wood and plaster; but an English traveller, Robert Dallington, who visited it in 1598, thought it "fairer built than London." In fact, in most respects it seems to have compared favourably with other European capitals. But in one matter it enjoyed an unenviable notoriety. Fynes Moryson, who was there in 1595, says that "the streets of the Ville" (the quarter north of the Seine) "are continually dirty and full of filth"; and Montaigne speaks of the odour of the Paris mud as the one defect of that fair city.

To remedy this insanitary condition of things, Henry IV, with the able assistance of François Miron, the Provost of the Merchants—who was virtually the Mayor of Paris—issued various regulations which made for cleanliness, paved and widened many of the streets, increased the water-supply, and constructed a large hydraulic pump known as La Samaritaine[1], which distributed water to the Louvre and the neighbouring districts. The evil was by no means abolished, for Thomas Coryate declared, in 1608, that "many of the streets are the dirtiest, and so consequently the most stinking, of all that ever I saw in any citie in my life[2]"; and James Howell wrote in 1620 that "this town is always dirty," and that the dirt "gives so strong a scent, that it may be smelt many miles off." However, so far as

---

[1] It was so called from the group of Our Saviour and the Woman of Samaria, which adorned the façade. For a description of it see Evelyn's *Diary*, December 24, 1643, and June 21, 1650, and for an illustration *Paris à travers les Ages*, I. 45.

[2] Malherbe, writing in October of the same year, says: "Il y a à cette heure un grand ordre à Paris pour les boues...mais j'ai peur...qu'il y fera crotté comme devant" (*Œuvres*, ed. Lalanne, III. 78).

regards the health of the inhabitants, Henry's sanitary measures had most important results. Whereas formerly the plague used to ravage Paris about every five years, after his reign it returned only once, namely in 1619.

Henry IV also did much in the way of building, replacing many of the old wood-and-plaster houses with brick ones. His chief works were the Pont-Neuf, which Henry III had begun but had abandoned after only two arches had been built; the triangular Place Dauphine, on the right bank of the Seine, between the Pont-Neuf and the Palais de Justice; and the Rue Dauphine, which formed the continuation of the bridge on the left bank. The new bridge, which thus connected the Ile with the Ville and the Université, speedily became the most crowded thoroughfare in Paris.

Another noteworthy memorial of this reign is the Place Royale, which was laid out on part of the site occupied by the old Palais des Tournelles and its park. The new square was surrounded by houses which by the uniformity of their architecture marked the æsthetic tendencies of an age of reason. So substantially were they built—of red brick with high-pitched slate roofs and with arcades in front—that the Place Royale, or, as it is called in republican times, the Place des Vosges, is little changed in outward appearance from what it was 300 years ago. It has a desolate, old-world air now, but when it was finished, two years after the death of Henry IV, it was regarded as the finest square, not only in France, but in Europe. Though Henry had destined it chiefly as a place of residence for merchants and lawyers and other non-noble classes, it speedily became the most fashionable quarter of Paris, and, beginning with the splendid fêtes given by Marie de' Medici in April, 1612, in honour of the announcement of the double marriage of Louis XIII with Anne of Austria and of his sister Elizabeth with Anne's brother, the future Philip IV of Spain, it was the scene of many interesting events and played a prominent part in the life of Paris throughout the seventeenth century. Here, in 1627, François de Montmorency, Comte de Bouteville, the father of the celebrated general, the Duc de Luxembourg, fought with the Marquis de Beuvron that fatal duel for which he suffered death on the scaffold; here, in 1643, the Duc de Guise, great-grandson of François de Guise, crossed swords with the Comte de Coligny, great-grandson of the Admiral, and wounded him so severely that he died shortly afterwards, partly of his wounds and partly of chagrin at his defeat; here Marion Delorme held her court and essayed the part of a Parisian Aspasia; here Mme de Sévigné was born; here lived Mme de Sablé and the Princesse de Guéméné, and other famous leaders of fashion.

Henry IV also resumed the building of the Tuileries, which Catherine de' Medici had abandoned in 1571, and completed the long gallery between that palace and the Louvre. Though during the greater part of his reign his Court was no more stationary than that of his predecessors, but rang the changes on Paris, Fontainebleau, Monceau, Saint-Germain, Blois, and Amboise, yet for the last four years of his life Paris, with Fontainebleau, seems to have been his favourite place of residence. Other measures— such as the reform of the studies and discipline of the Paris University (1600), the creation of new royal professorships, the reorganisation of the royal library, which Charles IX had moved from Blois to Paris, and with which Henry IV now incorporated the magnificent collection of Catherine de' Medici—all tended to make Paris the social and intellectual centre of the kingdom[1]. In spite of royal edicts, its population went on increasing, and a constant stream of aspiring provincials flowed to Paris and the Court to seek favour and fortune, while Paris fashions in language, in literature, in manners, permeated in their turn the provinces. Thus, in the words of M. Hanotaux, "was prepared that strong centralisation which is the form of French society in modern times[2]."

---

[1] A German traveller, writing in 1616, says: "To have seen the towns of Italy and Germany and other kingdoms is nothing; what makes a real impression is when a man says that he has been in Paris."

[2] *Tableau de la France en 1614*, p. 399.

Finally, there is another result of this work of reconstruction which must not be lost sight of in estimating its effect on literature. The measures for the furtherance of industry and commerce, the sanitary improvements and the rebuilding which took place in the capital, combined with the long era of peace to increase greatly the prosperity and importance of the *bourgeoisie*, not only among its higher ranks—the lawyers and politicians who had by this time formed themselves into a *noblesse de robe*—but also among the true *bourgeoisie*—the merchants and larger shopkeepers, and, above all, the great army of lesser public functionaries, of attorneys and notaries and registrars, which the system of selling judicial offices had multiplied to an alarming extent. "Never," to quote M. Hanotaux again, "has the French *bourgeoisie* been seen under a more favourable light than during the first years of the seventeenth century." Thus, although the literature of the first half of the century was in the main an aristocratic literature —that is to say, a literature adapted to the requirements and tastes of the aristocratic classes—it was to the *bourgeoisie* that France owed Corneille and Descartes and Pascal, and it was the *bourgeois* element which finally triumphed in the great literature of 1660, and produced Molière, La Fontaine, Boileau, Racine, Bossuet, and Bourdaloue.

CHAPTER III

MALHERBE AND THE CRITICAL SPIRIT

THE year 1605 is an important date in the history of French literature, for in that year François de Malherbe, the future legislator of the French Parnassus, came to Paris. He was then fifty years of age, having been born at Caen in 1555. But though a Norman by birth, he had resided since manhood chiefly at Aix in Provence, and had been living there continuously for the last six years. Here he had become intimate with Guillaume Du Vair, the First President of the Aix Parliament, who, though a year younger than himself, had attained far greater celebrity in the literary world. M. Brunot has shown that he exercised an appreciable influence on Malherbe, whose views on the subject of language and literary style bear considerable resemblance to those of his friend[1]. At any rate, when Malherbe arrived at Paris, his doctrines were already fully developed.

But, in spite of his fifty years, he had written very little poetry, and he had published still less—only eight pieces. Of these the earliest and longest, *Les Larmes de Saint-Pierre*, a free translation of portions of an Italian poem by Luigi Tansillo, was in Desportes's worst manner. Its only merit is its versification, which found favour with so good a judge as André Chénier. Malherbe had also published at this time his famous *Consolation à M. Du Perier*, but not in the form in which the modern reader is familiar with it. Some of the most admired stanzas, such as the fourth ("Mais elle étoit du mònde, où les plus belles choses") and the nineteenth ("La mort a des rigueurs à nulle autre pareilles"), are positively bad in the original

[1] *La Doctrine de Malherbe d'après son commentaire sur Desportes*, 1891.

version. But the last two, which are, perhaps the best that Malherbe ever wrote, are the same as in the later version.

> Le pauvre en sa cabane, où le chaume se couvre,
>   Est sujet à ses loix;
> Et la garde qui veille aux barrières du Louvre
>   N'en défend point nos rois.
>
> De murmurer contre elle, et perdre patience,
>   Il est mal à propos;
> Vouloir ce que Dieu veut, est la seule science
>   Qui nous met en repos.

The most ambitious of Malherbe's more recent efforts was an ode presented to Marie de' Medici on her passage through Aix as a bride in November, 1600. Like nearly all official poems, it is for the most part pompous and empty, but it contains at least three good stanzas, especially one inspired by the only theme which seems to have stirred Malherbe to genuine emotion—namely, the restoration of peace and prosperity to his country.

> Ce sera vous qui de nos villes
> Ferez la beauté refleurir,
> Vous qui de nos haines civiles
> Ferez la racine mourir;
> Et par vous la paix assurée
> N'aura pas de courte durée,
> Qu'esperent infidellement,
> Non lassez de notre souffrance,
> Ces François qui n'ont de la France
> Que la langue et l'habillement.

A month or two later his name was favourably mentioned to Henry IV by his fellow-Norman, the Cardinal Du Perron, who told the King that he had "brought French poetry to such a point of perfection that no one could come near him." Henry did not forget this. When Malherbe arrived at Paris he sent for him and gave him an order for a poem. The result was the *Prière pour le Roi Henri le Grand allant en Limousin.* It contains one of Malherbe's best stanzas.

La terreur de son nom rendra nos villes fortes;
On n'en gardera plus ni les murs ni les portes,
Les veilles cesseront au sommet de nos tours;
Le fer mieux employé cultivera la terre,
Et le peuple qui tremble aux frayeurs de la guerre,
Si ce n'est pour danser, n'orra[1] plus de tambours.

The poem was presented to the King towards the close
of 1605, and it was about this time that Malherbe's celebrated quarrel with Desportes took place. Desportes was
at this time the recognised head of French literature, but
for many years he had written no poetry except a translation of the Psalms. He showed great kindness to other men
of letters, and entertained them royally either at his
abbey of Bonport in Normandy, or at Vanves near Paris.
Malherbe, soon after his arrival in the capital, seems to
have been admitted to his circle. Dropping in one evening
—so the story goes—accompanied by his friend, Mathurin
Regnier, the nephew of Desportes, he found the soup already
on the table. The host received him with his usual courtesy,
and was about to leave the room for a copy of a new edition
of his translation of the Psalms which he wished to show
him, when Malherbe stopped him with the remark that he
had already seen his Psalms, and that they were not so
good as his soup. Desportes sat down again, but the two
men did not speak to one another during dinner, or ever
afterwards. It was the beginning of a complete rupture
between Malherbe and the followers of the old school of
poetry. Desportes and his friends criticised severely all
that Malherbe wrote, while he on his side declared that if
he were to set to work to criticise one of their productions,
the mistakes would make a bigger volume than the book
itself.

It was probably with this amiable intention that he proceeded to annotate a copy of Desportes's *Premières Œuvres*,
using an edition published at Paris in 1600. The copy thus
annotated is preserved in the Bibliothèque Nationale, and,

---

[1] This is the older and preferable reading. The ordinary reading *aura*
first appeared after Malherbe's death.

as Malherbe wrote no regular treatise on the art of poetry, it is our principal source of information with regard to his poetical theories. The notes are for the most part very brief, and are often contemptuous and not seldom rude. *Mauvaise imagination, ridicule imagination, drôlerie, sottise, froid, mal parlé, plébée, quel langage! je ne vous entends point,* are some of the more common flowers of Malherbe's criticism. But his two favourite words are *bourre* and *cheville*, both of which mean practically the same thing—namely, padding. Often a simple *nota* serves to call attention to some mistake or negligence, or without any remark a word is scored under, or whole lines are struck out. The pages, in fact, bear the appearance of a schoolboy's exercise after it has been looked over by an angry schoolmaster[1]. No volume of poetry was ever subjected to so searching a criticism. How far is it just?

Desportes, when he was imitating second-rate Italian poets, copied and even exaggerated their affectations and mannerisms. These faults are most conspicuous in his sonnets. But he also had a natural vein of considerable charm. He could put wit and sentiment into songs, such as his *Rozette pour un peu d'absence* and *O Nuit! jalouse Nuit*, which were on the lips of every gallant. In these he comes, perhaps, nearest to our Cavalier poets, especially to the easy grace of Suckling. Among his contemporaries he was reckoned a master of his own language; but, like nearly all sixteenth-century writers, he wrote carelessly and with little or no idea of self-criticism.

Thus an accomplished grammarian like Malherbe found much to criticise in his grammar and his syntax. For it was mainly as a grammarian, as a "tyrant of words and syllables," that Malherbe addressed himself to his task. He rarely objects to Desportes's affectations and conceits, he is apparently unconscious of his plagiarisms, and he has no praise for his undoubted merits as a song-writer. His

---

[1] M. Brunot gives facsimiles of some of the pages. All the notes, with the lines to which they refer, will be found in Lalanne's edition of the *Œuvres*, IV. 248–473.

own poetical taste may be judged by the fact that he set little value on Greek poetry, especially disliking Pindar, and that he considered Statius to be the greatest Latin poet. Rejecting the great principle for which Ronsard and the Pleiad had contended—that the style of poetry should differ from that of prose—he recognised no distinction between them save that of metre and rhyme. An enemy to all licence, he would have poetry conform as strictly as prose to the rules of grammar and syntax, and, confusing poetic truth with scientific truth, he judged poetry with his reason instead of with his imagination. We must therefore primarily consider him not as a critic of poetry, but as a critic of language. As such, his views, if narrow, were thoroughly sound in principle. The three qualities on which he chiefly insisted were purity, clearness, and precision. In the matter of purity he was especially rigid. He objected to provincialisms, to archaisms, to diminutives, to low words, to foreign words, to technical words—all of these being sources from which the Pleiad had drawn freely and legitimately for the purpose of enlarging their poetic diction. His standard of purity was usage—not the usage of the Court or the Bar, still less the usage of books, but that of ordinary educated society.

His crusade against obscurity and vagueness had more justification. Obscurity is a common fault with sixteenth-century prose-writers. They pack too many thoughts into their sentences, or wander from their main argument into pleasant digressions. The result is that they lose themselves in mazes of ill-constructed periods. Montaigne, with all his incomparable merits, is anything but a clear writer. Rabelais, when he pleases, can write with clear and straightforward brevity, but in his later Books he will sacrifice much, sometimes even sense, to a harmonious cadence. Precision is a still rarer virtue in the sixteenth century. Montaigne leaves his thought vague, flitting from metaphor to metaphor. Rabelais paints with a highly-charged brush, and will use two words, or a dozen, or a hundred, where a precise writer would use one. In fact, sharpness of outline, precision of utterance, are more easily to be found in the poetry of the period than in the prose—in such pieces, for instance, as Ronsard's *Quand vous serez bien vieille*, or Du Bellay's *Heureux qui comme Ulysse a fait un beau voyage*.

Malherbe, then, in advocating purity, clearness, and precision of language, was doing a real service to the prose of his country, though even here his intolerance and rigidity had an impoverishing effect upon the language. But the virtues which he preached are the virtues of prose, and not of poetry. Limit poetry to the words and expressions of ordinary educated conversation, insist that it shall be always logically clear and mathematically precise, judge it, in short, by the intellect and not by the imagination, and you deprive it of all the sensuous charm and the vague suggestiveness which are part of its very essence

The only characteristics, then, which Malherbe left to poetry to distinguish it from prose were metre and rhyme. Even as regards these he showed his habitual narrowness and severity. He insisted that rhymes should be rich, "not only to the ear, but to the eye," and he preferred difficult rhymes to easy ones. Of the numerous metres with which Ronsard had enriched French poetry he selected a limited number and rejected the rest. The only metrical novelty that can be ascribed to him is the creation of the French classical strophe of ten octo-syllable lines, which he uses for six out of his ten odes. But, as Faguet has pointed out, he merely perfected what Ronsard had begun, for already in Ronsard we find the same strophe, with the only difference that the older poet uses a line of seven syllables instead of one of eight.

Malherbe's own versification is remarkable for its firmness, its dignity, its feeling for movement and cadence. He has a particular affection for the Alexandrine. As we have seen, the *Prière pour le Roi* is written in six-line stanzas of that metre, while in the *Consolation à M. Du Perier* he uses it for the first and third lines of the stanza. But whatever the length of the lines, Malherbe's lyrics always move in the stately measure proper to the Alexandrine. The result is that he has only one note—a note eminently suited to that grave and impersonal form of lyric which alone he attempted, but wholly inadequate to express the varying passions and emotions of true lyrical utterance.

But as yet we have not taken into account Malherbe's chief claim to recognition. When one has pointed out his incapacity for judging poetry, when one has reprobated the narrowness and inflexibility of his views on language, there remains the fact that he was the first Frenchman to apply to literature the test of a reasoned criticism. Du Bellay and Ronsard had both embodied in treatises literary principles of great value. Sibilet, Peletier, and Vauquelin de La Fresnaye had each written an *Art of Poetry*, based on the practices of contemporary poets. There is some excellent criticism of a general character in Montaigne's *Essays*. But hitherto the theory had prevailed that poetry was chiefly a matter of inspiration; and though Du Bellay in his *Deffence* had written a chapter entitled "That Natural Genius is not sufficient for the man who would write an immortal poem," it was by learning and by imitation of the ancients, and not by a critical effort, that he urged his poet to cultivate his genius. The great defect of sixteenth-century poets, the chief cause of their errors of conception and execution, of their shortcomings in proportion and taste, is their lack of self-criticism. It is true that Ronsard, who, with the exception, perhaps, of Belleau, had a far larger measure of this quality than any of his followers, frequently revised his poems after their first publication, and that as a rule his alterations are not merely the substitution of one thought for another, but are improvements in the artistic expression of the original thought. Yet his work would have been maintained more consistently at the highest level had he brought his critical powers to bear upon it while the clay was still plastic and the inspiration still fresh. According to Racan, Malherbe's disciple and biographer, the arrogant critic treated Ronsard even more contemptuously than he did Desportes, having

struck his pen through more than half of his copy of
Ronsard. Racan asked him whether he approved of what
he had left. "No more," he replied, "than I do of the
rest"; and on a suggestion by another disciple that, if the
volume were found after his death, it would imply his
approval of what he had left, he proceeded to strike out
all that he had hitherto spared. This insolent treatment of
Ronsard was not, perhaps, intended to be taken quite
seriously, but in any case Malherbe's failure to recognise
the faultlessness of some of Ronsard's work, and his great
superiority over his followers in critical power, shows a
serious defect in his own critical capacity.

Malherbe's doctrines seem to have been chiefly dis-
seminated through a small band of disciples who used to
meet in his modest apartment and discuss with him the
principles of poetry. The names of seven have come down
to us, and possibly there may have been others; but only
two, Racan and Maynard, attained to any fame as poets.

The first writer to take the field on behalf of the old
school was Mathurin Regnier, the nephew of Desportes,
who, as we have seen, had been on friendly terms with
Malherbe when he first came to Paris. His ninth satire,
embodying his attack on the new doctrines, appeared, with
others, in 1608, but it was probably written somewhat
earlier. It is addressed to Nicolas Rapin, Grand Provost
of the Constabulary of France, who occasionally beguiled
his leisure by writing French and Latin verses.

The following lines form so admirable an exposition of
the points in dispute between the two schools that, well
known though they are, it will be useful to quote them
here:

> Contraire à ces resveurs dont la Muse insolente,
> Censurant les plus vieux, arrogamment se vante
> De reformer les vers, non les tiens seulement,
> Mais veulent deterrer les Grecs du monument,
> Les Latins, les Hebreux, et toute l'Antiquaille,
> Et leur dire à leur nez qu'ils n'ont rien fait qui vaille.
>   Ronsard en son mestier n'estoit qu'un aprentif,
> Il avoit le cerveau fantastique et rétif;

Desportes n'est pas net, Du Bellay trop facille,
Belleau ne parle pas comme on parle à la ville;
Il a des mots hargneux, bouffis et relevez,
Qui du peuple aujourd'huy ne sont pas approuvez.
 Comment! il nous faut doncq' pour faire une œuvre grande
Qui de la calomnie et du tans se deffende,
Qui trouve quelque place entre les bons autheurs,
Parler comme à sainct Jean parlent les crocheteurs!

This last line agrees with the story told by Racan, that whenever Malherbe was asked his opinion about some word, he would refer the questioner to the porters of the Port au Foin, saying that they were the masters of the language. But Regnier, perhaps wilfully, has understood the remark in too literal a sense. Malherbe certainly did not mean that poets were to use the language of street porters, for in his commentary on Desportes he frequently objects to words as low or plebeian. He rather meant that they should not cultivate, as the Pleiad had done, an erudite vocabulary which common people could not understand[1]. He was expressing the same sentiment as Montaigne when he says that he wishes he could use only those words which were used in the *halles* at Paris. He was opposing the theory which Jean Bastier de La Péruse, a member of the Pleiad school who died young, expressed in the following lines:

> Le vulgaire populace
> Ne merite telle grace,
> Et la grand' tourbe ignorante
> N'est digne qu'on les luy chante:
> Car Apollon ne veut pas
> Que celuy qu'il favorise
> Ses vers divins profanise
> Les chantant au peuple bas.

In other respects, however, Regnier fairly represents Malherbe's criticisms on the older school, on their want of *netteté* or polish, on their too great facility, on their erudite and heightened language. A few lines further on he pushes

[1] See Brunot, *op. cit.*, pp. 222–226.

the attack home, though still without mentioning Malherbe's name:

> Cependant leur sçavoir ne s'estend seulement
> Qu'à regrater un mot douteux au jugement,
> Prendre garde qu'un *qui* ne heurte une dipthongue,
> Epier si des vers la rime est breve ou longue,
> Ou bien si la voyelle à l'autre s'unissant,
> Ne rend point à l'oreille un vers trop languissant,
> Et laissent sur le verd le noble de l'ouvrage:
> Nul eguillon divin n'esleve leur courage,
> Ils rampent bassement foibles d'inventions,
> Et n'osent peu hardis tanter les fictions,
> Froids à l'imaginer, car s'ils font quelque chose,
> C'est proser de la rime, et rimer de la prose;
> Que l'art lime et relime et polit de façon
> Qu'elle rend à l'oreille un agreable son.

The last seven lines well indicate the fundamental difference between the two schools. While the Pleiad believed,
and rightly, that, apart from metre and rhyme, there is an
essential distinction between poetry and prose, Malherbe
maintained that poetry is only measured prose. The Pleiad
were also right in believing in inspiration—in what
D'Aubigné calls *fureur poétique.* But they were wrong in
trusting, as the majority of them trusted, to inspiration
alone. When a poet, says Regnier, feels himself borne up
by the strong wing of inspiration, he must

> Laisser aller la plume où la verve l'emporte,

and Regnier despised the art of correcting and polishing
his verse. But inspiration is sometimes treacherous, and, if
the poet has not art to sustain him, he is apt to tire in his
flight or fall ignobly to the ground.

Regnier only survived by five years the publication of
his vigorous defence of the Pleiad; but had he lived longer,
he could hardly have delayed, much less have averted, its
overthrow. Of its followers, only Pasquier, Du Perron,
Montchrestien, Scévole de Sainte-Marthe, Jean de La
Taille, and D'Aubigné were living at the time of Regnier's
death, and of these Pasquier, Sainte-Marthe, and La Taille

were very old men, while Montchrestien and Du Perron had long ceased to write poetry. In fact, the only active poet of the old school was D'Aubigné, whose long poem, *Les Tragiques*, printed at his private press in far-off Poitou, was unheeded by the Paris world.

But long before Regnier's death, long before even the arrival of Malherbe at Paris, Ronsard's school had ceased to produce much poetry. After the Massacre of St Bartholomew, poetry, like the other arts, had fallen upon evil days, and during the twenty years which elapsed between the death of Ronsard and the arrival of Malherbe in Paris little verse was written in France. In fact, the only poet of any note who continued to produce poetry was Bertaut. Moreover, though Desportes was regarded down to his death as the "Prince of French poets," like the rest of his school, except Bertaut and Du Perron, he was no longer read. It is significant that from 1597 onwards the older Pleiad poets, not excepting Ronsard, cease to be represented in anthologies[1]. In these, down to 1609, Bertaut and Du Perron fill the chief places, and both, especially Bertaut, are forerunners of Malherbe.

Thus, when Malherbe began his campaign, there had ceased to be any vitality in the older school of poetry. The success of his revolution, as of most literary revolutions, was due far more to the weakness of the defence than to the vigour of the attack. This is only natural. A literature which mirrors the tastes and ideas of one generation seems antiquated alike in form and substance to the next. The leader of the new movement succeeds because he has the youth of the nation at his back.

So Clément Marot, without any manifesto, without any abuse of his predecessors, peacefully succeeded to the sceptre which had fallen from the feeble hands of the *grands rhétoriqueurs*. So the Pleiad—though in this case after a sharp but short struggle—drove out the Marotic school, of which the only noteworthy representatives that

[1] See F. Lachèvre, *Bibliographie des Recueils collectifs de Poésies publiées de 1597–1700*, 3 vols., 1901–05.

were left had themselves helped to prepare the way for the new movement.

Malherbe thus became, in his turn, a successful leader of revolution, partly because there was no one to oppose him, but chiefly because his poetry represented the ideals of the rising generation. Frenchmen were weary of individualism and licence and disorder; they sighed for repose and authority and a strong central government. The day of high imaginings and adventurous quests was over; an era of sober reason and common sense had set in. Malherbe, with his odes in praise of Henry IV and Richelieu, with his robust patriotism, his feelings for national unity, his clear language, and his manly harmony, gave them exactly what they wanted. By the year 1609—the year after the publication of Regnier's defence—Malherbe's victory was assured. In an anthology published in that year—*Nouveau Recueil des plus beaux vers de ce temps*—Malherbe is represented by fifteen pieces. That his doctrine represented the spirit of the age may also be inferred from a treatise on the *Art of Poetry* which appeared in the following year, 1610. Its author, Pierre de Deimier, who was born at Avignon in 1570, had been a follower of the Pleiad, and he speaks of its leading poets, Garnier and Desportes, in terms of high respect. But though, so far as we know, he was not acquainted with Malherbe, his doctrine has many points of resemblance with that of his more famous contemporary. In one of his chapters, which he entitles "On Reason which ought to shine in all poetry," he insists, like Malherbe, that poetry must be probable, and finds fault with Homer, Virgil, Ovid, Dante, Petrarch, and Boccaccio for many violations of this principle.

But, if Malherbe's reforms succeeded because they accorded with the spirit of the age, we must not forget that Malherbe's character especially fitted him to lead a revolutionary movement. Positive, intolerant, arrogant, and undaunted by opposition, he at once dominated his followers by his force of character, and vanquished his opponents by his tenacity. The last story told of him by

Racan is that an hour before he died he reproved his nurse for using a word which was not good French, and that when his confessor reprimanded him he replied that he would uphold to his death the purity of the French language.

A further stage in his success was marked by the publication, in 1615, of a poetical anthology—*Les Délices de la poésie française*—in which the majority of the pieces are by him and his followers, though Du Perron and Bertaut are still well represented. It is true that the leading poets of the Pleiad school continued to be printed separately: a magnificent folio edition of Du Bartas was published at Paris in 1610–11; there was an edition of Desportes in 1611; the dramatist Garnier was frequently reprinted down to 1619; and Ronsard himself appeared in 1623 in a superb edition of two volumes folio. But these were the last efforts of a dying cause. The edition of Du Bartas was, in Sainte-Beuve's phrase, his tomb; after this he was only read in Protestant countries. An edition of Ronsard— the last for nearly two centuries—was printed at Paris as late as 1629–30, but on poor paper and from worn type. It is more significant that in none of the anthologies published between 1600 and 1626 is there a single piece of Ronsard's, and that in the *Séjour des Muses*, published at Rouen in 1626, the editor specially calls attention to the fact that he has inserted ten poems by Ronsard "in order to show the difference between the style of the past and that of the present." In the same year Toussaint Du Bray, the publisher of *Les Délices*, issued a new anthology, which was composed almost entirely of the poetry of Malherbe and his disciples[1]. Even Bertaut and Du Perron were excluded.

[1] It includes 19 pieces by Jean de Lingendes (1580–1616), whose most important poem, *Les Changements de la Bergère Iris*, was published in 1605, the year of Malherbe's arrival at Paris, and who firmly resisted the newcomer's censorship. He has been admirably edited by Mr E. T. Griffiths for the *Soc. des textes français modernes* and the Manchester University Press (1916), but neither his long pastoral, nor his much admired *Élégie pour Ovide*, nor anything else in the volume seems to me to have any real poetical value.

In the same year, 1626, died Théophile de Viau, the one poet of the period—except Saint-Amant—whose natural gifts might have enabled him to vie successfully with Malherbe. He was only thirty-five at the time of his death, and the last three years of his life had been spent first in prison and then in exile. After the success of his play, *Pyrame et Thisbé*, presented some time between 1617 and 1619, he had become a conspicuous figure in the free-living and free-thinking set known as the *libertins*. But he was a born poet, and had he condescended to improve his natural gifts by study and discipline, he might have been a great one. As it was, he occasionally produced verses equal to Malherbe's in harmony, and superior in imagination and feeling. The following stanzas from a poem entitled *Solitude*, but which should rather have been entitled *Solitude à deux*, are exquisite:

> Dans le val solitaire et sombre
> Le cerf qui brame, au bruit de l'eau,
> Penchant ses yeux dans un ruisseau,
> S'amuse à regarder son ombre.
>
> De cette source une naïade
> Tous les soirs ouvre le portal
> De sa demeure de crystal,
> Et vous chante une sérénade.
>
> Un froid et ténébreux silence
> Dort à l'ombre de ces ormeaux,
> Et les vents battent les rameaux
> D'une amoureuse violence.

Théophile, as he was called by his contemporaries, belonged to neither of the rival schools. He appreciated and imitated alike Ronsard and Malherbe, but he differed from Ronsard in being less influenced by classical and Italian models; and, while he recognised Malherbe's merit as a poet, he declined to bow to his poetical laws.

> Imite qui voudra les merveilles d'autrui;
> Malherbe a très bien fait, mais il a fait pour lui,
> Mille petits voleurs l'écorchent tout en vie.
> Quant à moi, ces larcins ne me font point d'envie,
> J'approuve que chacun écrive à sa façon,
> J'aime sa renommée et non pas sa leçon.

Like Regnier, he failed to recognise the fact that
poetry is an art, and that it cannot attain to perfection without discipline and self-criticism. The following
lines at once express his theory and testify to its
inadequacy:

> Mon âme imaginant n'a point la patience
> De bien polir les vers, et ranger la science.
> La règle me déplaît; j'écris confusément;
> Jamais un bon esprit ne fait rien qu'aisément[1].

A year before his death Théophile sent a letter of com-
mendation to a younger poet named Tristan L'Hermite
(1601–51), who later achieved fame by his tragedy of
Mariane (1636). His lyrical verse, though overpraised by
his enthusiastic admirer, M. Jacques Madeleine, has not
only the two great merits of individuality and sincerity,
but other more distinctively poetical qualities—a strong
sense of rhythm, a command of a great variety of metres,
a feeling for nature, and here and there touches of real
imagination. Five stanzas from Tristan's most admired
poem, *Le Promenoir des deux Amans*, and a sonnet en
titled *L'Amour divin* will serve as specimens.

> Croy mon conseil, chère Climène,
> Pour laisser arriver le soir,
> Je te prie, allons nous asseoir
> Sur le bord de cette fontaine.

> N'oy tu pas soupirer Zephire
> De merveille et d'amour atteint,
> Voyant des roses sur ton teint
> Qui ne sont pas de son Empire?

> Sa bouche d'odeurs toute pleine
> A soufflé sur nostre chemin,
> Meslant un esprit de Jasmin
> À l'Ambre de ta douce haleine.

[1] M. Lachèvre notes that there were about 70 editions of Théophile from
1627 to 1696.

Penche ta teste sur cette Onde
Dont la christal paroist si noir;
Je t'y veux faire apercevoir
L'objet le plus charmant du monde.

Tu ne dois pas estre estonnée
Si vivant sous tes douces lois,
J'appelle ces beaux yeux mes Rois,
Mes Astres et ma Destinée.

Mon âme, esveille toy du dangereux sommeil
Qui te pourroit conduire en des nuits éternelles:
Et chassant la vapeur qui couvre tes prunelles
Ne prends plus désormais l'ombre pour le Soleil.

Ne croy plus de tes sens le perfide Conseil,
C'est assez adorer des objets infidèles:
Servons à l'avenir des beautés immortelles,
Que l'on trouve toujours en un estat pareil.

Aimons l'Auteur du monde, il est sans inconstance,
Sa bonté pour nos vœux n'a point de resistance,
Nous pouvons en secret lui parler nuit et jour.

Il connoist notre ardeur et notre inquiétude,
Et ne reçoit jamais de traits de nostre amour
Pour les recompenser de traits d'ingratitude.

Tristan was of the school of Théophile in his lack of self-criticism. He hardly ever blotted and he seldom revised. It is, however, to a second thought that we owe his most beautiful stanza, the fourth of *Le Promenoir*:

L'ombre de ceste fleur vermeille,
Et celle de ces joncs pendans
Paroissent estre là dedans
Les songes de l'eau qui sommeille.

Another poet with a true lyrical gift who refused to range himself under the banner of Malherbe was Marc-Antoine de Gérard, Sieur de Saint-Amant (1594–1661), whose father held for twenty-two years a naval command under Queen Elizabeth. He was born in 1594 and was therefore four years younger than Théophile. Like Malherbe, he was a Norman. Though he has found some warm

and discriminating admirers—notably M. Livet, who has
edited his poems, and M. Durand-Lapie, who has written
his life[1]—he has hardly received due measure from historians of French literature. For he is not adequately
represented either by his bacchanalian drinking-songs, or
by his realistic pictures after the manner of Berni, or by
his heroi-comic verse inspired by Tassoni. It is in his
serious poems that we can best judge of his poetical gifts,
his genuine feeling, his vein of romantic imagination, his
felicity of language, and his true feeling for movement and
harmony. His first poem, entitled *La Solitude*[2] (1617),
which was greatly admired by his contemporaries, and
which called forth Théophile's poem of the same name,
La Pluie, La Nuit, Le Contemplateur, all contain several
stanzas of considerable beauty. He also wrote some
fine sonnets, notably a description of the Alps in winter,
and· one on the death of Charles I. But as with Théophile
and Tristan L'Hermite the Muses had given him along with
their other gifts the dangerous one of facility. Like them,
he did not know when to blot. He had more genius than
judgment. Had he taken to heart the true lesson of
Malherbe's teaching—the necessity of self-criticism—he
would have been a far better poet.

In 1627, the year after Théophile's death, Malherbe
wrote an *Ode for the King on his way to chastise the rebellion
of La Rochelle*, in which Richelieu's policy is commended in
terms of warm and intelligent appreciation. The poem has
been highly praised by Sainte-Beuve[3], and finds favour
generally with French critics; but to most English readers
it will seem that Malherbe has here definitely crossed the
line which divides poetry from prose, and that even the
harmony of his verse has become hard and almost metallic.

[1] *Œuvres complètes* (Bibliothèque Elzévirienne), 2 vols., 1855–56; *Saint-Amant*, Montauban, 1896. For Théophile and Saint-Amant see Rémy de Gourmont, *Promenades littéraires*, 1916, III.

[2] Mme de Sévigné, writing from her beloved Les Rochers, July 15, 1671, quotes the first stanza. The whole poem was translated by Mrs Katherine Philips, "The Matchless Orinda" (*Poems*, 1669, pp. 170 ff.).

[3] *Nouveaux Lundis*, XIII. 1859.

But in fairness I must quote those stanzas to which Sainte-Beuve has awarded special praise:

> Certes, ou je me trompe, ou déja la Victoire
> Qui son plus grand honneur de tes palmes attent,
> Est aux bords de Charente en son habit de gloire,
>   Pour te rendre content.
>
> Je la voy qui t'appelle, et qui semble te dire:
> "Roy, le plus grand des rois, et qui m'est le plus cher,
> Si tu veux que je t'aide à sauver son empire,
>   Il est temps de marcher."
>
> Que sa façon est brave et sa mine asseurée!
> Qu'elle a fait richement son armure étoffer!
> Et qu'il se cognoist bien, à la voir si parée,
>   Que tu vas triompher!

This was almost Malherbe's last poem. In July of 1628, soon after its publication, he visited the King's camp before La Rochelle. From there he brought back the germs of an illness, which proved fatal on October 16, thirteen days before the capture of the Huguenot stronghold. Two years later, in 1630, the first collected edition of his poems was published.

Of the little group of disciples who assembled in Malherbe's modest apartment to hear the words of wisdom that fell from his lips, only two, as I have said, attained to any fame as poets, Honorat de Bueil, Marquis de Racan, and François de Maynard. Of these their master said that Maynard was the best versifier, but had no *force*; while Racan had more *force*, but did not take sufficient pains with his work. If, as Petit de Julleville conjectures, Malherbe meant natural facility by *force*, the remark is a pretty accurate description of the two writers. Maynard's Ode, *La belle vieille*, which may be read in Professor Saintsbury's *Specimens of French Literature*, is admirably versified and does credit to Malherbe's teaching, but only a few of the stanzas are really poetical in expression. Sainte-Beuve is right in preferring to it the *Ode à Alcippe* (*Alcippe, reviens dans nos bois*)[1]. Racan's masterpiece,

---

[1] *Malherbe et son École* in *Causeries du Lundi*, VIII.

Tircis, il faut penser à la Retraite, written on a similar theme—the praise of country life—shows that he was a real poet, if not a very original one. But it is amusing to find a disciple of Malherbe plagiarising Desportes and Du Bartas with a freedom which even Desportes might have envied.

After the death of Malherbe lyric poetry showed little sign of vitality. Writers confined themselves either to *vers de société*, like Voiture, or to bacchanalian songs, like Saint-Amant. The true lyrical cry was hushed for nearly two centuries. The real disciple of Malherbe was the great dramatist who produced his first play in the year after Malherbe's death. If, on the one hand, Malherbe "killed lyricism," on the other he fashioned a splendid and powerful instrument for the classical drama. The position which he occupies in French literature may seem to Englishmen unduly high, but in the eyes of the best judges he holds it, not as a poet, but as a literary reformer, as the creator of the critical spirit in literature, as the man who helped to prepare the way for the great school of 1660.

CHAPTER IV

THE CATHOLIC REVIVAL

THE condition of the Church in France when she emerged from the Wars of Religion was deplorable. To the evils which had called forth the outcry for reform at the beginning of the century—the worldliness and non-residence of the Bishops, the ignorance of the inferior clergy, the decay of discipline in the monasteries—were now added the fruits of anarchy and religious warfare. The churches were in ruins, the services were abandoned, hundreds of parishes were without a pastor.

In 1596 the Bishop of Le Mans presented to Henry IV on behalf of the assembly of the French clergy a long statement setting out the pitiable condition of the Church. They said that three-quarters of the ecclesiastical benefices were without proper occupants; that of the fourteen archbishoprics six or seven were vacant, and of the hundred or so bishoprics thirty to forty; that of the sees that were filled many were in the hands of men who had obtained them by illicit means, or were incompetent, ignorant, or idle. The abbeys and monasteries, they complained, were in a still worse condition, being for the most part in the hands of laymen. In twenty-five dioceses of which they had made an examination there were about 620 in which either there was no Abbot at all, or the titular Abbot had been illegally appointed. To take a single instance: the Protestant Sully enjoyed the revenues—amounting to 45,000 livres—of four abbeys. In reply to these remonstrances, Henry declared that he would appoint in future none but competent persons to bishoprics and abbeys.

In 1605 the clergy held another important assembly, and not only renewed their complaints, but demanded the restoration of the elections to the Chapters, of which they had been deprived by the Concordat. In answer to this the King renewed his promises and issued in 1606 an important edict as a basis of Church reform. Nevertheless, in the following year he bestowed three of the four abbeys vacant by the death of the poet Desportes (whose vocation for the Church had been of the slightest) on his bastard by Mme de Verneuil, a boy of six, and at the same time requested the Chapter of Metz to elect him as Bishop. Though the Pope refused to nominate him, he promised him the next vacancy without a fresh election, and the result was that Henri de Bourbon became a Bishop before he was eleven. Another well-known instance of this kind is that of Jacqueline Arnauld, better known as La Mère Angélique, who became Abbess of Port-Royal before she was eleven.

On the whole little was actually accomplished in the way of Church reform during the reign of Henry IV except the removal of the grossest scandals and abuses. Church services, for instance, were re-established in over 300 towns. Towards the close of the reign, indeed, the necessary work of reforming both the regular and the secular clergy was taken in hand. But perhaps the measure by which Henry gave the greatest impulse to reform was the re-establishment of the Jesuits. This was done by an edict of 1603, which authorised them, under certain restrictions, to return to those towns in which they already possessed establishments, and to found in addition colleges at Lyons, Dijon, and La Flèche in Anjou. In 1608 Père Coton became keeper of the King's conscience, and for the remaining two years of the reign the Jesuits steadily increased in influence and power. In 1609 they were allowed to reopen their College of Clermont at Paris for education. Ultramontane doctrines began to triumph over Gallicanism. Under Jesuit influence the great history of De Thou was censured at Rome. In 1615 the assembly of the clergy passed an unanimously-signed declaration that they accepted the Council of Trent.

Whatever practical measures may be taken by a Government for the promotion of Church reform, nothing can be of any avail without a revival of the religious spirit in the hearts of the people. That this revival took place in France in a marvellous degree was due, in a large measure, to the efforts of certain private individuals. Among these were Pierre de Bérulle, a former student of the College of Clermont, who had wished to become a Jesuit, but who after a year's novitiate had been told that he had no vocation for that Order; Jean de Brétigny, the translator of the Life and works of St Teresa; Mme Acarie, "the strongest religious force of her time," whose practical ability was as remarkable as her mysticism[1]; and her cousin, Mme de Sainte-Beuve. The whole group were greatly influenced by the writings of St Teresa, and in 1603 Mme Acarie, with the help of Bérulle, introduced into France the Order of the Reformed Carmelites.

It was this religious group that François de Sales[2] found at Paris when he came there in 1602 on a mission from the Bishop of Geneva. Born at Sales, near Annecy, in 1567, he had studied at the College of Clermont from 1581 to 1588, and had there made the acquaintance of Bérulle. His fervent love of God found in this religious atmosphere of Paris much that was congenial to him; but he tempered its austerity by a sweet reasonableness, and he gave a practical turn to its mysticism by showing that a religious life could be lived in the world as well as in the cloister, and that in order to love God it was not necessary to become a Carmelite. His gentle firmness and his quick insight into human nature made him an ideal spiritual director, and it was by his work in this capacity even more than by his preaching that his influence was exercised. When he returned to Geneva, to the bishopric of which he succeeded in this same year, 1602, he continued to correspond with those whom he directed, and two-thirds of his extant correspondence consists of letters of spiritual advice. The correspondent to whom he was knit by the closest ties

[1] See H. Brémond, *Hist. litt. du sentiment religieux en France*, ii. 193–262.
[2] See F. Strowski, *Saint François de Sales, Introduction à l'Histoire du Sentiment religieux en France au XVIIe Siècle*, 1898.

of spiritual kinship was Mme de Rabutin-Chantal (Sainte Chantal), the grandmother of Mme de Sévigné. He treated with hardly less affection and confidence the Mère Angélique of Port-Royal, whose director he became in 1619. Another correspondent was Mme de Charmoisy, to whom he addressed a series of letters in 1607. A Jesuit Father to whom she had shown them having urged him to publish them, he revised them with certain additions, and published them in the following year (1608) under the title of *Introduction à la Vie dévote*. It is, more or less, a complete manual of Christian conduct, but it is specially adapted to the usage of persons in society. Never before did a book of devotion achieve such popularity. It captivated alike by the easy charm of its style, which unites the exuberance, the picturesqueness, the love of metaphor of the sixteenth century with the reasoning power, the lucidity, and the structural harmony of the seventeenth, and by the smiling amiability of its tone. Yet the standard of conduct which it prescribes is an exceedingly high one, and it is never lowered to meet the requirements of a mundane society. François de Sales no more than Montaigne places virtue "on the top of a rugged and inaccessible mountain," but he would have denied that it was accessible "by shady, verdant, and flowery walks," or "by a pleasant, easy, and smooth ascent[1]."

A modern, or perhaps I should say a northern, reader is struck by the large part allotted to love in this treatise of devotion. *Philothée* is repeatedly warned against the dangers of flirtation. In this St François de Sales was true to the spirit of his age, for it was in the very year in which he wrote these letters to Mme de Charmoisy that the first part of the *Astrée* was published. It is hardly too much to say that the human love purified and ennobled by suffering and constancy which is the principal theme of this famous

---

[1] Il a ramené la dévotion au milieu du monde; mais ne croyez pas qu'il l'ait déguisée, pour la rendre plus agréable aux yeux des mondains; il l'a amenée dans son habit naturel, avec sa croix, ses épines, avec son détachement et ses souffrances (Bossuet, *Panégyrique de Saint-François de Sales*).

romance was the starting-point of François de Sales's whole philosophy of religion; for his *Traité de l'Amour de Dieu* (1616) is based on the idea that the love of God exists in germ in the heart of every man, generated by the imperious desire of the Will to unite itself with the Good. Hence the love of God is the true source of all religious feeling and conduct. Thus religion and morality, the divorce of which is so striking in the writings of Montaigne and Charron, are reconciled in those of François de Sales. Christian conduct is no longer a superhuman ideal to which the ordinary man cannot be expected to conform; it is the natural aspiration of the human will towards the source of all goodness.

During the regency of Marie de' Medici (1610–17) the new religious spirit began rapidly to bear fruit. It showed itself in the founding of new religious Orders, especially for women, and in the introduction of Orders of Strict Observance from other countries. The Récollets, an Order of reformed Franciscans, had already been established in France in 1592, and in Paris in 1603, where their house enjoyed the especial favour of Marie de' Medici and Henry IV. They became one of the most active and influential Orders in the kingdom, and were the founders of the Church in New France (1615). For several years, with only six friars, they supported missions there from Acadia to the borders of Lake Huron, till they were compelled to call in the assistance of Jesuits and finally retired in favour of the more powerful organisation[1].

Among the most important and influential Orders for women was that of the Ursulines for the education of young girls, which Mme de Sainte-Beuve established at Paris in 1610. They, too, extended their work to Canada, where the romantic Mme de La Pelterie founded a convent at Quebec, with Marie de l'Incarnation for its first Superior (1639)[2]. Of equal importance was the contemplative Order of the Visitation, or Visitandines, which François de Sales

---

[1] See Parkman, *Pioneers of France in the New World.*
[2] Parkman, *The Jesuits in North America*, chap. xiv.

had instituted at Annecy with the help of Mme de Chantal, and of which she now established a branch at Paris. A special feature of its organisation was the inclusion of widows and of aged and infirm persons among its members.

Women also played a leading part in the reform of existing monasteries. The foremost names among the re-forming Abbesses, who were mostly quite young women, are Marie de Beauvillier, who reformed the Benedictine abbey of Montmartre (1598–1601), Marguerite d'Arbouze, the Abbess of Val de Grâce, another Benedictine abbey, which she reformed in 1619, and, better known than either of these saintly and practical women, Jacqueline Arnauld, the Mère Angélique, who in 1608 at the age of seventeen began the difficult task of reforming the Cistercian convent of Port-Royal.

In the supplement to Du Breul's well-known work on the antiquities of Paris, published in 1639, mention is made of thirty-six convents which had been erected in three of the principal quarters of Paris during the last five-and-twenty years. Among them was a new Jacobin convent built for the reformed Dominicans in the Rue Saint-Honoré, which was destined to become famous in the days of the Revolution. Numerous churches also were built or completed. Saint-Étienne-du-Mont, which had been begun in 1517, was completed in 1626, the foundation-stone of the western façade having been laid in the year of Henry IV's death by his divorced wife, Marguerite de Valois. The beautiful and elaborate rood-screen, carved by Pierre Biard, is also of this period. In 1616 Salomon de Brosse added a Renaissance façade to the Gothic church of Saint-Gervais, and in 1643 the great church of Saint-Eustache, the largest in Paris after Notre-Dame, was finally completed.

Another crying evil from which the Church in France had long suffered was the deplorable condition of the in-ferior clergy. They were not only grossly ignorant, but they lacked all sense of the spiritual side of their vocation. According to Bérulle, who turned his attention to this necessary side of Church reform, they were luxurious, ambitious, and idle. It was to stem this grave evil that in 1611 he founded the Oratoire, a congregation of secular clergy devoted to the work of training and educating the priesthood. It was approved by Pope Paul V in 1613. Modelled on a similar foundation of Filippo Neri, though differing from it in several particulars, it rivalled its Italian prototype in the success of its development. At the death of Bérulle in 1529 it numbered forty-three houses.

In 1623 it also undertook, by order of the Pope, the work of secular education. Numerous colleges were founded, and that of Juilly, about twenty miles north-east of Paris, which was regarded as the model establishment, attracted the young nobles in large numbers. The new features of Oratorian education were that in the lower classes French, and not Latin, was the general medium of instruction, that history was taught in French throughout, and that under the influence of Descartes special attention was given to mathematics, the natural sciences, and philosophy[1].

The education given in the Little Schools of Port-Royal, which were organised in 1646, was on similar lines, but I shall recur to it in a later chapter. The real rivals of the Oratory were the Jesuits, who, ever since their re-establishment in France, had been extending their educational system in all directions. In the year 1626 they had fourteen colleges and over 13,000 pupils in the single province of Paris. The success of their secondary education was, in a large measure, due to the combined efficiency and mildness of their discipline and to their care for the health and physical well-being of their pupils. Swimming, riding, and fencing were all included in the school life. Descartes, who spent nine years (1604–13) as a boarder in the recently founded college of La Flèche, always retained a warm affection for his Jesuit teachers, and looked back with

[1] See P. Lallemand, *Hist. de l'Éducation dans l'ancien Oratoire de France*, 1888.

pleasure on his schooldays, however much he criticised the system of instruction. This instruction was based on the study of Greek and Latin, but, owing partly to the general decline of Greek studies in France, and partly to the greater encouragement given by the Jesuits to Latin as the language of the Church, Latin soon greatly predominated. The pupils were obliged to talk in Latin, and the cultivation of a good Latin style in prose and verse was regarded as of first-rate importance. It was the style rather than the spirit of ancient learning that the Fathers laboured to instil into their pupils. With this object in view the Greek and Latin authors were read in carefully prepared extracts, and though subjects of "erudition"—that is to say, history, geography, and the like—were introduced into the ordinary lessons by way of commentary, they were only taught as independent subjects in extra hours. The normal length of the literary course was five years, one year for each grade—three of grammar, one of humanity, and one of rhetoric—but it varied according to the capacity of the pupil. In the larger colleges, such as La Flèche, it was succeeded by a three years' course of philosophy, which comprised logic, metaphysics, and mathematics.

It has become almost a commonplace with writers on education that the Jesuit system, owing to its excessive devotion to style and language, leads to superficiality, and that it has produced neither men of science nor men of real learning. But the names of Jacques Sirmond, Denys Petau, Adrien de Valois, Descartes, and Ducange, all of whom were educated in Jesuit colleges during the first fifty years of their establishment in France, show that this statement requires qualification. It is a striking testimony also to the flourishing condition of these colleges during the thirty years which succeeded the recall of the Jesuits that they produced a Corneille, a Molière, a Bossuet, a Condé, and a Luxembourg.

The Capuchins, stimulated by the ardent zeal of the celebrated Father Joseph, vied with the Jesuits in promoting the welfare of the Church. They founded convents

and organised missions in the heart of Protestant districts
—Poitou, Dauphiné, the Cevennes, Languedoc, Provence.
They sent missionaries to England, Constantinople, the
Greek archipelago, Asia Minor, Syria, Mesopotamia, Persia,
Egypt, Morocco. In short in the words of M. Fagniez,
the biographer of Father Joseph, "they meditated the
spiritual conquest of all the countries washed by the
Mediterranean or the Caspian Sea." They even dreamt of
a new crusade against the Turks[1]. As the result of this
many-sided activity on the part of the chief Catholic forces,
the Catholic revival in France now entered on a period
of triumphant conquest. At the same time French Protestantism began to decline, not only under the attacks of
its opponents, but owing to its own internal dissensions
and to the desertion of some of its chiefs. In 1622 the
aged Lesdiguières was converted to Catholicism and received the promise of the Constableship, vacant by the
death of Luynes in the preceding year. In the same year
the Protestants were forced to conclude an unfavourable
peace.

When Richelieu, on the fall of La Vieuville, became
Chief of the Council, or first Minister, in August, 1624, he
found two parties in the State—the "good Frenchmen,"
as the *politiques* now called themselves, who were in favour
of Protestant alliances, and the religious party, who advo-
cated a policy of active opposition to the Protestants both
within and without the kingdom. On the side of the former
were the Parliament, the Gallicans, and the mass of the
public; the Catholic policy was supported by the Jesuits,
the Ultramontanes, the Court, and all Richelieu's colleagues on the Council. The Queen-Mother, who was largely
under the influence of her director Bérulle, inclined in the
same direction. Richelieu himself was a practising Catholic,
and entertained a high idea of the authority and dignity of
the Church. But he was a Frenchman and a statesman
before he was a Churchman, and his ecclesiastical policy

[1] See G. Fagniez, *Le Père Joseph et Richelieu*, 2 vols., 1894, i. c. vi. pp.
273–278.

was consistently directed to one aim—the greatness and unity of France. He was determined that no party in the Church—neither Gallicans nor Ultramontanes, neither Jesuits nor Jansenists—should exercise a preponderating influence, but that all alike should bow in humble submission to the central authority. It was in harmony with this policy that he promoted the discipline of the Church by choosing, as a rule, men of ability and learning to fill bishoprics and abbeys. If he preferred those of good birth, it was because he believed them to be better suited to positions of authority. But he did not altogether abandon the old practice of appointing mere boys. Thus Henri de Lorraine, afterwards Duc de Guise, the hero of the fantastic expedition to Naples, who in his elder brother's lifetime was destined for the Church, held nine abbeys at the age of twelve, and became Archbishop of Reims when he was fifteen. Moreover, it was scarcely to the advantage of their dioceses that Richelieu employed the Cardinal de La Valette, Archbishop of Toulouse, as a general; François de Sourdis, Archbishop of Bordeaux, as an admiral; and his own brother, the Archbishop of Lyons, as a diplomatist.

Richelieu also gave much attention, though with but moderate success, to the difficult work of reforming the monasteries. He especially occupied himself with the Benedictines, and for that purpose had himself elected Abbot of its two principal Orders—Cluny and Cîteaux. To the former of these he united the new Congregation of Saint-Maur, which had been founded in 1618 on the model of the reformed Congregation of Sainte-Vanne, and he gave his warm approval and sympathy to the great work of ecclesiastical education, learning, and research which was being organised by the first Superior of the Congregation, Dom Grégoire Tarisse. In furtherance of this work, manuscripts and books were rapidly collected for the library of Saint-Germain-des-Prés, the headquarters of the Congregation, and the learned Dom Luc d'Achery was placed at its head. Here, in peaceful seclusion, he led for nearly half a century a life of laborious study. Here, in 1655, he in-

augurated with the first volume of his great *Spicilegium*
that splendid series of monumental works which the world
owes to the learning and enthusiasm of the Benedictines of
Saint-Maur. Dom d'Achery handed on the torch to perhaps
the greatest of all these princes of scholarship, the gentle,
humble, indefatigable Mabillon (1632–1707), whose journeys
in search of manuscripts resembled royal progresses; and
Mabillon in his turn handed it on to his pupil and biographer,
Thierri Ruinart. Contemporary with the latter are Denys de
Sainte-Marthe, the editor of *Gallia Christiana*; Bertrand de
Montfaucon, the editor of Athanasius and Chrysostom, and
the equal of Mabillon in his knowledge of palæography; and
Dom Martène and Dom Durand, the two companions of the
famous *Voyage littéraire*. The next generation was represented by Dom Rivet, who began the *Histoire littéraire de
la France*; Dom Bouquet, the first editor of the historians of
Gaul and France; and Dom Clément, who is chiefly famous
as the editor of a new edition of *L'Art de vérifier les dates*.
The last-named died in 1793 in his eightieth year—for,
happily, these learned Benedictines were all long-lived—
and thus carried on till the close of the eighteenth century
the traditions of his illustrious house.

Catholic learning was not by any means confined to the
Benedictines. The Jesuits especially realised that Catholicism could not flourish without the help of learning, and
that, if they wished to control the thought of Christendom,
they must meet the Protestants with intellectual weapons,
and produce men equal in learning to a Scaliger or a
Casaubon. The effect of this policy was that there issued
from Paris presses during the first half of the seventeenth
century a number of epoch-making editions of the Greek
and Latin Fathers, such as the Chrysostom of Fronton Du
Duc, the Tertullian and Cyprian of Nicolas Rigault, the
Eusebius of André de Valois.

Another sign of the Catholic revival was the publication
of numerous Lives of French saints. This work began in
1610 with the Life of St Louis. It was followed by Lives of
St Sigisbert, the brother of Clovis; St Isabella, the sister

of St Louis; St Martin, St Aldegonde, St Éloy, St Rade-
gonde, and others of lesser fame.

But the age was not contented with recording the lives
of past saints; it produced new ones. I have already
mentioned Sainte Chantal. An even more important
part in the Catholic revival of France was played by St
Vincent de Paul, one of the chief glories of the Gallican
Church. The son of a small farmer in the Pyrenees, he
took priest's Orders in the year 1600, and not long afterwards was captured by Moorish pirates and sold as a slave
at Tunis. He escaped, and returned to France in 1607.
The two great institutions which are associated with his
name and which owed their origin to his initiative are the
Priests of the Mission and the Sisters of Charity. Both
arose from a desire to alleviate the hardships and miseries
of peasant life. At Châtillon-les-Dombes, where he was
priest for some months in 1617, he founded an association
of women of all classes, who, without taking any vows,
gave voluntary help to the sick and poor. This grew into
the Congregation of the Filles de la Charité, which, with
the help of Mme Legras (Louise de Marillac)[1], was organised
in 1633. Other charitable institutions founded by St
Vincent were the Hospital for Foundlings, the Hospice du
Nom de Jésus for old men, and the Hospice de la Sal-
pêtrière, a species of workhouse where the poor were fed,
educated, and provided with work.

Another evil besides the material misery of the people
which had attracted Vincent's attention at Châtillon-les-
Dombes was the ignorance and coarseness of the country
clergy, which made them unfitted for the delicate task of
spiritual guidance. With a view to remedy this, he founded
the Congregation of the Mission for the purpose of evangelis-
ing the country districts. The members were first established in the Collège des Bons-Enfants (1627), and afterwards in the house of Saint-Lazare[2] (1632), whence their
name of Lazarists. Their work soon expanded beyond its

[1] Since 1920 la Bienheureuse Louise de Marillac.
[2] Near the Gare du Nord and the church of St Vincent de Paul.

original scope; for "M. Vincent," as he was always called, mindful of his former experiences, sent his missionaries not only to Tunis and Algiers to minister to Christian slaves, but into heretic countries to convert souls to Catholicism. Saint-Lazare was not only a seminary for missionary work, but a house of retreat and spiritual edification for clergy and laity alike. "Rich and poor, lackeys and great nobles, soldiers and bishops, ate at the same table, and shared in the same devotions."

In both of St Vincent's great foundations the association of a lay element was a special feature. The Filles de la Charité comprised not only *Sœurs* but *Dames*, who, in pursuance of the original idea of the society, were bound by no vows. In the terrible years of the Fronde both of these institutions did admirable work. Into Lorraine, Champagne, and Picardy, provinces in which the misery was at its highest, came the Lazarists and the "Grey Sisters" to distribute bread and alms, to heal the sick, and to console the dying. "The house of Saint-Lazare became the granary of France."

The better education of the clergy was still a pressing want. The Oratory had been diverted somewhat from its original object by the work of secondary education. Special training-schools were needed. In 1618 Adrien Bourdoise, a man of humble origin, who before taking Orders had earned a living in various menial employments, founded, with the approval of Bérulle, the community and training-school of Saint-Nicolas-du-Chardonnet. Bourdoise had a high conception of the dignity of the ecclesiastical profession, and of the order and decorum which the services of the Church demanded, but he was not a man of learning, and theological studies formed no part of the training of his seminary. Claude Lancelot, the well-known teacher of Port-Royal, who spent ten years in the community, having entered it at the age of twelve, says that at the age of twenty he had never read a line of the New Testament. One of his instructors had even said to him that the *Introduction to the Devout Life* was more useful to many people than the Gospel.

Bourdoise's initiative was speedily followed, and other seminaries for priests were established in Paris and elsewhere. In 1620 Charles de Condren, a man of saintly life and singularly attractive character[1], who was most active in promoting the education of the clergy, founded a seminary for the see of Paris in the abbey of St Magloire. But the institution which was destined to take the lead throughout France in the work of preparing men for the priesthood was that founded in 1641 by Jean-Jacques Olier, *curé* of Saint-Sulpice, under the name of the Congregation of Saint-Sulpice. Assisted by several associates, he carried on the work of his parish and his seminary with equal success. The two most famous pupils of the seminary—at least, in the annals of literature—were Fénelon, whose uncle was an intimate friend of the founder, and Renan, who has left an interesting account of his two years' residence at Saint-Sulpice in his *Souvenirs d'enfance et de jeunesse*.

Olier, stimulated by the success of his undertaking, went on to found similar institutions in the provinces, and even in distant Canada. The first European settlement on the island of Montreal (May 17, 1642) was due to his efforts to provide a home for a seminary of priests[2].

A similar foundation to Olier's was that of the Congregation of the Eudistes, as they were commonly called, after their founder, Père Eudes, a priest of the Oratory. Their first house was at Caen (1643), but they soon spread over Normandy and the neighbouring districts.

One fruitful result of the greater attention that was now given to the training and education of ecclesiastics was a marked improvement in pulpit oratory[3]. During the sixteenth century, apart from the grotesque exaggerations of the League preachers, sermons that aspired to eloquence were habitually disfigured by pedantry and bad taste, the former showing itself in the piling up of citations from ancient authors, and the latter in the unrestrained use of

[1] See Brémond, *op. cit.*, III. 284 ff.
[2] Parkman, *The Jesuits in North America*, chap. xv.
[3] See P. Jacquinet, *Des prédicateurs du XVIIᵉ siècle avant Bossuet*, 1863.

metaphor. Both vices were due to the same cause, the lack of true spiritual earnestness. With the Catholic revival pulpit oratory for the first time for two centuries began to be carefully cultivated by the Catholic clergy. The best preacher during the reign of Henry IV was Cardinal Du Perron. A man of learning and ability, and a master of the arts of controversy, he was also a skilled rhetorician, but he lacked the warmth and spiritual conviction of a true orator. Other preachers of note in his day were Jean Bertaut the poet, Bishop of Séez; Pierre de Fenoillet, Bishop of Montpellier, whom Henry IV appointed to be his preacher in ordinary; and Philippe de Cospéan, Bishop successively of Aires, Nantes, and Lisieux. A greater name is that of François de Sales, but, so far as can be judged from the imperfect condition in which his sermons have come down to us, he seems, like his contemporaries, to have gratified the popular taste for erudition and ingenuity. At the same time he was aware of better things, for in a treatise on preaching which he addressed in 1604 to the Archbishop of Bourges, a brother of Mme de Chantal, he urges the avoidance of those faults of conceit and bad taste which disfigured the ordinary preaching of his day.

The marked improvement in pulpit oratory, which began to take place about the time of the accession of Richelieu to power, was, in a large measure, due to the efforts of Cardinal de Bérulle and the Oratoire. The first famous preacher of this society—the most famous until the days of Massillon—was "the blind Father," Père Lejeune, who for forty years—from 1620 to 1660—gave his whole life to preaching and missionary work. His sermons, which testify to a long and careful study of the Fathers, especially of the most eloquent of all, St Chrysostom, are clothed in homely but expressive language, suited to the needs of a popular audience. Occupied almost entirely with the moral and practical side of religion, they abound in interesting pictures of manners. But there is no attempt at elaborate description or ingenious rhetoric; it is the language of a natural orator who speaks from heart to heart, from imagination to imagination, and who becomes eloquent from the depth of his moral fervour and from the sincerity of his utterance. Another member of the Oratoire, Père Bourgoing, who took a leading part in its institution and, on the death of Père Condren in 1641, became its third General, is fortunate in having had his funeral oration pronounced by Bossuet (1662). "The Gospel message came from his lips, living, penetrating, full of intelligence and fire....Eloquence followed him like a servant, not elaborately prepared, but born of the subject-matter itself." Unfortunately, these eloquent phrases must be regarded as descriptive rather of the ideal preacher than of Père Bourgoing. Another Oratorian, Père Senault, who succeeded Bourgoing as General, was the most fashionable preacher in Paris during the days of Mazarin and Anne of Austria. But he was cold and monotonous, too much of a rhetorician, too much under the influence of Balzac. For Bossuet, in his treatise addressed to the young Cardinal de Bouillon on the training of a Christian orator, exactly hits the mark when, after recommending Balzac as a good example of a finished style, he adds that "he must be soon thrown aside, for his is the most unsound of styles, because it is the most affected and the most constrained."

A preacher of a very different stamp to Senault was his Jesuit contemporary, Claude de Lingendes, who inveighed against the sins of society with passionate directness and an unshrinking description of particular sins. Unfortunately, his sermons have only come down to us in the Latin form which he used in preparing them. Of this Jesuit, at any rate, Bossuet could not have said that "he put cushions under the elbows of sinners." He is a worthy predecessor of the great Bourdaloue, who appears to have studied his sermons. His style is all the more remarkable because Jesuit oratory during the first half of the seventeenth century was, for the most part, as florid and meretricious as Jesuit architecture. Yet as early as 1619 a Latin treatise on eloquence had been published by a Jesuit, Père Caussin, in which the superiority of a pure and unaffected style to the pedantic and artificial oratory of the day was pointed out with admirable force.

The cause of simplicity was greatly helped by the advocacy of two great leaders of the Church—St Vincent de Paul and the Abbé de Saint-Cyran. Under the imperious influence of the latter there grew up at Port-Royal a school of simple and austere eloquence, of which the best exponent was Antoine Singlin, Saint-Cyran's assistant and successor in the spiritual direction of Port-Royal. It was under the influence of "M. Vincent," who summoned him to Paris in 1659, that Bossuet, whose Metz sermons are sometimes disfigured by pedantry and bad taste, adopted a more chastened style of preaching. His favourite model had been hitherto the African Tertullian with his rich and lurid rhetoric, but he now turned to the purer but hardly less picturesque beauties of St Chrysostom, and, falling into line with the severe taste of the school of 1660, became the great master of pure and manly oratory whom we know.

In nearly every form of activity which had for its object the promotion of the Catholic religion the efforts, due to the initiative of individuals, that have been briefly recorded above were seconded, and in some cases anticipated, by a remarkable society, of which the originator was Henri de Lévis, Duc de Ventadour. At first he only communicated his design to four persons, including Frère Philippe d'Angoumois, a Capuchin monk, and Père Suffren, the Jesuit confessor of Marie de' Medici and Louis XIII. These gradually admitted others to their conclaves, and a small committee was formed, which included, besides the founders, two bishops, the French Ambassador at Rome, and Charles de Condren, Bérulle's successor as General of the Oratoire. At the end of 1630 the society was definitely constituted, and for thirty-six years, until its dispersion in 1666, it carried on a remarkable work. Among its members were St Vincent de Paul, who joined in 1635 or 1636; Louis Abelly, Bishop of Rodez, his biographer; the Abbé Olier; and Bossuet, who during his sojourn at Metz (1652–59) was an active worker. But the membership was not confined to ecclesiastics; presidents and councillors of Parliament, advocates, officers of the royal household, great nobles, ambassadors, marshals, and even a prince of the blood (Conti), were enrolled in the ranks. The only class that was definitely excluded by the statutes were members of religious Orders and all priests who owed obedience to a General. The reason for this exclusion, which had been voted on the advice of the Capuchin, the Jesuit, and the Oratorian who were among the founders of the society, was that it would be difficult for those who owed implicit obedience to their superiors to attend the meetings of a secret society. For secrecy was a distinctive feature of the society, and from the beginning was regarded as essential to its success. It even had at first no name, and was simply spoken of by the initiated as The Company; that of *La Compagnie du Saint-Sacrement* was adopted later.

The work of the society, which rapidly developed and before long numbered fifty branches in the provinces, embraced nearly every department of religious life. It may be classified under five heads: works of charity, ecclesiastical discipline, missionary enterprise, repression of heresy, supervision of morals. Under the first head the Company anticipated and afterwards co-operated with St Vincent de Paul in measures for the material and spiritual welfare of convicts and other prisoners. During the terrible years of the Fronde it vied with the Lazarists and the Grey Sisters in providing food and medicines and nursing for the stricken peasantry. Part of its regular work consisted in giving relief to *les pauvres honteux*, that is to say, to the unemployed who were ashamed to beg. Relief, except in cases of emergency, was only given after careful investigation, so that its action closely resembled that of our modern Charity Organisation. As might be expected, it made religious conformity a condition of receiving relief, and thus the distribution of alms became a powerful weapon of propagandism. But it went much further than this. It organised an elaborate system of spiritual police, with its attendant evils of espionage and interference with family life. In the words of M. Allier, whose book on the work of this remarkable society has thrown so much light on the Catholic revival in France, "they had for their agents fanatics who loved souls to the point of ferocity, and who, in order to save them, recoiled from nothing, 'sanctifying by the purity of their intentions' what simple souls would call dirty actions[1]."

There were other ways, too, in which the Company exercised the functions of a spiritual and moral police. It put down scandals and disorders in churches, insisted on the reverent performance of Divine service, and, rightly believing that many of the abuses in Church administration were due to the non-residence of the clergy, procured an Order of Council commanding all priests to reside in their parishes (1644). But it by no means confined its activity to ecclesiastical reforms. All classes felt the pressure of its religious zeal. It laboured for the stricter observance of the feasts and fasts prescribed by the Church, and for the abolition of the orgies of the Carnival and other time-honoured festivals. It also waged crusades against the fashionable vices of the upper classes, swearing and gambling and duelling.

But in nothing was its zeal more unflagging than in the repression of heresy. All means towards this end were justified in its eyes. For the purpose of spreading the true faith it employed alike the vulgar arts of some platform charlatan and the lofty intelligence of a Bossuet. But it did not confine itself to persuasion. From 1632, and with unremitting activity from 1638, it made war on the Protestants, who were harassed, plotted against, and accused, if possible, of crimes. The Edict of Nantes, which protected the lives and liberties of the heretics, was held up to systematic denunciation, and no body of men did more to prepare the way for the revocation of that edict than the Company of the Holy Sacrament.

On the other hand, we must put to the credit side of its

[1] R. Allier, *La cabale des dévots*, 1627–66, Paris, 1902; A. Rebelliau in the *Rev. des deux mondes* for July 1, Aug. 1 and Sept. 1, 1903, and for Aug. 15, 1908.

account its work among the Christian slaves in Africa, and its missionary enterprises in China and Canada, of which latter country the Duc de Ventadour had acquired the vice-royalty by purchase[1]. In all of these it found a willing and able co-operator in St Vincent de Paul.

Such, briefly, was the vast sphere of religious activity which the Company had mapped out for itself. But clashing, as it did, with the interests and pleasures, and above all with the liberties of so many classes and individuals, it was inevitable that in the end it must provoke violent opposition. Men felt that, wherever they turned, a secret society—all the more oppressive because secret—was spying on them, denouncing them, interfering with them. It was especially the crusade against duelling which led to the ultimate downfall of the Company. Here the Christian code and the code of honour were brought face to face in sharp opposition. The Company had skilfully put forward as its leaders in this crusade men of high birth and proved valour, and it secured a triumph in a royal edict against duelling, by which the young King solemnly pledged himself to grant no indulgence to delinquents (1651). Three years later—during the Fronde it had been impossible to enforce it—it was renewed. But society was now thoroughly roused against the Company, or, as it began to be called, *La Cabale des Dévots*. The leaders, at any rate, were known, and were regarded—unjustly, but perhaps naturally—as hypocrites. Opposition came not only from classes, but from important individuals. That very mundane prelate, François de Harlay de Chanvallon, who had recently succeeded his uncle as Archbishop of Rouen, was its enemy. Most ominous of all, it had against it Mazarin, who brooked no interference with his political aims, least of all a subtle insinuating interference, which he felt everywhere but could not bring to light. And after Mazarin's death this enmity was inherited by Colbert, and was all the more embittered by the fact

[1] M. Allier gives good reasons for supposing that the foundation of Montreal was the work of the Company (*op. cit.*, pp. 145–150).

that the Company was favourably disposed to Fouquet. After Fouquet's fall the Company was doomed. In 1664 it seemed for a moment to have triumphed over its enemies, and it succeeded in stopping the representation of *Tartuffe*. But the end soon came. The existence of a secret society with so vast a conception of its sphere of action was wholly incompatible with the absolutism of Louis XIV. In 1666 the central committee met for the last time, and the Company was dispersed.

In their attempt to raise the general standard of morality and to make religion a stricter and more austere guardian of conduct the Jansenists resembled the Company of the Holy Sacrament. But their methods were different. While the Company warred against outward sin by calling in the forces of the law, the Jansenists attacked the human heart. Both were equally sincere in their zeal, but both showed an imperfect sympathy with human nature. The danger of the Company's methods was that they encouraged hypocrisy; of the Jansenist doctrine, that it bred aversion or despair. But, of Jansenism, and its noble offspring, Port-Royal, I shall have more to say in a later chapter.

Such were the remarkable achievements of the Catholic revival in France. Churches had been built, monasteries had been reformed, ecclesiastical discipline had been restored, and, above all, the spiritual indifference which the corrupt state of the Church had produced, and which, in its turn, chilled and paralysed all attempts at reform, had been converted into a warm and active religious zeal.

At first this revival of spiritual feeling had seemed likely, under the influence of Spanish mysticism, to spend itself in passive contemplation; but largely through the influence of St François de Sales and his friend Pierre de Bérulle, both of whom, like St Teresa herself, combined with mystical tendencies much practical common sense and a marked capacity for organisation, it was before long diverted into active channels[1]. Mysticism inspired action,

[1] Another instance of this combination is Marie de l'Incarnation, the Superior of the Ursuline Convent at Quebec (see Parkman, *op. cit.*, p. 272).

instead of paralysing it. This activity took chiefly two forms: first, in the promotion of works of charity, in which St Vincent de Paul was conspicuous; secondly, in the encouragement of education and learning. By the middle of the seventeenth century the French clergy, who at the beginning of it had been noted for their ignorance, had become the most learned in Catholic Europe. A few years more and they were also the most eloquent, not only in Catholic countries, but throughout Europe.

A marked change, too, had taken place in the whole attitude of the nation towards religion. During the sixteenth century it had been, indeed, neither sceptical nor indifferent. The Wars of Religion, culminating in the almost grotesque, but absolutely sincere, violence of the League, sufficiently show this. But the zeal was that of men who were attached to the forms rather than to the substance of religion, who recognised no connexion between religion and morality, but ruled their lives according to the easy precepts of the so-called Law of Nature. Ronsard and Montaigne are types of the orthodox Catholic of the sixteenth century. But in the seventeenth century this spirit, though it lingered still in certain places, was replaced for the great majority of Frenchmen by a sincere belief in Christianity and the Catholic Church. Men might sin, and did sin, strongly and repeatedly, but they repented. It is the belief in repentance which distinguishes Condé and Mme de Longueville, La Fontaine and Mme de Sablé, from the author of the essay *On Repentance*. A noteworthy and unfailing sign of the religious spirit of the age is that it produced two great religious painters in Philippe de Champaigne (1602–74)[1] and Eustache Le Sueur (1616–55). The great portrait painter, who was so closely associated with Port-Royal, and the painter of the Life of St Bruno, are, whatever their differences, alike in the absolute sincerity of their religious feeling[2]. Both were

[1] Among his chief portraits are Richelieu, Saint-Cyran, Arnauld d'Andilly, La Mère Agnès, and Le Maître de Sacy.

[2] See Lemonnier, *op. cit*.

laymen, and it is a noteworthy feature of the whole movement that laymen played in it a distinguished and important part. As we have seen, they were assigned a
definite place in some of the new Orders and Congregations,
especially in those founded by St Vincent de Paul.

There is one merit which the Catholic revival in France
did not possess—that of tolerance. In an age when liberty
of conscience was still in its infancy it could hardly have
been otherwise, and it is only natural that the Church of
Rome, with its claim to the exclusive possession of religious
truth, should be less tolerant than Protestantism. Even
the Anglican Church, in spite of Chillingworth and Hales
and Jeremy Taylor, was intolerant enough during the
seventeenth century. But the intolerance of Pierre de
Bérulle, who largely guided the Catholic movement in
France during the first thirty years of the century, had a
sharper edge than that of Laud. He would gladly have
seen the Protestants exterminated, and he rejoiced over
the death of Luynes, whom he believed to be lukewarm in
the work. Richelieu, on the other hand, as soon as he had
crushed the pretensions of the Protestants to independent
political power, showed himself tolerant in the matter of
religion. Mazarin was personally as tolerant as his predecessor, but he gave little attention to the Church. During
his ministry the most influential Churchman was Vincent
de Paul, who had the warm support of the pious but
narrow-minded Spaniard, Anne of Austria. Now, "M.
Vincent" was, as we have seen, an active member of the
Company of the Holy Sacrament, and as such may be
supposed to have approved of its policy and methods. It
is true that in 1666 the Company was compelled to dis-
perse; but this was not on account of the intolerance of its
policy or of the immorality of its methods, but because it
clashed with the absolutist ideas of Louis XIV. But its
spirit survived. Its seed had been sown in receptive soil,
and before long bore fruit in the revocation of the Edict of
Nantes.

CHAPTER V

THE HÔTEL DE RAMBOUILLET AND THE
ORGANISATION OF SOCIETY

I

WE have seen that the standard of purity to which Malherbe wished the French language to conform was usage, and that by usage he apparently meant the usage of polite society. But in the year 1605, when he first came to Paris, society, apart from the Court, hardly existed, and the Court of Henry IV, with its boisterous amusements, coarse habits, and poverty of intellectual interests, was hardly of a nature to exercise a refining influence on either language or manners. In fact, *dégasconner la cour* was one of Malherbe's professed aims. Meanwhile a lady of noble birth and high intelligence was gradually feeling her way towards the organisation of Paris society, towards the formation of that *vie de salon* which was destined to play so important a part in the development of French literature down to, and even beyond, the Revolution.

In the year 1600 Catherine de Vivonne, the daughter of Jean de Vivonne, Marquis de Pisani, at one time French Ambassador at Rome, and of Giulia Savelli, a member of the great Roman family which had furnished two Popes— Honorius III and Honorius IV—in the thirteenth century, being then barely twelve years of age, was married to Charles d'Angennes, eldest son of the Marquis de Rambouillet. Like other ladies of her rank, she at first frequented the Court, at which her husband had an official position, but, finding the freedom of its manners and language not to her liking, she gradually discontinued her visits, and finally, after the birth of her first child, Julie, in 1607, abandoned them altogether. At the same time she began to receive a select circle of friends in the Hôtel Pisani, which she had inherited from her father, and which was situated in the Rue Saint-Thomas-du-Louvre, a street running south from the Place du Palais-Royal. At first her receptions attracted but little attention, but from about 1615, the year of the marriage of Louis XIII with Anne of Austria, they began to exercise a perceptible influence, not only on society, but even on literature.

At this time Mme de Rambouillet was greatly occupied with the alteration of her house. The work was completed in June, 1618, and the house was henceforth known as the Hôtel de Rambouillet, her husband having become Marquis de Rambouillet on his father's death in 1611. It was a feature of the reconstructed hôtel that, in place of some of the immense reception-rooms customary in great houses of this time, it contained a suite of moderate-sized apartments, adapted to intimate conversation. We are also told that Mme de Rambouillet was the first person to use other colours than red or brown (*tanné*) for the decoration of her rooms. One of these rooms was hung with blue-green Flemish tapestry representing pastoral scenes. It was here that, according to the fashion of the day, she received her guests, seated on a bed in full dress. The bed, which was raised on a dais, faced the window, and the spaces between it and the walls on either side were called *ruelles*. Thus *tenir une ruelle* became a regular term for receiving one's friends. The guests sat round the bed on seats carefully regulated by their rank or sex—some in arm-chairs, some on chairs without arms, and some on stools—while the younger men and those of humbler rank had to content themselves with the floor. Later, Mme de Rambouillet had her bed placed in a recess or *alcôve*, whence the terms *alcôve* and *alcôviste* were applied to receptions of this sort and their frequenters.

Among the leading beauties who frequented the Blue Chamber in its early days were the Princesse de Condé, who, as Charlotte de Montmorency, had been the object of Henry IV's undignified passion; Mme de Sablé (Madeleine de Souvré), famous for her wit as well as for her beauty;

her friend, the fantastic and virtuous Anne d'Attichy, afterwards Comtesse de Maure; the Princesse de Guéméné (Anne de Rohan); and Mme de Combalet, Richelieu's favourite niece, who kept house for him after her husband's death, and whom he created, in 1638, Duchesse d'Aiguillon. More occasional visitors were Richelieu himself, and his young friend the Cardinal de La Valette, a son of the Duc d'Épernon, who, in spite of his red hat, obtained some distinction as a military commander. They had both been introduced by the pious, eloquent, and witty Bishop of Lisieux, Philippe de Cospéan, whose friendship with M. and Mme de Rambouillet dated from the early days of their marriage, when he was a theological student at the Sorbonne. Other old friends were M. de Chaudebonne and Arnauld d'Andilly, who had been secretary to M. de Rambouillet at Rome, and with him, at a somewhat later date, came his younger brother Henry, Abbé of Saint-Nicolas of Angers, who, when Bishop of Angers, was regarded as one of the most virtuous and enlightened of French prelates. It was a special feature of the hôtel that men of letters and men of fashion met there on equal ground. Malherbe was a visitor at least as early as 1613, and he brought with him soon afterwards his friend and disciple, the Marquis de Racan. From this period, too, or a little later, dates the intimacy of Ogier de Gombauld, one of the original members of the French Academy, and the author of a pastoral romance, called *Endymion*, which was supposed to be an allegory of his romantic passion for the Queen-Mother, Marie de' Medici.

In 1615 another visitor was added in the person of the Neapolitan poet Giambattista Marini, who had arrived in Paris with an immense reputation. There he composed and published his epic poem of *Adone*, which appeared in 1623, just after his return to Italy. A year or two before this the poet Saint-Amant had made his first bow in the Blue Chamber.

Of Mme de Rambouillet herself, the incomparable Arthénice (Malherbe's anagram of her name Catherine), we have a portrait by Mlle de Scudéry, which, allowing for a certain amount of flattery, may be accepted as a faithful one. She was tall and well made, with a beautiful delicate complexion and fine eyes, the charm of which lay in their gentle calm rather than in their fire. Her dignified presence and uniform tranquillity of temperament imposed respect on all. But if "her passions," as became one who helped to inaugurate the age of reason, "were always in subjection to her reason," she was of a gay disposition and loved amusement. Though she was extremely modest about her learning, she had considerable information on various subjects and was well read in Italian and Spanish. Thus, alike by her personal appearance, her character, and her attainments she was admirably fitted for the position of hostess to a select circle of cultivated men and women. Above all, she had the gifts which more than any other have contributed to the success of famous salons—of Mme de Tencin's, and Mme Geoffrin's, and Mme Recamier's. She ruled her guests without appearing to rule them; she guided conversation instead of dominating it; she strove to please rather than to shine. In two words, she had tact and sympathy. Doubtless at the outset she had no idea beyond that of collecting her friends around her; but gradually it must have dawned upon her that here was an opportunity for organising polite society more thoroughly and with higher aims than had ever been before attempted.

One of these aims was refinement. In the days of Francis I, as we learn from the *Heptameron*, men allowed themselves in the presence of women the same licence of language which they used among themselves. The language of the drawing-room differed little, if at all, from that of the camp. It is true that some of the ladies in the charming and instructive conversations which form the epilogue to the stories of the *Heptameron* protest against this practice; but the practice continued till the days of Mme de Rambouillet. Montaigne's *Essays*, in which the language is sometimes of the frankest, were addressed as much to women as to men.

Refinement was not Mme de Rambouillet's only aim. She wished to raise the intellectual standard of society as well as the moral one. It was towards this end that the world of fashion and the world of letters met in her salon on a footing of perfect equality. Intellectual conversation was encouraged. Poems and other pieces were read by their authors before publication, and subjected to criticism. Malherbe, doubtless, expounded his theories, though with less asperity and dogmatism than in his own lodgings. Thus gradually the connexion between society and literature was strengthened. Society became literary and literature became social. The hôtel began to be recognised not only as a social tribunal, but as a court whose decisions carried weight also in literature.

This formation of a social ideal for the intercourse of men and women of the world was greatly assisted by a work which was published in the very year (1607) in which Mme de Rambouillet finally withdrew from the Court. This was the famous pastoral romance of *L'Astrée*, the influence and popularity of which were more widespread and of longer duration than those of any book of its kind. It was praised enthusiastically on its appearance by François de Sales, and by his friend and neighbour Pierre Camus, Bishop of Belley. Sixty years later the learned Bishop of Avranches, Pierre-Daniel Huet, spoke of it as "the most ingenious and most polished work of its kind that had ever appeared." About the same time La Fontaine declared that he used to read it as a boy, and that he still read it as a grey-bearded man. As late as 1734 the Abbé Lenglet-Dufresnoy said in his *Bibliothèque des romans* that it still retained its reputation, and the statement is borne out by the tributes of the Abbé Prevost and Jean-Jacques Rousseau.

The author of *L'Astrée*, Honoré d'Urfé, was a younger son of a distinguished family, which had held estates since the twelfth century in the district of Le Forez between the upper waters of the Allier and the Loire. He was a Leaguer, and, when Le Forez submitted to Henry IV, he retired to the Court of his relative the Duke of Savoy, and, taking up his residence at Annecy, devoted himself to literature. Among his earliest productions was a pastoral poem entitled *Sireine*, the plot of which is borrowed from the famous Spanish pastoral romance, Montemôr's *Diana*. The First Part of *L'Astrée* appeared, as we have seen, in 1607, with a dedication to Henry IV, who was the least likely man in the world to bear a grudge towards his former opponent. "Accept her, Sire, not as a simple shepherdess, but as the work of your hands, for truly you may be called its author. She is a child of peace, and it is to your Majesty that all Europe owes repose and tranquillity." We learn from Bassompierre's *Memoirs* that it was read to Henry on three nights in succession when he was suffering from an attack of the gout. The Second Part was published in 1610, and the Third, dedicated to Louis XIII, in 1619. When the author died in 1625, he left behind him the completed manuscript of the Fourth Part, and some notes for the Fifth and concluding Part. Accordingly in 1627 his friend and secretary, Balthazar Baro, published not only a fourth volume, but a fifth, which was of his own composition. Thus for twenty years the public patiently followed the fortunes of Celadon and Astrée, until at last the glamour of their long and romantic attachment faded into the light of common matrimony.

The sources of D'Urfé's inspiration are tolerably obvious. His model was, of course, Montemôr's *Diana*; but the immense length of his work, with its many subsidiary episodes (each part, containing twelve books, is rather more than half the length of *Middlemarch*), is suggestive of *Amadis*, to which it also owes the adventurous character of many of the episodes and the actual details of one or two. The numerous verses—sonnets, madrigals, and songs —which, after the manner of *Diana*, are interspersed throughout the narrative, show strongly the influence of Desportes, who, when he died in 1606, the year before the publication of *L'Astrée*, was still regarded as the chief French poet. There are also unmistakable traces of the two

Italian pastoral dramas, Tasso's *Aminta* and Guarini's *Il pastor fido*, which were no less popular in France than *Diana*.

In all this D'Urfé shows himself dominated by the literary influences which prevailed in his youth; it is in his subject, or rather in his treatment of it, that the novelty and originality of his work appear. For his subject, practically to the exclusion of every other topic, is love—love dissected and analysed in all its phases and aspects. The perfect lover is "Love's Phœnix," Celadon, in whose love for Astrée Petrarch's sonnets, Bembo's *Gli Asolani*, the whole literature on the topic of spiritual love which was so abundant in France between 1540 and 1550, the sonnet-sequences of Ronsard and Du Bellay and Desportes, all find their embodiment. Thus *L'Astrée*, with its refinement, its moral elevation, and especially its glorification of woman, made a strong appeal to Mme de Rambouillet and all those who under her influence were striving to refine the relations and intercourse between the two sexes. Since Malherbe had banished imagination from poetry, the human heart, from which it cannot be banished, welcomed all the more its appearance in a new form. In other and more particular directions too the romance left its impress upon the Hôtel de Rambouillet: in the spirit of psychological analysis and in the long conversations in which this is embodied, in the feeling for nature, and in the exaggerated sentiment and high-flown language with which the various lovers express themselves. It has been said that *L'Astrée* is a mirror of the Blue Chamber; it is a truer view that the Blue Chamber is a mirror of *L'Astrée*[1].

II

The twenty years from the death of Malherbe (1628) to the outbreak of the Fronde (1648) may be regarded as the most flourishing of the Hôtel de Rambouillet. At its opening Mme de Rambouillet was only forty, and still a

[1] For an appreciative account of *L'Astrée* see G. Saintsbury, *A History of the French Novel*, 2 vols., 1917–18, I. 167–175.

woman of considerable beauty. Among her contemporaries, besides the Princesse de Condé and Mme de Sablé, whose names have already been recorded, her most habitual visitors during this period were Mme Du Vigean, who was deaf but pretended not to be, Mme de Clermont d'Entragues, and Mme Aubry, the wife of a rich president of the Paris *parlement*. Before long their daughters were old enough to accompany them, and to form a new generation, of which the leader was Julie d'Angennes, Mme de Rambouillet's eldest daughter. Born, as we have seen, in 1607, she was now of an age to take a prominent part in the entertainment of her mother's guests. "Since Helen," says Tallemant des Réaux, "few women have been praised more generally for their beauty, and yet she was never beautiful." He admits, however, that she had a fine figure, and in her younger days, so he is told (when he first made her acquaintance she was thirty-six), a good complexion[1]. If she had not the equable temperament and noble character of her mother, she was clever, romantic, and of a high spirit. In the congenial task of organising the amusements of her friends she had a brilliant assistant in Angélique Paulet, daughter of Charles Paulet, the inventor of the tax known as *la Paulette*. Though *la belle Lionne*, as she was called from the ruddy gold of her hair, was no longer in her first youth, having been born in 1590 or 1591, her beauty and her wit, her singing and her dancing, had lost little or nothing of their attractions. Among the unmarried ladies, most of them considerably younger than Julie, were Henriette de Coligny, who, as Mme de La Suze, acquired some fame as a poetess, the two daughters of Mme de Clermont d'Entragues, and the two Mlles Du Vigean, Anne and Marthe, of whom the younger is celebrated as the object of Condé's devoted but unhappy passion.

---

[1] *Les Historiettes*, ed. Monmerqué, 10 vols., 1861. Vol. III. is mainly devoted to the frequenters of Mme de Rambouillet's salon, but notices of some of them will be found in other volumes. As pointed out above, Tallemant only knew the salon in its later days, but his information was good, though some allowance must be made for his love of scandal. "Il ne ment pas," says Sainte-Beuve, "mais il médit avec délices."

Three soldiers, all of more or less distinction, also belonged to Mme de Rambouillet's more intimate circle, and in their visits to Paris between two campaigns greatly contributed by their jests and good sayings to the gaiety of her salon. These were the Marquis (afterwards Duc) de Roquelaure; Arnauld de Corbeville, a first cousin of Arnauld d'Andilly, a Colonel of Carbineers and a brilliant improviser of burlesque verse, whom Mme de Rambouillet called her *poète carabin*; and the Comte de Guiche, brave, handsome, and debauched, who became a Marshal of France in 1641, and succeeded his father as Comte de Grammont three years later.

But the most brilliant stars among the younger guests during the years 1635–42 were Condé, then the Duc d'Enghien, and his sister, Geneviève de Bourbon, afterwards so celebrated as the Duchesse de Longueville. Condé, who had received a classical education at the Jesuit college at Bourges before he devoted himself to military studies, was a good judge of literature, and even dabbled in poetry; while his sister, indolent and frivolous, was of dazzling beauty and had a reputation for wit. Her name naturally suggests that of her lover, La Rochefoucauld, who, with Saint-Évremond, was another *habitué* of the salon.

Of the men of letters pure and simple who frequented the hôtel during its period of splendour the chief was Vincent Voiture. The son of a wine-merchant of Amiens, he was presented to Mme de Rambouillet by M. de Chaudebonne in 1625, being then in his twenty-seventh year, and before long, by his audacity, his invention, and his wit, he made himself indispensable to her guests. "If he was one of us," said Condé, "he would be insupportable." But though he had few virtues and most vices, and though his temper was somewhat fitful and his impertinence sometimes so outrageous that even his firm ally Julie was disgusted with it, he generally contrived to save the situation by his ready wit. He had considerable natural ability, but his ambitions lay in the direction of social rather than of literary success. He published nothing during his life-time[1], though the letters which he wrote from Spain and elsewhere to Mme Rambouillet, Mlle Paulet, and others, as well as those in which he informed absent members of the circle of its doings at Paris, were certainly destined for more eyes than those of the recipients. In any case, they throw an interesting light on the character and habits of the Rambouillet society. Apart from the care and excellence of their style, they display in a remarkable degree three characteristics of a successful letter-writer—the art of saying nothing as if it were something, the art of adapting oneself to the tastes of one's correspondent, and the art of paying egregious compliments without being offensive.

As a writer of *vers de société* he has perhaps been over-praised. It is only occasionally, as in the well-known *rondeau* on making a *rondeau*, or in the song to Sylvie, which in its graceful impertinence reminds one of his contemporary, Suckling, that his workmanship is skilful enough to atone for his lack of emotion and imagination, and his somewhat imperfect sense of harmony.

"There is a man here shorter than you by a cubit, and a thousand miles more gallant." So wrote Julie to Voiture during his absence in Spain in the service of Gaston d'Orléans. The little man in question was Antoine Godeau —*le nain de Julie*, as he came to be called—whose wit, gaiety, and natural gift for poetry might well have made Voiture tremble for his supremacy. But he took Orders, and so greatly impressed Richelieu by his sermons that within a year the Cardinal conferred on him the see of Grasse. He had dedicated to his patron a poetical para-phrase of the *Benedicite*, and it was said that the great man seasoned his gift with the words: *Vous m'avez offert Benedicite, je vous donne Grasse.* Contrary to expectation, the little man made an excellent bishop and resided with

---

[1] His works were first published in 1650; by 1663 there had been 15 editions, besides two of his *Nouvelles Œuvres*; before the end of the reign of Louis XIV there had been 38 altogether. Since then there have only been six complete editions.

praiseworthy regularity in his beautiful but remote Provençal diocese, where he kept up his intercourse with his friends by a frequent correspondence.

Other men of letters who were more or less regular visitors at the hôtel were Sarasin, whose reputation as a wit and a writer of occasional verse equalled Voiture's, but whose lack of discretion prevented his being a serious rival; the Abbé Cotin, a *précieux sans le savoir*, and Gilles Ménage, the Trissotin and Vadius of Molière's *Les Femmes Savantes*; Conrart, who set up for a man of fashion, and gave agreeable parties at his country villa; the modest, unassuming Vaugelas, with his Savoyard accent; and, above all, Chapelain, who belonged to the more intimate circle, and whose letters[1], especially for the years 1638 to 1640, are a precious source of information for the doings of Mme de Rambouillet and her friends. We shall meet these latter three again as members of the new Académie Française, to the success of which they all largely contributed. To a somewhat later period belong Georges de Scudéry and his more famous sister Madeleine (1637), and Tallemant des Réaux (about 1643), who became the chronicler of the hôtel. He tells us, indeed, that the greater part of the information contained in his *Historiettes* was supplied to him by Mme de Rambouillet; but, considering the character of some of it, we may regard this as an exaggeration. However, as far as concerns the hôtel itself, he is doubtless a fairly faithful historian.

Such were the men of letters who habitually made their bow in Mme de Rambouillet's salon, but among the more occasional visitors there were two even more illustrious. Corneille used to visit the hôtel on the somewhat rare occasions when he came to Paris to produce a new play, and late on one memorable evening Bossuet, then a lad of sixteen studying theology in the College of Navarre, was invited to give a specimen of his precocious talent for preaching. His sermon, which surpassed the expectation of his audience, but which did not end till near midnight,

[1] Ed. P. Tamizey de Larroque, 2 vols., 1880–83 (*Doc. inédits*).

provoked from Voiture the remark: "I never heard anyone preach so early or so late."

From Voiture, Tallemant, and Chapelain we get plenty of information as to the amusements of the Rambouillet circle. One of Voiture's best letters is the description of a supper-party which Mme Du Vigean gave in honour of the Princesse de Condé at La Barre, a little beyond Épinay, where she had a country house. They drove there from Paris, starting about six o'clock, the party consisting of Mme Du Vigean, Mme la Princesse and her daughter Mlle de Bourbon, Mlle de Rambouillet, Mlle Paulet, Mme Aubry, M. de Chaudebonne, and Voiture. We hear of a thick wood, into which the daylight penetrated for the first time with the "most beautiful princess in the world," a long avenue, at the end of which was a fountain, twenty-four violins, and a recess in which was discovered a youthful Diana of eleven or twelve, who bore a remarkable resemblance to Mlle de Bourbon. Then they danced, and Voiture sang a Spanish song, and everybody said that the only thing wanting to their happiness was the presence of Mme de Rambouillet and the Cardinal de La Valette (Voiture's correspondent). Then they sat down to an excellent supper, which was followed by more dancing and by fireworks. Finally they started on their return journey by the light of twenty torches, and reached Paris about three in the morning.

To dress up girls as goddesses or nymphs and arrange them on rocks or other points of vantage in the middle of a beautiful landscape was a favourite amusement with Mme de Rambouillet and her friends, and was doubtless a tribute to their admiration for *L'Astrée*. Tallemant tells us how Mme de Rambouillet delighted the Bishop of Lisieux with a surprise of this kind at her country seat of Rambouillet, and he says that "one of her greatest pleasures was to surprise people." She also liked to be surprised by her friends, and in the *Memoirs* of Antoine Arnauld, the eldest son of Arnauld d'Andilly, there is a charming account of how, during the siege of Corbie (1636), he and one of his

uncles, and his cousin, Arnauld de Corbeville, who were all
serving in the Carbineers, paid a surprise visit to Rambouillet, and found there Mme de Clermont d'Entragues
and her daughters; and how they acted Mairet's tragedy
of *Sophonisbe*; and how, the time for learning their parts
being so short, some of these, including that of the heroine,
were shared by two performers, and how Mlle Paulet sang
to her theorbo; and how, nearly all being actors, there
were no spectators except M. and Mme de Rambouillet,
Mme de Clermont, one of the Arnaulds, and M. de Pisani.
Sometimes these surprises took a more alarming shape.
For instance, one day Voiture, seeing two bears with their
keepers in the street, silently introduced them into the room
where Mme de Rambouillet was reading, with her back to
a screen. All of a sudden she heard a noise, and turning
round, saw the two bears peering over the screen. In these
practical jokes and other forms of horse-play, which
throughout the seventeenth century commended themselves to the taste of the most civilised society in Europe,
Voiture found a willing ally in the Marquis de Pisani, Mme
de Rambouillet's son, a young man of lively wit and high
courage, who, hunchback though he was, served under
Condé in all his campaigns, till he met a soldier's death at
the battle of Nördlingen (1645).

Admiration for military virtues ran high in the Hôtel
de Rambouillet. Julie had a special cult for Gustavus
Adolphus, who, in January, 1631, signed a treaty with
France, and in the following September avenged the sack
of Magdeburg by the great victory of Breitenfeld. Soon
afterwards Voiture dressed up some lackeys in a Swedish
costume and despatched them with a letter to Julie, in
which the Lion of the North professed to lay his laurels at
her feet, and signed himself her *très passionné serviteur*.
In February, 1635, Louis XIII took the field against Spain,
and the Rambouillet circle followed the fortunes of the
French troops with the most lively interest. The recapture
of Corbie, which commanded the Somme, from the
Spaniards in 1636 prompted Voiture to send to a friend a

long appreciation of Richelieu's foreign policy, in which
for once he lays aside his ordinary frivolous tone and
writes like a man of sound judgment and enlightened
patriotism.

If Voiture represents the lighter and more frivolous side
of the hôtel, Jean Guez de Balzac, whose name is frequently
associated with his, exercised a decided influence on its more
serious occupations. Yet this influence was exercised from
a distance, for he hardly ever set foot in the famous Blue
Chamber. From 1631 he lived in retirement, either at his
château of Balzac, four miles from Angoulême, or at
Angoulême itself, a hypochondriacal and disappointed
man. For, though since the publication of the first instalment of his letters in 1624 he had enjoyed a great reputation,
which he nursed with elaborate care, he looked for a more
substantial recognition of his merits—a red hat, a bishopric,
or at least an abbey. However, he continued to write his
elaborate letters, numbering among his correspondents all
the learned men in France. Chapelain and Conrart were
his chief correspondents in the Rambouillet circle, but his
letters were read to the whole circle, and their publication,
when collected in a volume, as they were from time to
time, was hailed as a great literary event. The first four of
his *Dissertations politiques* (his dissertations only differ
from his letters in their greater length), three of which are
on the subject of the Romans, are addressed to Mme de
Rambouillet, whom he had once compared to the mother
of the Gracchi. One of his most admired productions was
a letter of consolation which he wrote to the Cardinal de La
Valette, who was in command in Piedmont when the
Piedmontese rose against the French. It was, as usual,
read aloud in the Blue Chamber, and some of the chief
habitués being absent, the reading was repeated a few days
later. On the first occasion the audience objected to the
word *besogne* as a synonym for *travail* or *ouvrage*. They
agreed that it was "low." The criticism is significant, for
it shows that already, to use Victor Hugo's expressive
phrase, "words were being penned up into castes," the

plebeian ones to be "marked with an F (*familier*) by Vaugelas in the Dictionary."

Pronunciation was also a favourite subject of discussion. Were you to say *Roume* or *Rome*, *houme* or *homme*, *sarge* or *serge*? "The great Arthénice," we are told, was in favour of *sarge*, and she was at first supported by Vaugelas; but yielding to the opinion of his three principal advisers, Conrart, Chapelain, and Patru, he declared in his *Remarques* for *serge*. In another "remark" he gives his approval to the word *débrutaliser*, which Mme de Rambouillet had invented, but which has never passed into currency. Even Voiture took an interest in questions of grammar and correct expression, and in a letter to his friend Costar gives his opinion on various points about which the latter had consulted him. *Courre*, he says, is more usual than *courir*, and more fashionable (*plus de la Cour*); but *courir* is not bad, and is a useful rhyme for *mourir* and *recourir*. Some say *chaire* without being laughed at, but *chaise* is better. *Deformité* has been dead for ten or twelve years; the right word is *difformité*. One of his best-known letters is a witty defence of the conjunction *car*, about which a regular battle was raging. The chief opponent of this harmless monosyllable was Marin Le Roy, Sieur de Gomberville, who has a somewhat more enduring title to fame as the author of *Polexandre*.

The *Astrée* had been followed by a long succession of romances; but *Polexandre* (1629–37) was the first which can be said to have rivalled its popularity in any degree with the Rambouillet circle. In Gomberville's hands the pastoral romance was transformed into the heroic romance, with prodigious adventures, which take place in every quarter of the globe and are woven together in an inextricable plot. An even greater popularity was enjoyed by the romances of Gautier de Coste, Seigneur de La Calprenède, a gentleman of Périgord. He wrote three in all—*Cassandre*, *Cléopâtre*, and *Faramond*—but only the first (1642–45) belongs to the period that we are now considering. It represents the high-water mark of the heroic novel from the artistic point of view. Rivalling *Polexandre* in multiplicity of adventurous incident, it differs from it in having a definite historical background. Its whole tone reflects the warlike period upon which France had entered under Richelieu.

The same glorification of the heroic spirit is shown in Corneille's plays; Don Rodrigue is the hero as lover, Horace the hero as patriot, Auguste the hero as monarch, Polyeucte the hero as martyr. Thus, as might have been expected, the *Cid* and its successors were greeted with enthusiasm in Mme de Rambouillet's salon. But *Polyeucte*, which Corneille read there in 1642, the year of the publication of the first part of *Cassandre*, found less favour. It was listened to with outward signs of approbation, but Voiture was charged with the delicate task of explaining to the author the real sentiments of the hôtel. The choice of a Christian subject had displeased his critics; it had offended the piety of some and the worldliness of others, while many disapproved of it as a departure from the classical tradition. Possibly, too, in the eyes of these sentimentalists the love-making seemed cold. Corneille, however, defended his choice, and produced his play at the Hôtel de Bourgogne in the winter of 1642–43.

On May 19, 1643, the young Duc d'Enghien, to the surprise of Europe, annihilated the hitherto invincible Spanish pikemen at Rocroi, and made France the first military power in Europe. It may be imagined what rejoicing there was in the Hôtel de Rambouillet, and what a letter of flattery Voiture addressed to the hero. Before the end of the year Turenne, who had just been appointed a Marshal of France, joined Enghien on the Rhine, and the following year saw the whole left bank of that river from Breisach to Coblentz in French hands. In 1645 Enghien and Turenne defeated the Bavarians at Nördlingen. The appearance of a French translation of Gracián's *El Héroe* in this year must have seemed singularly opportune.

III

In July, 1645, an event took place which largely contributed to the decline of the famous salon. This was the
marriage of Julie to Charles de Sainte-Maure, who by the
death of his elder brother in 1638 had become Baron de
Montausier and had since been created a Marquis. He had
fallen in love with Julie at first sight in 1635, but it was
not till four years later, when, after distinguishing himself
in the war, he was made governor of the newly acquired
province of Alsace, that he openly declared himself as a
suitor for her hand. He was a man of considerable literary
culture, a buyer and a reader of books. He was greatly
attached to Chapelain, with whom he corresponded regularly, and he hated Voiture, of whom he was perhaps
jealous. For the next three years he carried on his suit
and his military duties with equal tenacity. It was probably on January 1, 1642, though the date is not quite
certain, that he presented to his mistress the famous
Guirlande de Julie, which figures in every account of the
Hôtel de Rambouillet, and which Tallemant describes as
"one of the most illustrious compliments that was ever
paid by a lover." It consisted of twenty-nine flowers
painted on vellum, with eighty-six madrigals, two sonnets,
and two epigrams, beautifully written by the calli-
grapher, Nicolas Jarry, round the flowers. The manuscript
was bound in Levant morocco, ornamented with Julie's
monogram. Among the poets who contributed to the
madrigals were Chapelain, Godeau, and Desmarests.
Montausier himself wrote sixteen. Voiture alone refused
his help, and was probably delighted that Julie remained
obdurate. Towards the close of 1643 Montausier was made
a prisoner on the field of Düttlingen, and after a captivity
of ten months returned to Paris a hero. Having abjured
Protestantism and been rewarded by the devout Anne of
Austria with a marquisate, he besieged Julie with re-
doubled energy. Mlle Paulet, Mme de Sablé, and the
Duchesse d'Aiguillon, all urged her to relent. Even the

Queen Regent, even Mazarin, let fall a word in Montausier's favour. But Julie, though she liked his admiration, was not really in love with him, and she preferred her position as the "princess" of the Hôtel de Rambouillet to that of the wife of the governor of a province. At last, when her mother reproached her with her hardness, she gave way. The marriage took place on July 15, 1645, when the bride was nearing her fortieth year, the ceremony being performed by her faithful "dwarf," the Bishop of Grasse.

The marriage left a great blank in Mme de Rambouillet's salon, for Julie had to accompany her husband to Saintonge, of which he was now governor. Less than three weeks after the marriage Mme de Rambouillet's only remaining son, the Marquis de Pisani, was killed, as we have seen, at Nördlingen. In the following year (1646) she lost her old friend, Philippe de Cospéan, Bishop of Lisieux. Voiture too, who, though she herself had no great liking for him, had largely contributed to the success of her salon, was now growing infirm with gout, and more and more uncertain in temper. He died in 1648. On January 6 of the following year Civil War began. For the next four years, save for the ten months which intervened between the War of the First Fronde and that of the Second, Paris was in a state of tumult, and there was little leisure or opportunity for the amenities of social intercourse. When peace and order were restored to the capital in October, 1652, the gaps in Mme de Rambouillet's circle had been increased by the deaths of her husband and her old friend, Angélique Paulet. Mme de Rambouillet herself was now well over sixty, and for the last thirty years had been delicate. Though she still continued to welcome her intimate friends, her Blue Chamber was no longer a centre of fashion and literature. She had done her work, and she had done it well.

In the first place, she had helped to achieve for women an influence in French society which they were never again to lose. And, so far as she was concerned, this influence was exercised in the direction of decency in language and delicacy in thought. Further, her idea of bringing together nobles and *roturiers*, men of fashion who wished to be cultivated and men of cultivation who wished to be fashionable, had the effect of making her salon a sort of tribunal for literature as well as for society. The refinement which was exacted in conversation and social intercourse began to impress itself also upon literature. Grossness was banished, at any rate from the higher kinds of literature.

But this process of refinement was only part of a general organisation of society. Under the humanising influence of the Hôtel de Rambouillet, a social code, unwritten but enforced by the strongest of sanctions, was gradually evolved. Its individual laws were called *les bienséances*, and the whole code *la bienséance*. It is "the least of all laws," says La Rochefoucauld, who, as we have seen, had served his apprenticeship in the Blue Chamber, "and the best obeyed." The man who conformed to this code was the *honnête homme* of whom we hear so much in the literature of the seventeenth century. In fact, La Roche-foucauld, in his reflections on society, premises that he will confine his remarks to the *commerce des honnêtes gens*. And it is from these remarks that we get, perhaps, the best idea of the nature of this social code to which the *honnête homme* had to conform. It was not merely a collection of rules which concerned outward behaviour only, and which could be observed mechanically. The *honnête homme* had, in the first place, "to find his pleasure in that of others, to treat with consideration their self-love, and never to wound it." "The intercourse of *honnêtes gens* cannot subsist without a certain amount of mutual confidence." "You must anticipate the pleasures of your friends, seek out ways of being useful to them, spare them heart aches, and, when these cannot be averted, show them sympathy." In expressing these views La Rochefoucauld was largely influenced by the Chevalier de Méré, who while La Rochefoucauld was writing his *Maximes* (1659–64) was regarded as the *arbiter elegantiae* of Paris society, and whom he must have frequently met in the salon of their common friend Mme de Sablé. Méré having, like La Rochefoucauld, little other religion, made a religion of *honnêteté*, which required for its practice a *cœur juste* and an *esprit bien fait*[1].

A special feature of the meetings in the Blue Chamber was the care with which conversation was cultivated. Here again La Rochefoucauld may be cited as an authority, and here again we find him insisting that the secret of excellence in this art, as in the other arts of society, is the spirit of consideration for others, the readiness to listen as well as to talk[2]. The conversation often took the form of a discussion on some special question, whether of literature, or politics, or religion; or they discussed some problem of psychological lore, after the pattern of the conversations which abound in *L'Astrée* and *Le Grand Cyrus*. The essential thing was that the question should be treated with *esprit* and distinction. It was Voiture's recognised pre-eminence in the kingdom of *esprit* that earned for him the name of *El rey chiquito* (the little king), but he had rivals who pressed him hard in Mme de Sablé and Mme Aubry, in Mlle Paulet and Julie, in Godeau and Arnauld de Corbeville.

Such was the nature of the work for which France is indebted to Mme de Rambouillet. Her example was followed by other ladies, such as the Princesse de Condé, Mme de Rohan (a daughter of Sully), the Duchesse d'Aiguillon, and especially Mme de Sablé, whose receptions began at least as early as 1644 and were continued after 1652 in her house in the Place Royale, where she went to live with her friend Mme de Maure. Another aristocratic salon which attained to distinction after the Fronde was that of Mme Du Plessis-Guénégaud, whose hôtel was on the site of the present Hôtel de la Monnaie. It was here that the sixth and seventh of the *Lettres Provinciales* were read for the first time.

---

[1] For Méré (1604–84) see Sainte-Beuve, *Portraits littéraires*, III. 85 ff.; F. Strowski in *Pascal et son temps*, 2me *partie*, 1907, pp. 248–267; and E. Chamaillard, *Le Chevalier de Méré*, Niort, 1921. Méré wrote three treatises, not published till 1676–77, entitled *Les Agréments, De l'Esprit*, and *De la Conversation*.

[2] Je suis convaincu que du temps où l'hôtel de Rambouillet donnait le ton à la bonne compagnie, l'on écoutait bien et l'on raisonnait mieux (D'Argenson, *Mémoires*).

But down to the outbreak of the Fronde the Blue Chamber had no serious rival within its special sphere. Yet when the civil disturbances closed its doors, there were already signs that its best work had been done. For everything human carries within it the seeds of its own decay, and the Hôtel de Rambouillet did not escape the common lot. The very cohesion and solidarity which make a select *coterie* so powerful for the propagation of new ideas render it peculiarly sensitive to the insidious attacks of affectation and other forms of bad taste. The germs of that *préciosité* which disfigured French literature during the years from 1650 to 1660 are to be found, beyond a doubt, in Mme de Rambouillet's salon, but how far they had developed into actual disease is a question which will be discussed more conveniently in a later chapter.

CHAPTER VI

THE ACADÉMIE FRANÇAISE

WE saw in the last chapter how a private individual's reception of her friends led to the formation of a distinguished circle, the opinions of which carried great weight, not only in social, but also in literary matters. We shall now see how another group of friends, meeting like the former in a private house, was developed by the pressure of external agency into a public institution, charged primarily with the care of the French language, but exercising a certain influence over the whole domain of literature.

The origin of the Académie Française has been related with such simple charm by one of its early members, Paul Pellisson, that I cannot do better than give it in his own words[1]: "About the year 1629 some private individuals who lived in different quarters of Paris, finding it highly inconvenient in that great town to pay frequent and fruitless visits to one another, determined to meet on one day of the week at the house of one of their number. They were all men of letters, and of a merit much above the ordinary: M. Godeau, now Bishop of Grasse, who was not yet in Orders; M. de Gombauld; M. Chapelain; M. Conrart; M. Giry; the late M. Habert, Commissary of the Artillery; his brother the Abbé de Cerisy; M. de Serizay; and M. de Malleville. They met at the house of M. Conrart, which was the most convenient for their reception, and was in the heart of the town, all the others living at almost equal distances from it. There they conversed familiarly, just as they would have done on an ordinary visit, about all sorts of things—public affairs, the latest news, literature. And

---

[1] *Relation contenant l'Histoire de l'Académie Française,* Paris, 1653. Edited, with Olivet's continuation, by Ch. Livet, 2 vols., 1858.

if any one of the company had written a book, as often happened, he showed it willingly to all the others, and they freely gave their opinions on it. Their discussions were followed, sometimes by a walk, sometimes by a meal, of which they partook in common. They went on in this way for three or four years, and, as I have heard several of them say, it was with extreme pleasure and incredible profit. So that when they talk even to-day of that first age of the Academy, they speak of it as of an age of gold, during which, with all the innocence and all the liberty of the early centuries, without publicity, and without pomp, and without any laws but those of friendship, they tasted together all the sweets and charms of mental intercourse and the life of reason.''

But this golden age was not to continue. The obligation to secrecy which they had at first maintained was broken by M. de Malleville, who spoke of the meetings to M. Faret, who had recently published his *L'Honnête Homme, ou L'Art de plaire à la Cour* (1630), a characteristic work of the age, which became very popular, and was translated into Spanish, Italian, and English. Having obtained permission to be present at one of the meetings, he, in his turn, imparted the secret to Desmarests de Saint-Sorlin and the Abbé de Boisrobert, Richelieu's factotum and jester. Desmarests came to several meetings, and read the first volume of his novel *Ariane*. Boisrobert also obtained permission to be present, ''and when,'' says Pellisson, ''he had seen the way in which the works were examined, and that it was not an interchange of compliments and flatteries, in which each bestows praises in order to receive them, but that they boldly and frankly pointed out every fault, even to the least, he was filled with joy and admiration. He was at that time at the height of his favour with Cardinal Richelieu, and his chief care was to refresh the mind of his master after the stress of public business, sometimes by those agreeable stories which he told better than anybody, sometimes by relating to him all the news of the Court and the town; and this diversion was of such service to the

Cardinal that his first physician, M. Citoys, was wont to say to him: 'Monseigneur, we will do all we can for your health, but all our drugs are useless, unless you mix with them a little Boisrobert.' In the course of these familiar conversations M. Boisrobert, who told the Cardinal everything, did not fail to give him a favourable account of the little assembly which he had seen, and of the persons who composed it; and the Cardinal, whose mind was naturally turned to great things, and who loved beyond everything the French language, which he wrote extremely well, after having praised their intentions, asked M. de Boisrobert if these gentlemen would not be willing to become an incorporated body, and meet regularly, and under public authority. M. de Boisrobert having answered that in his opinion this proposition would be received with joy, he commanded him to make it, and to offer to these gentlemen his protection for their body corporate (which he would have established by Letters Patent), and for each individually the proof of his affection in all circumstances."

This offer was received by the friends with considerable perturbation, and two of their number—Serizay and Malleville—who were respectively attached to the household of the Duc de La Rochefoucauld and the Maréchal de Bassompierre, both enemies of the Cardinal—were of opinion that they should excuse themselves to him as best they could. But Chapelain pointed out that, though they would have gladly continued their meetings without any publicity, yet as things had turned out they had no choice but to accept the Cardinal's offer. This view prevailed, and it was agreed "that M. de Boisrobert should be asked to thank the Cardinal very humbly for the honour that he did them, and to assure him that, though they had never looked so high, and were much surprised by the intentions of His Eminence, they were all resolved to comply with his wishes."

The first step towards the formation of the Academy was the enlargement of their body. Accordingly they at once added eighteen new members, including Faret, Desmarests, and Boisrobert, which, with eight of the original

nine (for one, Giry, had withdrawn), brought the number
up to twenty-six. They then determined to appoint three
officers—a Director and a Chancellor, who should change
from time to time, and a permanent Secretary. The first
Director was Serizay, and the first Chancellor Desmarests,
both chosen by ballot, while Conrart was unanimously
elected to the office of Secretary. Thus equipped, they held
their first regular meeting on March 13, 1634, at Desmarests's hôtel in the Rue Clocheperce, as Conrart's recent
marriage had, says our historian, rendered his house less
convenient than formerly for their meetings. At their
second meeting (March 20) they adopted the name of
Académie Française. Meanwhile they had been working
at the statutes. These were completed by the end of the
year, and submitted, with a draft of the proposed Letters
Patent, to the Cardinal. In February, 1635, he gave his
approval to them; in the previous January Séguier, the
Keeper of the Seals, had affixed the Royal Seal to the
Letters Patent. It was a work of much greater difficulty
to procure their registration by the *Parlement* of Paris,
always inclined to regard Richelieu's proposals with suspicion, and, in spite of the Cardinal's personal intervention,
it was not till July 10, 1637, that the long-delayed registration conferred on the new Academy a complete legal status.
Meanwhile, before the end of the year 1634 nine new
members had been elected, making the total thirty-five.
Three more were added in 1635, including the Chancellor
Séguier, who had expressed a wish to be elected, and one
more, Giry, in 1636. In the course of the three following
years four members died, and it was not till February,
1639, that the number of forty was completed.

Of these earliest Academicians—for so they determined
to style themselves—several have already been mentioned
in these pages—Racan and Maynard as disciples of Malherbe, and Gombauld, Godeau, Chapelain, Saint-Amant,
Balzac, Voiture, and Vaugelas in connexion with the Hôtel
de Rambouillet. Desmarests and Boisrobert will find a
place in the chapter on Comedy. Desmarests, like Bois-

robert, was a protégé of the Cardinal's, and was one of
"the five authors" whom he employed to write his plays.
Among the five were also two other members, Guillaume
Colletet and Claude de L'Estoile; the former a bad poet,
but with some claim to the regard of posterity as the author
of the well-known Lives of the poets; the latter a son of the
diarist Pierre de L'Estoile, who wrote little himself but
had the reputation of being a severe critic of others.
Another member who was a protégé of the Cardinal's was
Jean Sirmond (a nephew of the learned Jesuit, Jacques
Sirmond), who wrote pamphlets for him and whose style
he highly commended. François de La Mothe Le Vayer,
who is now chiefly known as a sceptic philosopher, was a
voluminous writer on manifold subjects, and had published
three works before his election in 1639. On the other hand,
Conrart, Serizay, Bautru, and Bourzeys had published
nothing. Finally, Abel Servien, a distinguished diplomatist
and one of the Secretaries of State, and Séguier, the
Chancellor, formed a link between the men of letters and
the political world. Of the members elected between 1639
and 1660 the best-known are Olivier Patru (1640), a lawyer,
who sustained his reputation as the French Quintilian by
writing speeches, which were equally celebrated for the
purity of their style and the failure of their advocacy;
Pierre Du Ryer, the dramatist (1646); Corneille (1647);
Tristan L'Hermite (1649); Georges de Scudéry (1649);
Pellisson (1653); and the Abbé Cotin (1655).

Four members of the Academy demand a special notice
here—Pellisson, its historian, Conrart, its first Secretary,
Chapelain, and Vaugelas. Paul Pellisson was in his twenty-
ninth year when he published, in 1653, his *Histoire de
l'Académie Française*, written from the official records
which his friend Conrart had placed at his disposal. It was
so well received by the members that they conferred on
him the unique privilege of being present at their meetings,
and promised him the first vacancy which should occur.
There was one before the end of the year. In the same year
he began to attend the Saturdays of Mlle de Scudéry, and

a romantic friendship sprang up between him and his hostess, which was maintained on both sides with unshaken fidelity. The lady was extremely plain; while of poor Pellisson, who was pitted with small-pox, it was said that he abused a man's privilege of being ugly. In 1657 he became first clerk to Fouquet, and having been arrested with him in 1661, spent five years in the Bastille. There he wrote, and found means to circulate, an elaborate defence of his master, which, while it does honour to his fidelity, lacks the charming simplicity of his *History of the Academy*. After his release from prison, while his old master still languished in the fortress of Pinerolo, he entered the service of Louis XIV, became a courtier, abjured Protestantism, and, having taken Orders, was rewarded with rich benefices. His successor in the Academy, Fénelon, rightly pronounced that his chief title to fame was his history of the society to which he had belonged for forty years.

Valentin Conrart was, like his friend Pellisson, born a Protestant, and, unlike Pellisson, remained one all his life. A man of some wealth, he had a fine library, which was remarkable for not having a single Greek or Latin book in it. Indeed, he knew neither Greek nor Latin; but, on the other hand, he was a master of Italian and Spanish. His social virtues, his talent for friendship, his knowledge of the world, and his conciliatory manners, made him an ideal secretary for a body which in becoming a learned society did not cease to be a club. One duty, however, of a secretary he seems to have performed indifferently well. On his death in 1675 it was discovered that no record of the Academy's proceedings had been preserved for the years previous to 1672. As we know that Pellisson used the minutes down to 1652 for the purposes of his history, we must conclude that Conrart kept them in a desultory fashion, and finally lost them. He was, after all, not quite the ideal secretary.

If the new Academy owed much to the tact and courtesy of Conrart, it owed even more to the zeal and energy of his friend, Jean Chapelain. The son of a notary, who numbered among his clients the family of M. de Rambouillet, he was educated by his mother's desire for the profession of letters, and acquired a thorough knowledge of Latin, Italian, and Spanish, with a certain amount of Greek. In 1623, when he was twenty-eight, though he had published nothing, he was held in sufficient repute as a literary critic to be asked by Marini to write a preface to his poem of *Adone*, which, as we have seen, was published at Paris. This added to his reputation, and about the year 1627 he was introduced to the Hôtel de Rambouillet, and acquired the confidence and esteem of most of its *habitués*. An ode to Cardinal Richelieu (1633) made his fame as a poet, while the *Sentiments de l'Académie sur le Cid* (1637), which was in the main his work, established his authority as a critic. In 1656 he published the first twelve cantos of an epic poem, *La Pucelle*, upon which he had been engaged for nearly thirty years. The fragment was received with enthusiasm, and went through four French editions and two Dutch ones in eighteen months. But then the ardour of the public began to cool, and Chapelain's friend, Mme de Longueville, expressed the general opinion when she said: "Cela est parfaitement beau, mais cela est bien ennuyeux." In 1663 Chapelain's name stands at the head of a pension list as "le plus grand poète français qui ait jamais été et du plus solide jugement." But in the following year a serious attack was made on his poetic renown. The assailant was Boileau, then a young and unknown writer, whose intolerance of poetical mediocrity was stimulated by a private grievance. But, though it came to be recognised that *La Pucelle* was a ridiculous poem, nothing availed to shake the author's position as "the head of the French Parnassus," and as Colbert's trusted adviser in the delicate task of distributing pensions to men of letters.

Partly owing to this position, Chapelain carried on an immense correspondence, not only with his own countrymen, especially with Balzac, Conrart, and Godeau, but with learned men of other countries. This correspondence, extending from 1632 to 1673 (the year before his death), but with a regrettable gap from 1640 to 1659, has come down to us, and is, as we have already seen in the preceding chapter, of great importance for the literary history of the period.

Of Chapelain's character we have two very different estimates in the flattering portrait by Mlle de Scudéry and in the malicious sketch from the pen of Tallemant. The truth seems to be that he was at bottom an honest and upright man, loyal and helpful to his friends, but that he had in a marked degree a defect which La Fontaine declares to be characteristic of his countrymen—that of *la sotte vanité*. In Chapelain's case it took the form of literary vanity—in dress he was a sloven—and as he lacked the support of Balzac's perfect self-confidence, being at heart a modest man, it led him into ways hardly consistent with his reputation for probity. He complimented other authors on their works in the generous terms of a complimentary age, and he expected to be paid back in his own coin. He nursed his reputation as a mother nurses her firstborn, and, if anyone lifted so much as a finger against it, he pursued him with rancorous enmity.

At the second meeting of the Academy (March 20, 1634), when its functions and occupations were under discussion, Chapelain gave it as his opinion that it ought "to labour for the purity of the language, and make it more capable of the highest eloquence," and that for that purpose it should compose a Dictionary and a Grammar, followed by treatises on Rhetoric and Poetry, "to furnish rules for those who wished to write prose or verse." But during the rest of the year the Academicians were busy in drawing up statutes, and, after these were definitely settled and approved, they could find nothing better to do than to listen to a weekly discourse from one of their number. This lasted for about a year, "when," says our historian, "the majority began to grow weary of a practice which, after all, resembled somewhat the declamations of their youth; besides, the Cardinal let it be known that he expected something more solid from them." So they began to talk about the

Dictionary and the Grammar, when "Fortune raised up for them another piece of work, which they had not expected." This was the famous inquiry into the merits of the *Cid*.

The great success of that play had aroused a considerable amount of jealousy among some of Corneille's rivals, and the haughty tone of his *Excuse à Ariste*, with its

Je ne dois qu'à moi seul toute ma renommée,

in which he replied to their covert manœuvres, gave the signal for a more open attack. The first onslaught was made by Georges de Scudéry with his *Observations sur le Cid*. Though published anonymously, it betrayed the writer by its style, and Corneille replied with a *Lettre Apologétique*, in which he showed that his prose was hardly less admirable than his verse. Then Scudéry appealed to the new Academy, and the Cardinal, who had probably encouraged him from the first, expressed a wish that the Academy should pronounce judgment between the disputants. This the more judicious members were unwilling to do, and various objections were raised. But the Cardinal insisted, and his factotum Boisrobert persuaded Corneille with some difficulty to write a letter, in which he said that he would accept the jurisdiction of the Academy, "if it would amuse His Eminence." Accordingly, on June 16, 1637, three Commissioners were appointed to examine the *Cid* and the *Observations sur le Cid*. Only one, however, seems to have sent in a report. This was Chapelain, whose draft, after being submitted to Richelieu and carefully considered by the Academy, was published in December, 1637, as *Les Sentiments de l'Académie française sur la Tragicomédie du Cid*. In its final form it was still in the main Chapelain's work, and, as I have said, established his authority as a critic.

It is as a critic that Chapelain holds a definite place in the history of French literature. He not only forms a link between Malherbe and Boileau, but his reign almost exactly fills the gap between the death of Malherbe (1628) and the publication of Boileau's *Art Poétique* (1674). It is true that down to 1654 he had a masterful, though friendly, colleague in Balzac, but Balzac's authority did not extend beyond the domain of prose. In poetry and the drama Chapelain reigned supreme.

We have seen that Malherbe introduced the critical spirit into French literature, but that, except for his curt annotations to Desportes's poems and a few critical dicta handed down by his disciples, he produced no actual criticism. Moreover, such principles as can be adduced from his isolated remarks are those of a grammarian, or, at most, of a rhetorician. Chapelain took a wider view of criticism than his predecessor, and far surpassed him in his knowledge of the literatures of other countries. He had thoroughly studied Latin, Spanish, and Italian, and his studies doubtless included the numerous Italian writers of poetics who flourished in the sixteenth century. Greek literature he seems to have known chiefly at second-hand. Certainly his references to Aristotle's *Poetics* show that he had not read that work in the original. To form a complete estimate of his critical powers we ought to include his preface to the unfortunate *Pucelle* and the scattered critical remarks in his letters. But his chief contribution to criticism is the *Sentiments sur le Cid*, and from this we may get a fair measure not only of his own powers, but of the literary doctrines which prevailed in France during the thirty years which preceded the advent of Boileau. La Bruyère, writing just half a century later, speaks of it as one of the best pieces of criticism that had ever been written on any subject. It is certainly not that, for, while it is moderate in tone and sensible in substance, it shows little or no feeling for the charm and beauty of the *Cid*; and, above all, it does not betray the faintest consciousness that, whatever were the *Cid's* defects, it was not only far superior to any drama which had appeared before in France, but marked a new departure in dramatic art. Perhaps, however, this is more than we have a right to expect from contemporary criticism.

The *Sentiments* takes the form of an examination of Scudéry's criticisms, and deals for the most part with special points in the play. These do not concern us here; our business at present is rather with the broad principles which Chapelain from time to time enunciates. At the outset he justifies the action of the Academy by declaring that a popular success is no proof of the merit of a work of art, unless it is confirmed by the approbation of "the experts, who are the true judges." This is an important truth, and one upon which the very existence of criticism may be said to rest. At first it seems to leave open the question who the "experts" are. Are they those who practise the same art, or are they the critics? But presently the use of the term "the learned" as equivalent to "the experts" makes this point clear. It is not Scudéry or Mairet who are "the true judges" of the *Cid*, but Chapelain. And it is in Chapelain's favour that his judgment is not a mere expression of his personal impressions and sentiments. He gives solid reasons for all his decisions. His view that the dramatic writer when dealing with a historical subject should prefer probability to truth, *le vraisemblable* to *le vrai*, shows that he, to some extent, understood the difference between artistic and scientific truth. His great error was that he treated principles as hard-and-fast rules. A work, he held, could not be good if it offended against the rules. The question was not whether the *Cid* had given pleasure, but whether it ought to have given pleasure—that is to say, whether it conformed to the rules. But his faith in the rules went even further than this. He believed that a knowledge of them sufficed for the production of a poem. He says, in the preface to his *Pucelle*, that it was an attempt to see whether his knowledge of the theory of epic poetry, "without any great elevation of mind," would not help him to produce a successful specimen of it. Other writers since Chapelain have had the same illusion, but no one has ever given such naïve expression to it.

Yet, for all Boileau's contempt, he is, as I have said, a link in the chain between Malherbe and Boileau. When he speaks of a certain rule as "based on the authority of Aristotle or, *better still, on that of reason,*" he is anticipating Boileau's *Aimez donc la raison.* When he reproaches Corneille with sinning against the laws of Nature by crowding the action of the *Cid* into twenty-four hours, we are reminded of Boileau's

> Que la nature donc soit votre étude unique,
> Auteurs qui prétendez aux honneurs du comique.

Thus Chapelain, by his support of the Dictionary, by his general ideas on criticism, and, as we shall see in the next chapter, by his championship of the unities, contributed largely to the formation of the classical ideal.

The publication of the *Sentiments sur le Cid* left the Academy free to take up the long-delayed project of the Dictionary. It was decided that Chapelain and Vaugelas, who had offered to the Academy his "admirable and curious observations on the language," should each draw up a plan for the conduct of the work. Vaugelas's was very short, but Chapelain entered into considerable detail. The Dictionary was to be "the treasury and storehouse of simple terms and accepted phrases." It was to be based on citations from dead authors, a list of which, both for verse and prose, was afterwards drawn up and approved by the Academy. The earliest poet on the list is Marot and the earliest prose-writer Amyot. One notices, but one can hardly be surprised at, the omission of Rabelais. Chapelain also proposed, among other things, that there should be marks to denote the words appropriate to poetry or prose, and that the words suited to the grand (*sublime*), medium, and low styles should be similarly distinguished. Chapelain's plan was adopted in February, 1638, but the worthy Academicians soon became alarmed at the labour which the examination of so many authors seemed to entail, and the historical basis was abandoned in favour of a simple register of words and phrases in common use. Even with this modified plan it was not till a year later, when Vaugelas was appointed by Richelieu to superintend the

work at an annual stipend of 2000 livres, that a beginning
was made.

It is remarkable that this man, whose enthusiasm for
the French language and long study of it made him the
fittest person for the post, was not a Frenchman by birth.
Claude Favre, Seigneur de Vaugelas, was a native of Savoy,
the son of Jean Favre, first President of the Savoyard
Senate, a man of high character and considerable learning.
Born in 1595, the same year as Chapelain, he had come to
Paris as a boy and had lived there ever since. He was a
welcome visitor at the Hôtel de Rambouillet, but, owing
to his shyness and awkwardness, he never played a prominent part either there or in the other salons which he
frequented. But he profited by his opportunities to pursue
in silence that study of the French language into which he
had been early initiated by Malherbe. Even under his
zealous superintendence the Dictionary advanced but
slowly. It was not till the middle of October, 1639, that
the letter A was completed. After the death of the Cardinal
(December, 1642), who had from time to time applied the
spur to the unwilling Academicians, the work progressed
even more slowly[1]. Vaugelas died in 1650, and was succeeded, but not replaced, by Mézeray. In 1651 they had
only reached the letter I, and Pellisson despaired of the
work ever being completed. The end, however, came at
last, and in 1694, a year after Pellisson's death, the great
Dictionary of the Academy saw the light.

The principles upon which the Dictionary was based had
already been enunciated by Vaugelas in the preface to his
celebrated *Remarques sur la langue française*, published in
1647[2]. There he had laid it down that the only true authority in matters of language was "usage, the master and
lord of living languages." But there is a bad usage and a
good usage, that of the majority and that of the *élite*. He

[1] Depuis six ans dessus l'F. on travaille,
Et le Destin m'auroit fort obligé
S'il m'avoit dit: Tu vivras jusqu'au G.
(Boisrobert, Ep. vi. à M. de Balzac, written in 1646.)
[2] Ed. Chassang, 1880.

further defines "good usage" as "the spoken language of
the better portion (*la plus saine partie*) of the Court, when
it is in conformity with the written language of the best
contemporary authors." And he adds: "When I say the
Court, I include women as well as men, and also several
persons in the town in which the Prince resides who by
their intercourse with frequenters of the Court share in its
polite tone." Elsewhere he says that in questions of doubt
it is generally better to consult women and those who have
not studied than those who are learned in Greek and Latin.
Lastly, he points out that of these two sources of authority,
the Court and the good authors, the Court is by far the
more important, but that, in order to establish an irrefra-
gable authority, the two must agree. His *Remarques*, which
are merely a collection of notes on pronunciation, ortho-
graphy, and grammar, put together without any attempt
at arrangement, are based entirely on these principles. He
is, he says, not a legislator, but a mere registrar; not a
judge, but a simple witness.

It will be seen that in regarding usage as the sole test of
correctness in language Vaugelas was following closely in
the footsteps of Malherbe. He differed from him only in
this, that, whereas Malherbe required that language should
be intelligible to the Paris populace, Vaugelas excluded
from consideration all but the Court and those connected
with it. This narrowing of the point of view, this exaggerated deference to the authority of the Court, which Vaugelas
shared with nearly all his brother Academicians, is in
accordance with the centralising spirit of the age, with its
love of correctness and uniformity. The weight which
Vaugelas attaches to the opinions and practice of women
testifies to the influence of the Hôtel de Rambouillet, which,
as we have seen, made for refinement and purity in language
as well as in manners. It should be noticed that in the
very year following the publication of the *Remarques* French
was established as the ordinary, though not the official,
language of diplomatic intercourse. This triumph, however,
was not obtained without some sacrifice. In its efforts

after lucidity the French language lost much of its picturesqueness, and it impoverished its vocabulary[1].

Pellisson tells us that, when the Academicians had nothing particular to do, one of them would read a portion of some work which he intended for publication and submit it to the criticism of his colleagues, and that this was sometimes so minute and so severe that the Cardinal had on several occasions to exhort them to greater leniency. Thus, during the interval between the acceptance of Chapelain's plan for the Dictionary and Vaugelas's appointment as editor they spent nearly three months in examining Malherbe's *Prière pour le Roi Henri le Grand allant en Limousin*, and even then did not reach the last four stanzas.

It was only to be expected that the Academy, as the creation of the great Cardinal, should come in for its full share of the public attention, and that, while the Cardinal's supporters praised it to the skies, his enemies should treat it with ridicule. Of the numerous satires to which it gave rise the best known is Saint-Évremond's *Comédie des Académistes*, which, though not published till 1650, was written at least as early as the beginning of 1638. It contains some happy touches, as, for instance, the quarrel between Godeau and Colletet (a hit at the log-rolling propensities of men of letters of the day), and the scene in which Chapelain is represented as composing ridiculous verses with great elaboration.

We are now in a position to consider what were Richelieu's aims in founding the Academy, and how far they have been realised. At the beginning of 1634, when his project first took shape, he had been first Minister for more than nine years, and ever since the Day of Dupes (November 10, 1629) he had been the virtual ruler of France. During the whole of this period he had applied himself to the task of unification and centralisation. Every force which in any way interfered with the unity of the State or with the orderly administration of affairs had been mercilessly crushed. Princes of the blood, nobles, governors of pro-

---

[1] On a appauvri, desséché et gêné notre langue (Fénelon).

vinces, financial and other subordinate officers, had all alike been compelled to recognise the indivisible authority of the Crown. No regard for long-established custom or tradition, no feeling for justice or humanity, was allowed to prevail over the public interest. *Raison d'État* was a sufficient justification for every arbitrary act. As regards Richelieu's foreign policy, its aim had been simply and clearly defined in a memorandum laid before the King on January 13, 1629, as "a perpetual intention to arrest the course of the progress of Spain"; and, though in 1634 open war against Spain had not yet been declared, the whole of Richelieu's policy had been directed to the furtherance of this intention. But in 1634, if not from the first, Richelieu contemplated something more than the arrest of Spanish progress. His aim was not only to depose Spain from the primacy of Europe, but to transfer this primacy to France. And with his instinct for large and fruitful ideas he saw all the advantages that would accrue to his scheme from an extension of the influence of the French language. In the Letters Patent of the Academy Louis XIII is made to say that "his very dear and much beloved cousin, Cardinal de Richelieu," had represented to him "that the French language, which up to the present time has suffered from the negligence of those who ought to have made it the most perfect of modern languages, is more capable than ever of reaching this perfection." And in the twenty-fourth statute it is laid down that "the principal function of the Academy shall be to labour with all possible care and diligence at giving fixed rules to our language, and rendering it pure, eloquent, and capable of treating the Arts and the Sciences." Further, we have seen with what insistence Richelieu constrained his reluctant Academicians to work diligently at the Dictionary.

But doubtless Richelieu was moved by another aim than that of promoting the ascendancy of the French language. He saw in the proposed Academy a means of organising and centralising literature, as he had already organised and centralised government. Moreover, by becoming its patron and protector, he would be able to exercise the same supervision over literature that he exercised over every department of the State. For Richelieu had a weakness which is often found in men of absolutist tendencies: he was jealous of all action and all thought that was not in some measure under his own control. But literature, however rigorous the censorship of the Press, will always find a means to escape the autocrat. Napoleon could not silence Mme de Staël. It was therefore a brilliant idea on Richelieu's part to organise a body of literary men, which should be regarded with respect by the literary world, and which should at the same time be a State institution. Sainte-Beuve ascribes an even more comprehensive aim to Richelieu. The urgency with which he requested the Academy to pass judgment on the *Cid* shows, in Sainte-Beuve's opinion, that he meant to establish it "as a *haut-jury*—as a high literary tribunal which should take cognizance of the most important contemporary productions." There was also, as Sainte-Beuve admits, a more personal motive for this request. Richelieu disapproved of the *Cid* for various reasons, for its Spanish theme, for its sanction of duelling, for the readiness with which both hero and heroine are prepared to sacrifice the interests of the State to their private feelings. Neither can he have been pleased to find one of his "five authors" scoring an independent success, and proudly declaring that he owed nothing to anyone's favour. Thus both as a Minister and as a patron of literature, if not as a dabbler in literature himself, he wished to see the proud *Cid* brought before the judgment-seat. Whether he also had the motive attributed to him by Sainte-Beuve must remain a matter of conjecture. But one thing is certain: the Academy accepted most unwillingly the task imposed upon them, and the experiment was never repeated. No one asked it to give an opinion on the *École des Femmes* or *Phèdre*. It is only at most during the second half of the eighteenth century that the Academy can be described as "a sovereign organ of opinion," and Matthew Arnold in adopting unreservedly this phrase of Sainte-Beuve's has greatly exaggerated the Academy's influence on literature. Rather Guizot is right when he says that "the direct influence of the French Academy in general on literature has only been feeble and limited. It has represented literature rather than guided it."

Two reproaches have been directed against the composition of the Academy in its early days. It has been said that it excluded some of the most illustrious names in French literature, and that it admitted chiefly obscure nobodies. As regards the first charge, there was a special reason for each notable omission. Descartes was living abroad, Pascal was a Solitary, Molière was an actor, La Rochefoucauld was invited to become a member but declined. Further, the Academy has never professed to be an assembly of the forty greatest men of letters in France. It was in its origin a literary club, and so, to some extent, it has practically remained. When Villemain was reproached with the exclusion of certain writers of genius because they were "unclubbable," he replied: "Songez donc qu'il faut vivre avec eux." From the very first the Academy included a sprinkling of members who had published nothing, and even some who had no pretensions to be men of letters. Of the latter class were Servien, the Minister of State, and Séguier, the Chancellor; while in 1652 Séguier's grandson, the young Marquis de Coislin, a lad of sixteen, was elected at the Chancellor's request. The second reproach, as to the obscurity of the first Academicians, is due to ignorance. Many of them have naturally passed into oblivion with time, but, as a matter of fact, they included practically all the chief men of letters of the day. It was this rather than any deliberate intention to make the Academy a high literary tribunal which conferred on it the authority that it possessed. But, true to its original design, the Academy has exercised this authority chiefly in the domain of language. The result is that French prose and poetry have been kept singularly free from the caprices and mannerisms of individuals. A French Carlyle is as impossible as a French Browning.

CHAPTER VII

CORNEILLE AND CLASSICAL TRAGEDY

I

THE production of the *Cid* is an important date in the history of French literature, for it marks the beginning not only of classical tragedy, but of the whole classical drama. It is true that it still shows certain imperfections, survivals from Renaissance tragedy, which Corneille afterwards removed in *Horace*; but the changes which it wrought in dramatic construction are so important and so fundamental that its claim to be considered the first French classical drama cannot be seriously disputed. In order to realise clearly the truth of this we must go back a little.

French Renaissance tragedy, which began with Jodelle's *Cléopâtre* in 1552, was lyrical and rhetorical, but essentially undramatic. Its chief representative was Robert Garnier, and it reached its high-water mark in that writer's *Juives*, a play which, mainly by virtue of its subject, the Jewish Captivity, attains a high measure of impressiveness and tragic dignity, but is hardly more dramatic than the earlier tragedies by the same author. The reason for this undramatic character of Renaissance tragedy was twofold: it was due partly to the excessive influence of Seneca, and partly to the want of stage experience on the part of the writers. Such representations of their plays as took place— M. Lanson has drawn up a fairly imposing list of them— were confined to private houses or the colleges either of the Universities or the Jesuits. The actors were amateurs and the audiences were uncritical.

The only regular theatre, at any rate in Paris, at this time was the Hôtel de Bourgogne, where ever since the middle of the sixteenth century the Confrères de la Passion had been producing before popular audiences, though with

indifferent success, various forms of the irregular drama—
profane mysteries, historical plays, and even the forbidden
religious mysteries, concealed under the name of tragedies.
In the year 1599 the Confrères leased their theatre to a
certain actor-manager named Valleran Lecomte, who had
in his employ as a playwright one Alexandre Hardy. It
was Hardy who first taught French tragedy to be dramatic.
A man of considerable learning and a great admirer of
Ronsard, he did his work as hack writer to a dramatic
company—his name did not even appear on the play-bills
—with great industry and considerable ability. During his
more than thirty years' service with Valleran Lecomte he
is said to have produced about 700 plays, all in verse, of
which he edited thirty-four for publication (1624–28)[1].
These included eleven tragedies and thirteen tragi-
comedies. He himself seems to have preferred tragedy, and
down to about the year 1610 he chiefly cultivated this form
of the drama. Guided by his dramatic instinct, he soon
abandoned the choruses of the Renaissance drama, though
he retained other characteristics, and he introduced a larger
amount of movement and incident. On the other hand,
while the plays of Garnier and Montchrestien are remarkable for the dignity and imaginative beauty of their verse,
Hardy's language is rough, bombastic, and obscure. It
has, however, a real merit—it shows a certain feeling for
the requirements of the stage, and this is a quality which
almost as much as the power of constructing a plot reveals
the born playwright. Anyone who wants to get an idea of
Hardy's capacity for tragedy cannot do better than read
the play of *Mariamne*, which was produced some time
during the first decade of the seventeenth century[2].

The play opens, after a fashion which had become common in Renaissance tragedy, with the appearance of the
ghost of Aristobulus, the murdered brother of Mariamne,
who in a soliloquy of some power predicts the fate that
awaits Herod. In the second scene Pherore (Pheroras) and

[1] *Le Théâtre d'Alexandre Hardy*, ed. E. Stengel, 5 vols., Marburg, 1883–84.
[2] In vol. II. of Stengel's edition.

Salome, Herod's brother and sister, hint to him that his
wife Mariamne has suborned his cup-bearer to poison him.
In the first scene of the second act Mariamne's nurse tries
in vain to persuade her to moderate her hatred for Herod,
or at any rate to adopt a more prudent attitude towards
him. A page then enters and summons Mariamne to
Herod's presence. In the second scene Salome persuades
Herod's cup-bearer openly to accuse Mariamne. The cup-
bearer's hesitation and the crafty skill with which Salome
finally overcomes his scruples are portrayed with considerable dramatic power. The third act consists only of a single
scene, the most dramatic in the whole play. First Salome
and Pherore inflame Herod against Mariamne; then the
cup-bearer demands a private interview with Herod, who
returns to the stage in a frenzy of rage, having heard and
believed the cup-bearer's story. Mariamne now enters, and
Herod accuses her openly, while she in her turn reproaches
him with having ordered her death in the event of his own
when he was summoned to appear before Mark Antony.
His rage now turns against Soesme (Soëmus), to whom he
had given the order, and from whom Mariamne had heard
of it. His jealousy suggests that he is Mariamne's lover,
and he accordingly sends for him and his confidential
eunuch. Both, however, declare Mariamne's innocence.
The fourth act opens with Mariamne in prison, where the
Provost comes to summon her to the King's presence. In
the second scene the cup-bearer accuses Mariamne to her
face before Herod, and this is followed by an effective
dialogue between Mariamne and Herod, in which she defies
him and bids him do his worst. In the single scene which
forms the fifth act a messenger relates Mariamne's death,
and Herod, who before had been mad with jealousy, now
becomes mad with grief.

The dramatic superiority of this unliterary production
over the tragedies of the sixteenth century appears in
various ways. The interest is sustained to the end, and the
principal antagonists are brought face to face—two features
which are conspicuously absent in Renaissance tragedy.

Further, as M. Rigal points out, we have the beginnings of
true psychological tragedy in the characters of Herod,
Mariamne, and Salome[1]. The action of the play is determined by Herod's jealousy, Mariamne's scorn, and Salome's
Machiavellism. Salome, in fact, is a sort of female Iago,
and the whole play reminds one of *Othello*, which was
written at most only a few years earlier. Lastly, it should
be noticed that the unities are adhered to with considerable
strictness. The unity of action is complete, and, though
nothing is said about the time, it may be regarded as more
or less coinciding with the performance of the play. The
unity of place is not absolute, but the action is, at any
rate, confined to different rooms, including the prison, in
the same palace. In fact, the treatment of the unities is
just what one would expect from a writer of dramatic
instincts who did not trouble his head about any rules,
but who simply conformed to the principle of concentration
which he had learnt from the ancient drama.

Tragedy was never really popular with the frequenters
of the Hôtel de Bourgogne, who liked bustle and incident
and spectacular effect; and about the year 1610 Hardy, at
the bidding of his manager, abandoned it for tragi-comedy,
or, in other words, exchanged classicism for romanticism.
For the term "tragi-comedy," which originally denoted
simply a tragedy with a happy ending, had come to be
used for an irregular kind of drama which blended the
characteristics of tragedy and comedy. Not only was the
ending a happy one, but persons of inferior condition were
admitted as heroes and heroines, and the grave and lofty
style of tragedy was lowered, as occasion required, to a
familiar or even slightly comic note. Moreover, the subject,
instead of being taken, as almost invariably in tragedy,
from antiquity, was drawn from medieval or contemporary
sources, such as epic poems or novels. Under the influence of these sources, and also, as M. Lanson has acutely
pointed out, impelled by the necessity of a happy ending,

[1] *Alexandre Hardy et le Théâtre Français à la fin du XVIᵉ et au commencement du XVIIᵉ siècle*, 1889.

a greater amount of incident was introduced. Thus it was partly owing to tragi-comedy that classical tragedy learnt to be more dramatic.

This class of play, which had been happily inaugurated in the sixteenth century by Garnier's *Bradamante*, is represented in Hardy's work by such plays as *Elmire, ou l'Heureuse Bigamie; Fregonde, ou le Chaste Amour; Gésippe, ou les Deux Amis*. The treatment of these is very different from that of *Mariamne*. The unities are abandoned; in *Gésippe* there are even two distinct actions. There is no attempt at psychology in the characters, but there is plenty of incident, including, when the plot requires it, improbable incident. Many of the scenes must have been effective on the stage. In short, Hardy's tragi-comedies are melodramas.

For a few years Hardy was without a rival in the production of plays of this type. But about the year 1617 Théophile de Viau produced his *Pyrame et Thisbé* (printed in 1623), which had a great success. It resembles Hardy's plays in form, but the treatment is rather more lyrical, and the style, as one might expect, is, in spite of a certain affectation, infinitely superior. About two years later, in 1619, Racan, the disciple of Malherbe, produced on the stage, under the title of *Arthénice*, a play which was printed in 1625, probably in a greatly enlarged form, as *Les Bergeries*. Written under the influence of Hardy's pastoral plays and of *L'Astrée*, it is remarkable, not for any dramatic merits, but for the beauty of its verse and the sincerity of its expression, which includes a real feeling for Nature and country scenes.

"After Théophile had performed his *Thisbé*, and Mairet his *Sylvie*, M. de Racan his *Bergeries*, and M. de Gombauld his *Amaranthe*, the stage became more celebrated, and several persons endeavoured to give it new support. The poets no longer made any difficulty about allowing their names to appear on the play-bills of the actors; for formerly no author's name had been given—it was simply stated that that author had written for them a comedy of such and such a name." This statement of Charles Sorel in his *Bibliothèque française* is somewhat loose as regards chronology, for more than a decade elapsed between the production of *Pyrame et Thisbé* and that of *Amaranthe* (*circa* 1628), but it roughly expresses the facts.

In 1622 the Comédiens du Roi, as the company of Valleran Lecomte was now called, quarrelled with the Confrères de la Passion, and left the Hôtel de Bourgogne. They did not return to it till the end of 1628, and during part of this interval, if not for the whole, they played in the provinces. As the veteran Hardy remained in their employment down to his death in 1631 or 1632, their absence from Paris must have left the field open to new authors. Accordingly between 1625 and 1630 several young dramatists produced plays in their own names—Jean Mairet, whose pastoral play of *Sylvie* was performed with great success in 1626, Jean Rotrou, Pierre Du Ryer, Georges de Scudéry, and Pierre Corneille. The two latter, with others of less note, made their début in 1629, and in the same year a new company of actors, that of Le Noir, established themselves in Paris. Henceforward the activity of the stage was stimulated by a rivalry between the theatres as well as between the authors[1]. This was the period of the struggle between the partisans of the classical and the irregular drama. It lasted till the year 1634, when the victory of the classical party may be said to have been assured, though it was not till a few years later that the law of the unities was completely established.

In 1628 a somewhat remarkable contribution was made to the cause of the irregular drama. In that year was printed—it does not seem ever to have been acted—a play entitled *Tyr et Sidon*, by Jean de Schelandre. It had been originally published in 1608 as *Tyr et Sidon, tragédie, ou les funestes amours de Belcar et Méliane*, the subject being

---

[1] During the thirty years from 1630 to 1659 inclusive about 400 new plays were produced at Paris (see the *Histoire du théâtre français* of the brothers Parfaict).

taken from Ronsard's *Franciade*[1]. It was now transformed under the influence of Hardy into a tragi-comedy of two parts, *Amours de Leonte et Philoline* and *Amours de Belcar et Meliane*[2]. It is chiefly the first part which contains new matter; a comic element, generally coarse and indecent, is introduced, and there is a total disregard of the unities of time and place. In the second part there are romantic incidents and some picturesque and touching scenes, which would be effective on the stage. But happy expressions and touches are varied by exhibitions of bad taste, and the characters are either exaggerated or colourless. On the other hand, the versification is greatly improved in the revised play; it has a firmer cadence, showing a study of Malherbe, and the language is better adapted to the stage[3]. The original version is dedicated to our James I, and the whole play reminds one of the Elizabethan drama, more especially of the plays which Fletcher wrote after the death of Beaumont. Was Jean de Schelandre acquainted with the English drama, or is the resemblance to Fletcher due to a common study of Lope de Vega?

The remodelled play is preceded by a remarkable preface from the pen of François Ogier, a man of some learning, and a friend of Balzac. In it he defends the irregular drama on the ground of its greater variety and therefore greater interest. Without making a regular attack on the unities, he points out that the ancients have not always observed the rule of twenty-four hours, and claims the right of freedom for the moderns. But the weight of opinion was against him. The *honnêtes gens* and the men of letters, with Chapelain at their head, who frequented the Hôtel de Rambouillet were almost unanimous in favour of the regular drama. The chief strength of the irregular cause lay in the support of the Hôtel de Bourgogne, which was given partly from conservatism, but chiefly from practical con-

---

[1] Ed. J. Harazti (*Soc. des Textes français modernes*), 1908, from a copy in the *Bib. de l'Arsenal*. The only other known copy is in the British Museum.

[2] *Ancien théâtre français* (Bib. Elzévirienne), VIII.

[3] See a reference to *Tyr et Sidon* in J.-J. Jusserand, *Shakespeare in France*, 1899, p. 499, n. 2.

siderations as regards scenery. Recently, however, a new company had arrived in Paris, which was hampered by no traditions, and which was only too glad to throw in its lot with the younger playwrights, and to adapt its stage to the tastes of the Court. In 1634 this company, of which the principal actor was the famous Mondory, established itself in the tennis-court of the Marais, in the Rue Vieille du Temple, and their theatre was henceforth known as the Théâtre du Marais.

It was on this stage and in the same year, 1634, that Jean Mairet produced his tragedy of *Sophonisbe*, which is sometimes spoken of as the first example of classical tragedy in France[1]. The subject was a favourite one with dramatists. Trissino, whose play was twice translated into French, Montchrestien, Marston, and Corneille in his later years, all tried it, and all without success. The story, as told by Livy, is as follows: Sophonisba was the wife of Syphax, the Berber king of the Massaesyli, who in the final struggle between Rome and Carthage at the close of the Second Punic War had espoused the Carthaginian cause. In a battle on the Great Plains he was defeated and taken prisoner, and his rival Masinissa, king of the Massyli, occupied his capital, Cirta (the modern Constantine). At the threshold of the royal palace he was met by Sophonisba, who prostrated herself at his feet, and implored that, whatever happened, she, the daughter of Hasdrubal, the Carthaginian general, might not fall into the hands of the Romans. Inflamed by her beauty, Masinissa not only promised to fulfil her request, but married her out of hand. On hearing of this, Scipio, the Roman commander, insisted on her being given up to him. Thereupon Masinissa, having no other way of keeping his promise, sent her a cup of poison, which she fearlessly drank. In the story as thus presented there are some obvious difficulties for the modern dramatist, and Mairet has got rid of the two chief ones by making Syphax fall in the battle, and by making Masinissa commit suicide, though as a matter of fact he lived to a

[1] Ed. K. Vollmöller, Heilbronn, 1888.

green old age. He also avails himself of the statement of
Appian and other historians that Sophonisba had been
originally betrothed to Masinissa. Mairet's first act consists of three scenes—the first between Syphax and
Sophonisba, the second between Syphax and his general
Philo, and the third between Sophonisba and her confidante,
Phenice. We learn from these scenes that Syphax has
intercepted a letter from Sophonisba to Masinissa, the
commander of the opposing army, in which she briefly but
clearly hints at her love for him. Sophonisba explains this
as a ruse which she had adopted as a means of securing
Masinissa's protection in case of need against the Romans,
but Syphax declines to believe her. In the first scene of
the second act Sophonisba appears with her two confidantes.
The battle is going on outside the walls of Cirta, and they
bring her reports of its progress. In the second scene a
messenger arrives to announce the death of Syphax and
the defeat of his troops. In the third the messenger brings
fresh information that the town is on the point of sur-
rendering to Masinissa. Sophonisba bids him kill her with
his sword, but he refuses to obey her, and the chief
confidante advises her to try instead the effect of her
charms upon the young conqueror. In the second and
third scenes of the third act, Sophonisba, after some re-
luctance, consents to adopt this plan, and in the fourth she
carries it out with such success that Masinissa is completely
captivated and insists on marrying her the same evening.
The opening of the fourth act finds the newly married pair
rejoicing in their happiness, and Sophonisba now explains
that she had been in love with Masinissa ever since her
betrothal to him by her father. A soldier enters and summons Masinissa to Scipio's presence. Both lovers fear the
worst, but Masinissa promises Sophonisba that she shall
never be taken to Rome as a captive. In the third and
fourth scenes the blow falls. Scipio is inexorable; Masinissa
must give Sophonisba up to him; the welfare of the Roman
State demands it—*raison d'état*. In the second scene of the
fifth act Laelius announces to Masinissa Scipio's unshaken

resolution. At this point a messenger arrives with a letter
from Sophonisba, in which she asks Masinissa in case of
failure to send her the present that he had promised her
(scene 3). Masinissa obeys and sends her a cup of poison,
which she drinks and immediately expires (scene 5). While
he is in conversation with the Roman generals, her death
is announced by a messenger, who adds that she is lying in
the neighbouring apartment. They lift the tapestry which
separates the two rooms, and Masinissa at the sight of the
dead body breaks forth into an outburst of grief (scene 7).
Scipio and Laelius retire, and in the final scene Masinissa,
after a soliloquy of considerable power and pathos, in which
he calls down the vengeance of the gods upon Rome, stabs
himself with his dagger.

The weakness in the construction of this play is evident.
The first act serves no purpose but the doubtful one of con-
ciliating the spectators in favour of Sophonisba, as the
young and beautiful wife of an old man to whom she had
been married against her will. The second act is better, and
Mairet in representing the battle as actually taking place,
instead of merely narrating the result by means of a messenger, shows a true dramatic sense. The third act is also
dramatic in intention. The interview between Masinissa
and Sophonisba is skilfully prepared, and but for the crude-
ness of its execution it might have been a really great scene.
At this point the interest shifts. Hitherto we have been
interested in the result of Sophonisba's attempt to captivate
Masinissa; during the two remaining acts the question is
whether she will escape falling into the hands of the
Romans. Thus the problem which is solved by the *dénouement* is not stated till the beginning of the fourth act. But
in English eyes a far worse fault than this weakness of
construction is the weakness of the two principal characters.
There is no psychological objection to Masinissa falling in
love at first sight, but it lessens the dramatic possibilities
of the scene, and the gallantries of the Hôtel de Rambouillet
are a poor substitute for the impassioned love-making of
Romeo and Juliet. In the last two acts Masinissa makes no

active effort to save Sophonisba. Even his appeals to Scipio have no dramatic quality in them, and it is not till the final scene that he really rises to the occasion. Sophonisba's character is, it must be admitted, a difficult problem for the dramatist. How is he to win the sympathies or admiration of the spectators for a woman who of her own free will marries a man who has just defeated and slain (though not, indeed, with his own hand) her first husband in battle? Mairet might either have made her, as Corneille does, an ardent patriot, who sacrifices her womanly feelings to her inherited hatred of the Romans, or he might have treated her as a second Cleopatra and made her passion for Masinissa her primary motive. But he seems to have hesitated between these two courses, with the result that, like Masinissa, she drifts rudderless to her fate. She is always talking about her destiny, she is changeable and irresolute, and it is only by her determination not to fall into the hands of the Romans that she wins our sympathy at the last. It is clear that Mairet had only a confused idea of what was meant by dramatic action. From the dramatic point of view he has made little advance upon the tragi-comedies of the period. Though there is a praiseworthy absence of melodrama, the plot is still worked out more or less mechanically, instead of by and through the characters. In fact, as a drama, *Sophonisbe* is inferior to Hardy's *Mariamne*. On the other hand, the style is vastly superior, and though it is sometimes marred by conceits and other signs of bad taste, it shows, on the whole, a sustained dignity. Such as it was, Mairet's *Sophonisbe* had a great success. Tragedy supplanted tragi-comedy and pastoral drama in the popular favour. In the same year Rotrou made his début in tragedy; in the following year (1635) Benserade and Corneille; and in 1636 Georges de Scudéry and Tristan L'Hermite. The last named achieved a great success with his play of *La Mariane*[1], in which

---

[1] Ed. J. Madeleine (*Soc. des textes franç. mod.*), 1917. I cannot agree with the editor and M. Bernardin that the play is superior to Hardy's either in construction or in characterisation.

Mondory acted the part of Herod. But none of these productions was a masterpiece, or even marked any real improvement in dramatic construction. It was not till the
winter of 1636–37 that Corneille showed the French stage
a more excellent way.

II

Pierre Corneille, the son of an advocate of the Parliament of Rouen, who held the post of Inspector of Waters
and Forests, was born at Rouen in 1606. After being
educated in the Jesuit College from 1615 to 1622, he became an advocate in 1624, and four years later his father
purchased for him two legal posts, which were practically
sinecures. In 1629 or early in 1630 he began his dramatic
career with the comedy of *Mélite*[1]. This was followed by
Clitandre, a tragi-comedy full of absurd adventure (1631),
and by four more comedies (1631 or 1632–33). Then came
his first tragedy *Médée* (1635), written more or less in imitation of Seneca's play of that name. Such alterations as he
has introduced are not for the better. Jason is a poor
creature, and Medea is a somewhat vulgar sorceress. But
some of the lines, and even one or two whole speeches,
especially in the scene between Jason and Medea in the
third act, presage the *belles tirades qui font frissonner* of his
great plays. In 1635 or 1636 he returned to comedy with
L'Illusion Comique, and then, either in December, 1636, or
in January, 1637, he produced on the stage of the Marais
the tragi-comedy (as he first called it) of the *Cid*. It
is founded on a Spanish play, Guillen de Castro's *Las
Mocedades del Cid* (The Youthful Exploits of the Cid), a
play in two parts, of which only the first is used by
Corneille. The Spanish play is thoroughly romantic in
character and full of episodes, while the loves of the Cid
and Chimène do not form the central motive. Of Corneille's

---

[1] See H. Carrington Lancaster, *The dates of Corneille's early plays*,
Modern Language Notes, 1915. I have adopted most of his dates.

play, well known though it is, I will give an analysis, because a careful study of its construction is essential to a right understanding of the claim made for the *Cid* that it is the first modern French tragedy.

The play in its original form opens with a scene between Don Gomez, Comte de Gormas, the father of Chimène, and Elvire, her *gouvernante*, in which the Count signifies his approval of Don Rodrigue as a suitor for his daughter's hand. In the second scene Elvire tells Chimène the result of this conversation. Chimène is filled with joy, but, like Romeo just before his entrance to the house of the Capulets, she feels a presage of coming evil:

> Et dans ce grand bonheur je crains un grand revers.

Then follow three scenes, afterwards reduced to one, in which the Infanta confesses her love for Don Rodrigue. They contribute nothing to the action, and Corneille himself afterwards admitted that the introduction of the Infanta into the play was indefensible. Scene 6 (3 of the revised play) is the celebrated scene between Don Gomez and Don Diégue, the Cid's father, who has just been chosen in preference to Don Gomez as Governor to the Prince of Castile. The boastful and arrogant tone of the two Spanish grandees, and the gradually rising tide of their wrath till it culminates in the famous blow given by the Count to Don Diégue, are admirably depicted. A soliloquy by Don Diégue follows, and then the Cid enters and in a short but effective scene his father bids him avenge the insult. The act closes with the well-known lyrical monologue of the Cid:

> Percé jusques au fond du cœur.

Writing in 1660, Corneille said that the affectation in these stanzas, which chiefly consists in the abuse of antithesis (a common defect at the time), was inexcusable. Though lyrical in form, the soliloquy is essential to the action, for in it the Cid makes up his mind to follow the course which determines the development of the rest of the play. Here

THE *CID* 117

we may pause to notice the admirable character of this first act, apart from the Infanta scenes, as an exposition (to use the French term) of the play. In a few short scenes a simple act, springing naturally from the characters of the two rival nobles, and followed by a deliberate choice on the part of the hero, which is equally in keeping with his character, sets the whole tragedy in motion. The interest of the spectators is aroused to an intense pitch, which is never lowered till the fall of the curtain.

In the first scene of the second act Don Arias appears before the Count with a command from the King to make up his quarrel with Don Diégue. The Count's self-confidence and obstinacy are well portrayed, and combine with his attitude to the Cid in the following scene to deprive him of our sympathy. Then follow three scenes in which the Infanta forms an abortive plan to stop the duel, and two short scenes, afterwards thrown into one, between the King and some of his nobles. They serve to keep the spectators in suspense while the duel is being fought. In scene 7 Don Alonse arrives to announce the Count's death, and is speedily followed by Chimène and Don Diégue, who in a splendid scene respectively implore the King for justice. In the speech of Don Diégue, in which he invites the King to punish him as the real offender, we have for the first time a *tirade* in all its splendour of impassioned rhetoric.

At the beginning of the third act the Cid comes to Chimène's house to submit himself to her vengeance. He is received by Elvire, who conceals him on the arrival of Chimène with Don Sanche. In the next scene Don Sanche, who is in love with Chimène, offers himself as her champion in case of the King's refusal to do her justice. Then follows an admirable scene between Chimène and Elvire, in which Chimène reveals the opposing sentiments by which she is torn and her determination to sacrifice her love to her filial duty. The Cid here emerges from his hiding-place and in a scene of great beauty implores Chimène to kill him with his sword. She confesses her love for him and admits that, though she will do her best to avenge her father, her one wish is to fail. The fifth scene consists of a short soliloquy, more or less lyrical in character, by Don Diégue; and in the sixth he urges the Cid, instead of brooding over his sorrows, to take the command against the Moors, who are on the point of attacking Seville, and by defeating them to compel the King to pardon him.

The fourth act opens with a scene between Chimène and Elvire, in which the latter relates the rumour of a great victory gained by the Cid. The Infanta arrives and confirms the report, and tries to persuade Chimène to give up her desire for vengeance. But she is obdurate. Here for the first time the Infanta really helps on the action of the play. In the third scene the Cid is received by the King and gives an account of the battle. Chimène then appears, and the Cid having retired, the King, to test her feelings, tells her that the Cid has died of his wounds. She betrays her love by nearly fainting, when the King undeceives her and urges her to forgive the Cid and give him her hand. Chimène, still unyielding, asks the King that, as he will not do her justice, she may choose a champion to fight with the Cid. In the event of his victory, she promises to marry him. The King consents; Don Sanche, claiming Chimène's promise, is selected as her champion; and the King decrees, in spite of her protestations, that she shall be the prize of the victor.

In the first scene of the fifth act the Cid pays another visit to Chimène's house, in order to bid her farewell before he falls in the duel with Don Sanche. For, as he explains, he does not intend to defend himself:

> Je cours à mon supplice et non pas au combat.

Chimène first tries to persuade him that he ought to fight for the sake of his honour, and then, when that argument fails, bids him fight because she loves him:

> Sois vainqueur d'un combat dont Chimène est le prix.

This is enough for the Cid, and he bursts forth in the well-known lines:

> Paroissez, Navarrois, Maures, et Castillans,
> Et tout ce que l'Espagne a nourri de vaillants;
> Unissez-vous ensemble, et faites une armée,
> Pour combattre une main de la sorte animée:
> Joignez tous vos efforts contre un espoir si doux,
> Pour en venir à bout c'est trop peu que de vous.

This scene, as well as the preceding visits of the Cid to Chimène (iii. 1–4), was much blamed by the critics of the day as an offence against *les bienséances*. In the *Sentiments de l'Académie sur le Cid* Chapelain declared that Chimène's morals "sont du moins scandaleuses, si en effet elles ne sont pas dépravées." And Corneille himself says in his *Examen* of 1660 that, though these scenes pleased the public at the time, he would be chary of introducing similar ones. But Chapelain admits that the first scene of the fifth act is well executed, and it is certainly very effective. Moreover, Chimène's betrayal of her hope that the Cid will prove victorious is thoroughly natural. Whether it is equally natural that the Cid should go and see her just before the duel is another question.

The second scene consists of a lyrical soliloquy by the unfortunate Infanta, who is the one absolutely unselfish person in the play; yet nobody wants her, not even the spectators. It is followed by an equally unnecessary dialogue between her and her *gouvernante*. The fourth scene finds Chimène waiting with Elvire for the result of the duel. Though she had urged the Cid to do his best because she was the prize of victory, she is still resolute in her determination not to marry him.

> Et, quoi qu'à sa victoire un monarque ait promis,
> Mon honneur lui fera mille autres ennemis.

Then Don Sanche appears with a sword in his hand, and Chimène immediately jumps to the conclusion that he has killed the Cid and turns on him with fury. She rushes into the King's presence and begs that, instead of marrying

Don Sanche, she may end her days in a cloister. The King points out her mistake, and bids her no longer resist his command to marry the man whom she so evidently loves (scene 6). In the final scene the Cid again offers to give himself up to Chimène's vengeance, and she once more protests, though now with weakening resolution, against the King's command. The King compromises by giving her time to consider the matter:

> Prends un an, si tu veux, pour essuyer tes larmes,

and he bids the Cid meanwhile command his army against the Moors.

> Espère en ton courage, espère en ma promesse;
> Et, possédant déjà le cœur de ta maîtresse,
> Pour vaincre un point d'honneur qui combat contre toi,
> Laisse faire le temps, ta vaillance et ton roi.

Judged according to the strict standard which came to prevail later in French classical tragedy, the *Cid* shows certain defects in the conduct of the play. The introduction of the Infanta, who has practically no influence on the action, but is merely a sympathetic spectator of it, is a survival from the lyrical tragedy, or tragedy of passion (to use M. Lanson's phrase), of the sixteenth century. There are other lyrical elements in the *Cid*, such as the soliloquies of Don Diègue (i. 7, and iii. 5), of which the former entirely and the latter to a great extent are mere expressions of personal emotion, and not, as Shakespeare's soliloquies generally are, revelations of some struggle or fresh development within the breast of the speaker. So, too, the fine scene between Chimène and the Cid in the third act ends with a lyrical duet which is strongly suggestive of opera. On the other hand, the lyrical form of the Cid's monologue at the end of the first act may be defended, though not its highly artificial character. Strong emotion may find a natural outlet in lyrical expression, but not in an elaborate arrangement of antithetical language. There is also, as Brunetière points out, an epic element in the *Cid*, which would not have commended itself to Corneille's more mature judgment. The Cid's narrative of his victory over the Moors is told at too great length, because we already know the result. In the Spanish original the battle is represented on the stage. In a Greek or a Renaissance play it would have been narrated by a messenger. Either method is legitimate, but the hero's recital of his exploits at this point checks the movement of the drama and consequently chills the interest of the spectators. Lastly, leaving for the present the whole question of the unities, it may be noticed that the monologue of Don Diégue, in the fifth scene of the third act, and that of the Infanta in the second scene of the fifth act, are violations of the rule of the *liaison des scènes*, according to which one actor at least had to remain on the stage at the end of every scene in order to connect it with the following one.

But all these shortcomings are as nothing compared with the fact that Corneille completely transformed the French stage, and introduced a pattern of drama which was to last practically unchanged for nearly two centuries. The Greeks had based their tragic drama upon two fundamental principles: first, that action is necessary to its structure; and second, that this action must proceed from within and not from without—that it must be developed, not mechanically, but through the characters[1]. It was Corneille's great merit that he thoroughly grasped the importance of these principles. Both, indeed, had been acted on by Hardy, but the second, at any rate, as we see from Mairet's *Sophonisbe*, had not been definitely established. In *Sophonisbe* the characters are the sport of fate and circumstance; in the *Cid* they work out their own destiny. The Count strikes Don Diégue because he has an overweening sense of his own importance. The Cid fights with the Count because, like a true Spaniard, he holds "the point of honour" dearer even than his love. Chimène, in spite of her love, cries for vengeance on him, because she is true to her sense of duty

---

[1] See for classical tragedy the admirable chapter, entitled "Plot and Character," in S. H. Butcher's *Aristotle's Theory of Poetry and Fine Art*, third edition, 1902.

to her father. The Cid takes the command against the Moors because he has a heroic soul, and he is victorious over Don Sanche because he knows that Chimène still loves him. So the plot is worked out, naturally, logically, to its final *dénouement*.

The fashionable public who crowded day after day to hear the *Cid* were naturally unaware that it marked the opening of a new and splendid era in French drama. They probably failed to recognise the superlative merits of its construction. But they felt to the full its all-pervading charm. Like *Romeo and Juliet*, the *Cid* is emphatically a play of youth. Our sympathies are with the lovers as entirely as were those of the spectators in the days when

> Tout Paris pour Chimène a les yeux de Rodrigue.

It matters not to us any more than it did to them that her actions are contrary to *les bienséances*. We are as little shocked by her reception of her lover in her house as we are by Juliet's conversation with Romeo from her balcony. Her manners may be "scandalous, not to say depraved," but we know that her heart is pure. We respect her filial affection, we admire the constancy with which she demands her lover's punishment, we approve her wish to retire to a cloister when that punishment becomes impossible; but in the struggle between love and duty our sympathies are wholly on the side of love.

It has been said that the style of the *Cid* shows traces of preciosity, but this is chiefly apparent in the lyrical monologues of the Cid and the Infanta. Corneille had little natural gift for lyrical poetry, and in consequence he nearly always becomes artificial when he attempts it. But otherwise the style of the play is of transcendent merit. In *Médée* Corneille is sometimes familiar, sometimes bombastic, but here he is completely master of his instrument. It is not an imaginative style—it would, indeed, be difficult to find a single image in the whole play—but it is always dignified, clear, and expressive, and ever and anon it stirs our blood as with a trumpet-call. To come to details, M.

Lanson points out that the language is more archaic than that of Pascal, Molière, or Bossuet, and that the construction is remarkable for its logical character. Corneille's heroes and heroines are skilled dialecticians, a feature which is due to his Norman blood, and not, as some suppose, to his profession as an advocate, for he pleaded rarely and without success. In his treatment of the Alexandrine he follows the technique of Malherbe, but with complete ease and mastery. His versification has a manly harmony, producing its effects rather by the expressive movements of its cadences than by the musical quality of its sounds.

III

Homely, domestic, simple, not to say ordinary, in appearance, with little or no conversation, Corneille, on his occasional visits to Paris before he came to reside there permanently in 1662, cut a poor figure in Paris society, especially at the Hôtel de Rambouillet, where wit and conversation played so prominent a part. Yet the majority of its *habitués*, especially the ladies, applauded the *Cid*, and were on Corneille's side in the famous controversy. We have seen how reluctantly he accepted the jurisdiction of the Academy. When the *Sentiments* at last appeared, though he affected indifference, he complained of its severity and pondered deeply over its criticisms. It was doubtless during the two years which elapsed between its publication and the production of *Horace* that he first began to make a careful study of the laws and principles of the drama.

Among the questions which occupied Corneille's attention during this period of meditation that of the unities was naturally one. It had been much discussed in the course of the controversy between the partisans of the regular and the irregular drama. In the preface to *Tyr et Sidon*, already referred to, Ogier had pointed out some of the faults into which dramatists had been led by following the rule of twenty-four hours, as the unity of time was called. He added that the ancients themselves had not always observed the rule, and that even if they had, that was no reason for imposing it upon the moderns. This, as we have seen, was in 1628. In 1630 Mairet, who had been asked by the Cardinal de La Valette and the Comte de Caraman to write a pastoral play "according to the strict rules observed by the Italians in such plays," produced the "pastoral tragi-comedy" of *Silvanire*, a remodelled version of D'Urfé's play of the same name, in which he observed the rule of twenty-four hours, and believed—though he was mistaken—that he had also observed the unity of action. Corneille, coming to Paris soon after the first representation of the play, in order to see his own comedy of *Mélite* performed, learnt for the first time, he tells us, of the existence of the rule of twenty-four hours. Mairet's play was more or less of a failure, but in 1631 he published it with a preface, in which he warmly supported the unities, and especially the unity of time. "If the same actor," he says, "who was at Rome at the end of the first act is found at Athens or Cairo at the beginning of the second, it is impossible that the imagination should not be chilled."

Meanwhile Chapelain, who, according to the *Segraisiana*, "was the cause why they began to observe the rule of twenty-four hours," had, on November 29, 1630, written to his friend Godeau, the Bishop of Grasse, a long letter on the subject, which was doubtless intended for circulation, and which in all probability Mairet had read when he wrote his preface. The gist of Chapelain's cumbrous and involved argument is that he bases his support of the rule on the theory of *vraisemblance* or verisimilitude. Starting with the absurd postulate that "imitation in all poems ought to be so perfect that no difference should appear between that which is imitated and that which imitates," he thinks that the ancients kept to the rule of twenty-four hours because they believed that, if they extended the action beyond the length of a natural day, they would render the play improbable (*non vraisemblable*) in the eyes of the spectators. He then proceeds to answer certain objections of Godeau's, and among them the extremely pertinent one that it is just as difficult to imagine that twenty-four hours have passed during a representation which at the most occupies three as it is to imagine that ten years have passed. Chapelain is of course unable to answer this, except by saying that ten years is much longer than a day; but he adds that the time of twenty-four hours is only a maximum, and that ordinarily the action is completed in twelve hours[1].

In the *Cid* Corneille has adhered to the rule, but he admits in his *Examen* of the play that its incidents are, in consequence, unduly crowded. The Cid, he says, after fighting all night against the Moors, deserved two or three days' rest before fighting a duel. Chimène, having once demanded justice from the King, should not have importuned him a second time on the following morning; she ought to have waited patiently for a week, "*but the rule of twenty-four hours did not allow it. That is the inconvenience of the rule.*" From this naïve confession of his difficulties we may suppose that Corneille accepted Chapelain's criticism in the *Sentiments*—namely, that in his fear of sinning against the rules of Art he had sinned against those of Nature.

At the time of the production of the *Cid* the unity of time was, as we have seen, understood to mean twenty-four hours; but Aristotle's remark that the action of a tragedy is generally confined within one revolution of the sun was soon to be interpreted more strictly. Chapelain, who in his letter to Godeau had not mentioned Aristotle, says in the *Sentiments* that Aristotle only allows for the action of a play the time between sunrise and sunset. If he had read Aristotle in the original he would have seen that he is only stating the general practice of Greek tragedy, and not laying down a hard-and-fast rule.

The unity of place, at least in a strict sense, took somewhat longer to establish. This was chiefly owing to the resistance of the Hôtel de Bourgogne. In the old days of the Mystery plays the system of scenery was that of simul-

---

[1] For an admirable defence of Shakespeare's violation of the unities of time and place see Johnson's *Preface to Shakespeare* (*Works*, v. 119 ff.).

taneous scenes. In other words, the various scenes were all
put on the stage at the same time, forming a series of
compartments, and when an actor wished to go from Paris
to Athens, or from Rome to Jerusalem, he walked out of
one compartment and into another. The comparatively
confined stage of the Hôtel de Bourgogne did not admit of
so many scenes as the huge temporary stages on which the
Mystery plays were performed, but the old system still
continued in force[1]. Naturally the actors were unwilling to
make a change which involved the sacrifice of their stock
of scenery, and it was equally natural that the system of
simultaneous scenes should seem absurd to the partisans
of the regular drama, and especially to those who held the
theory of verisimilitude. The English stage got over the
difficulty by having practically no scenery at all, and giving
full rein to the imagination of the spectators; but in France
it was reason and not imagination which at this time held
sway in art. The establishment of the new theatre in the
Marais helped greatly to break down the resistance of the
Hôtel de Bourgogne. In *Sophonisbe*, which was produced
at the Marais, the scenery was confined to several rooms in
the Palace of Syphax. In the *Examen* of the *Cid* Corneille
tells us that the unity of place gave him as much trouble
as the unity of time. The action is confined to Seville, but
it shifts between the King's apartments and those of the
Infanta in the royal palace, Chimène's house, and the street.
Scudéry objected that all these were represented by a single
scene almost without change, so that "the spectators...do
not know where the actors are." M. Rigal explains this to
mean that the scene was divided into compartments in the
old fashion, but that the divisions were not clearly defined,
and the actors practically disregarded them[2]. It was only
a step from this to abolish the compartments altogether.

[1] See J.-J. Jusserand, *Shakespeare in France*, for illustrations (*a*) of the
mansions for the performance of a Passion play at Valenciennes in 1547
(p. 63); and (*b*) of the scenery of a play at the Hôtel de Bourgogne in 1631
(pp. 71, 75). (*a*) is also reproduced in Petit de Julleville, *Hist. de la langue
et de la litt. française*, vol. II.
[2] *Le théâtre français avant le période classique*, 1901, p. 290.

This final victory of the unity of place was helped by the practice of seating some of the spectators on the stage, which we first hear of in connexion with the *Cid*, but which from this time became customary.

One effect of Corneille's meditation on the rules of his art was that in his next play, *Horace*, produced in the early months of 1640, he adhered strictly to all the three unities. Another result was that he took his subject from the fashionable source of Roman history, instead of from the romantic drama of Spain. Moreover, in *Horace* we have no superfluous character like the Infanta—for Sabine, if not strictly necessary to the development of the piece, forms an admirable contrast to Camille—no lyrical or epic elements, nothing that interferes with the logical sequence of events. The dedication to Richelieu, though possibly it was not so intended, is a delightful piece of irony. Corneille tells the great man that he has "ennobled the aim of dramatic art," because authors, in writing for his amusement, render no little service to the State, and thus contribute "to the preservation of a health which is so precious and so necessary to it"; and that he has facilitated their study of its laws because they can read on his face whether he is pleased or not. "I have often," he adds, "learnt more there in two hours than my books could have taught me in ten years." Whatever Richelieu may have thought of this dedication, he should have been moved by the more delicate flattery of the play itself. Not only does it conform to the unities as strictly as his own play of *Mirame*[1], but it glorifies the sacrifice of natural affection to the welfare of the State in a manner that must have been highly acceptable to the absolutist Minister.

Horace was succeeded later in the same year (1640) by *Cinna, ou La Clémence d'Auguste.* Corneille's contem-

---

[1] Written in collaboration with Desmarests de Saint-Sorlin. It was published in 1646 in a superb folio edition, with five engravings—one for each act—which indicate, by the identity of the scenery and the varying position of the sun, that the unities of time and place have been strictly observed in the play (see, for a reproduction of two of the plates, Petit de Julleville, *op. cit.*, IV. 358).

poraries, he tells us, generally regarded it as his masterpiece, but they were probably prejudiced in its favour by
its strong political character. It was an age, as Voltaire
says, "when every man wanted to be a statesman." Moreover, the clemency of Augustus must have seemed the most
desirable of political lessons to not a few of the "illustrious"
spectators, budding Cinnas and Maximes, who gave their
suffrages in its favour[1]. A more disinterested criticism
rates it less high. The transference of interest and sympathy
from the conspirators to Augustus, indicated by the double
title of the play, is, from a strict point of view, a fault of
construction. It is a more important defect in English eyes
that Cinna is the most unheroic and irresolute of prota-
gonists, and that he is completely overshadowed by Émilie.
The main interest of the play lies in the admirable picture
of the struggle which takes place in the breast of Augustus,
and which culminates in the lines:

> Je suis maître de moi, comme de l'univers:
> Je le suis, je veux l'être. O siècles! ô mémoire,
> Conservez à jamais ma dernière victoire.

Here speaks the superb Stoic[2]. In Corneille's next play,
Polyeucte, produced in the winter of 1642–43, he drew a
companion picture of Christian virtue. We have seen that
this choice of a Christian subject offended the taste of the
Hôtel de Rambouillet, and it may be admitted that a
Christian martyr is not a good "tragic hero" in the Aristo-
telian sense, because his fate is not tragic. But then,
Corneille does not pretend to give us "tragic heroes"; his
heroes, as a rule, excite, not pity or terror, but admiration.
Apart from the many and obvious beauties of *Polyeucte*[3],
there is no play of Corneille's, except *Nicomède*, which
shows so careful a study of normal human character.
Sévère and Pauline, and, on a lower and almost comic

---

[1] *Examen de Cinna.*

[2] In act v. scene 1, Augustus's speeches to Cinna are borrowed largely
from Seneca's *De clementia*.

[3] There is an excellent appreciation of *Polyeucte* by Faguet in his *Dix-
septième siècle*.

plane, Félix, are characters whom Corneille might have encountered in that salon where he read his play to an inappreciative audience.

Moreover, the subject of Christian martyrdom, though neither Corneille nor his audience was aware of it when the play was first produced, possessed an interest of poignant actuality. On the last day of September, 1642, the first martyr of the Jesuit Mission to Canada, René Goupil, a layman attached to the mission, had, after enduring horrible tortures, laid down his life for the faith. The news reached France about a year later, and on Christmas Day of 1643 Isaac Jogues, a Jesuit who had been Goupil's companion and had undergone similar tortures, was landed by an English ship on the coast of Brittany. His fame spread to Paris and he was summoned to the Court, where Anne of Austria kissed his mutilated hands, while her ladies thronged round him to do him homage[1].

Polyeucte was produced before the publication of Arnauld's *La Fréquente Communion* had aroused the interest of society in the dispute between the Jesuits and the Jansenists. But Jansen's *Augustinus* had been published, first at Louvain (1640) and then at Paris (1641), and the fact that the third edition appeared at Rouen (1643) may be taken as a sign that the work had awakened some interest in Corneille's native city. At any rate, the question of grace makes its appearance in the very first scene of his play, and it is interesting to notice that on this thorny subject Corneille follows the Jesuits and the Dominicans in distinguishing between *sufficient* and *efficacious* grace:

> Sa grâce
> Ne descend pas toujours avec même efficace[2].

But the application which he makes of this distinction is free from any theological subtlety, for it is quite natural that the inspiration which Polyeucte derived from his baptism should be in danger of growing colder and less efficacious with lapse of time.

[1] Parkman, *The Jesuits in North America*, chap. xvii.
[2] Cf. act ii. scene 6.

It is a long descent from *Polyeucte* to *La Mort de Pompée* (winter of 1643-44), in which the characters are simplified beyond measure and the dramatic interest is slight. On the other hand, it is full of fine declamation and political discourse. "Look upon the *Cinna* and the *Pompey*," says Dryden, whose own plays are stuffed with politics; "they are not so properly to be called plays as discourses of reason and state."

In the following winter (1644-45) Corneille produced the tragedy which he regarded as his best work—namely, *Rodogune*. The fact that he so regarded it is a sign that in his later years he attached more and more importance to plot. It was not merely that, like Aristotle, he regarded the plot as "the end" and "the first principle of tragedy," but that he revelled in a plot which was at once improbable and complicated. In the preface to *Héraclius* (winter of 1646-47), which has a most intricate plot of his own invention, he goes so far as to say that "the subject of a fine tragedy ought not to be probable." In accordance with this view he has greatly added to the improbability and complication of the plot of *Rodogune* by improving upon the story as he found it in Appian. From the point of view of the plot the play is well constructed, for it increases in interest up to the tremendous climax of the fifth act. But the plot is everything; it shapes the characters instead of being developed by them. The two brothers are wanting in energy; they are paralysed by the horror of their situation. Rodogune is ambiguous; she is meant to be gentle and charming, but for the sake of the plot she is made to promise her hand to the prince who will avenge her on his mother. Cléopâtre, who, as Corneille confesses, ought to have given her name to the play, is too inhuman to appeal to the imagination. *Rodogune*, in short, is a romantic melodrama.

Corneille was a versatile playwright, and was fond of making experiments. Two such experiments we have in *Don Sanche* (1649 or 1650) and *Nicomède* (summer of 1651). *Don Sanche* is a *comédie héroïque*, a name which Corneille invented to denote a play which deals with persons of high condition, but in which the hero does not fall into any peril. The first act, which is imitated from a Spanish play, is, as Lemaître says, *d'un panache étonnant*, and we welcome it as a happy return to the field which Corneille had explored with such success in the *Cid*. But, in spite of the romantic setting, the play is thoroughly classical in construction. Here, again, the plot is too complicated, while the characters, with the exception of the hero and possibly Isabelle, are uninteresting.

Nicomède was a more successful experiment. Produced in the very middle of the Fronde, it is, like *Rodogune* and *Héraclius*, a study in political intrigue, and, as in those plays, the plot is complicated and difficult to follow. The strength of the play lies in the characters, and in the extremely clever scenes in which, like brilliant swordsmen, they match themselves against one another. All the characters—Prusias; Arsinoé, the typical second wife; Flaminius (really Flamininus), the typical diplomatist; Attale; Laodice —are alive, even if they are no more than types. But Nicomède has a certain individuality. After the hero as lover, the hero as patriot, the hero as monarch, the hero as martyr, we have now the hero as *frondeur*, but a *frondeur* who is justified by the plots against his life. The public saw in many of the lines allusions to the great Condé, who had been released from prison a few months before the production of the play and who was now preparing for open war. But it is doubtful whether Corneille intended such allusions, and it is quite unlikely that in the character of Nicomède he meant to portray Condé. Nicomède is too perfect, too complete an example of that exaltation of the will which Corneille carried to excess in his later plays, to win our entire sympathies. He irritates us by the impassive air of superiority, the calm indifference, and the lofty irony with which he meets his enemies. He is a hero of grave comedy rather than of tragedy, and the whole play has nothing tragic in it. Prusias is a comic character, and the scene between him and Arsinoé

in the fourth act has been aptly compared to that between
Argan and Bélise in *Le Malade imaginaire* (i. 8). The style
throughout, which is a model of easy, nervous, dignified
language, without poetry or passion, differs very little from
that of the graver scenes in Molière's comedies. We know
that Molière studied the play, for during his visit to Rouen
in 1658, where he doubtless made Corneille's acquaintance,
it was given several times by his company, and it was the
play which he selected for their first performance when they
established themselves at Paris in the autumn of 1658.
Possibly, too, Pascal, who was at Paris when *Nicomède* was
produced, may have learnt something from the easy distinction of its style and its effective use of irony[1]. *Nicomède*
was Corneille's last real success. His next work, *Pertharite*
(1652), was a complete failure, and, discouraged by its
reception, he wrote no more plays for seven years.

During this temporary retirement from the stage he
again applied himself to the consideration of the problems
of his art. He pored over Aristotle and his commentators;
he read Minturno and Castelvetro and Heinsius, and he
carefully studied many ancient and modern plays. The
results of his labours were given to the world in 1660,
partly in the *Examens*, a series of criticisms on his own
plays, and partly in the *Trois Discours*. Three years before
this the Abbé d'Aubignac had published his *La Pratique du
Théâtre*, which he had begun to write as far back as 1640
at the urgent request of Richelieu, and which aspired to be
a complete manual of the theory and practice of dramatic
art. Written from the point of view of a bigoted and unintelligent partisan, its advocacy of the rules is carried to
an exaggerated pitch almost amounting to caricature, and
must have helped to repel Corneille from the strict paths
of the regular drama. At any rate, in the *Examens* and the
Discours he shows himself more of a heretic than he had
done in his plays. He justifies his own violations of the
rules by ingenious, if not always ingenuous, pleading, and,

[1] Scarron gives high praise to *Nicomède* in *Le roman comique*, ii. 79. It
was a favourite with Napoleon.

mindful of what he had written in the dedication of *La Suivante*, that "to know the rules and to understand the secret of skilfully taming (*apprivoiser*) them to suit one's own dramatic art are two different sciences," he conducts his case with all the subtlety and tenacity of a Norman. He even advocates still greater licence. He would extend the twenty-four hours to thirty, and the place from a single room or street to a whole town; and he actually goes so far as to suggest that both time and place should be left to the imagination of the spectators.

Had Corneille been equally bold in practice, had he not always had the fear of the rules before his eyes, he might perhaps have invented a form of drama which, while keeping to the concentration of the classical type, would have admitted rather more freedom in the treatment. For he was a great playwright with an instinctive knowledge of stage-construction, and even the less successful of his many experiments have not been wholly without influence on his successors. But though he never again conformed so strictly to the classical pattern as he did in *Horace*, all his plays belong fundamentally to the classical type, to that type of which he was virtually the creator in the *Cid*.

IV

Corneille's most apt pupil was Pierre Du Ryer[1], his senior by a year, whose masterpiece, *Scévole*[2], was produced in 1644 by that ill-fated company, the Illustre Théâtre of Molière and the Béjarts. Written under the unmistakable influence of the *Cid*, *Horace*, and *Cinna*, it is an admirable example of the Cornelian method. It shows how it is possible to construct an interesting and moving tragedy out of the simplest plot, with few characters and without any outward action. Not even by Corneille has the rhetorical idea of the Roman character, which was so much in fashion with Paris society at this period, been presented with greater force and dignity. Moreover, Du

---

[1] See H. C. Lancaster, *Pierre Du Ryer*, Washington, 1912.
[2] *Théâtre français*, 12 vols., 1737, vol. III.

Ryer has not fallen into Corneille's error, the result of the criticisms on the *Cid*, of relegating love to the background. On the other hand, his characters are simplified and generalised even to a greater degree than Corneille's. Scaevola is the patriot hero, but without the brutality of Horace; Junia is the patriot heroine, but without Émilie's vindictive spirit; Porsena is the generous enemy, but he is more easily moved to clemency than Augustus; Aruns, like the Cid, is torn between love and loyalty, but he has even less hesitation than the Cid in declaring for loyalty.

If Du Ryer was Corneille's aptest pupil, Jean Rotrou[1] was his most original one. He was a prolific writer, who, when he died in 1650, had produced thirty-six plays, of which nine were tragedies and the rest tragi-comedies and comedies in about equal proportions. Born four years after Corneille, he began his dramatic career a year before him, and for a short period was *poète à gages* to the Hôtel de Bourgogne, probably succeeding Hardy. He wrote nothing of any merit before the *Cid*, but his comedy of *Les Sosies* ran contemporaneously with it, and with equal success, and in 1637 he produced his best tragi-comedy, *Laure persécutée*. The hero and heroine arouse our interest and sympathies at the outset, and there are some good scenes, especially one in which the jealousy of the hero is depicted. But the plot is of the mechanical type, and the characters degenerate into puppets. At the end of the fourth act the action has not advanced a step, and the *dénouement* is finally brought about by that favourite method of melodrama, a recognition. The play, in fact, is a sentimental melodrama. Rotrou's earlier tragedies have little merit, but towards the end of his life he wrote three which show distinct traces of Corneille's influence, and are much superior to the rest. The earliest, *Saint-Genest* (1645), which, like *Polyeucte*, is a story of Christian martyrdom, is somewhat wanting in action, but it is well constructed and has some scenes of considerable beauty. For Rotrou is superior to Corneille in the representation

---

[1] *Théâtre choisi*, ed. F. Hémon, 1883.

of the more tender emotions, and is more of a poet. *Venceslas* (1647), which, like *Saint-Genest* and the great majority of Rotrou's plays, is imitated from the Spanish, retained its popularity to the close of the eighteenth century, and even in the nineteenth had not altogether disappeared from the stage. The subject is an exceedingly promising one, and might have been made into a noble tragedy. But in Rotrou's hands, owing to his unskilful treatment of the character of Ladislas, the virtual hero of the piece, and to the repulsive *dénouement*, which is a caricature of that of the *Cid*, it becomes little better than a melodrama.

In *Cosroès* (1648)—the subject, a family political intrigue at the Persian Court, is almost identical with that of Corneille's *Nicomède* (1650)—Rotrou has learnt his lesson better. There is no fault to find with the construction of the first two acts. In the third, however, a certain weakness appears, while in the fourth recourse is had, quite unnecessarily, to the melodramatic device of a change at birth. On the other hand, the *dénouement*, though a bloody one, is the logical result of the unscrupulous ambition of Palmiras dominating the weaker nature of Siroès. The character of Palmiras, however, is not sufficiently accentuated, and three at least of the minor characters are wholly superfluous. Rotrou does not fall into Corneille's error of making his heroes too strong and perfect; but they lack consistency, and consequently they fail to sustain the interest which they arouse on their first appearance. Rotrou's style, though neither correct nor pure nor clear, has plenty of life, and he has a considerable command of both pathos and dignity. In short, he can write strong and effective scenes, but not a complete play. With these qualities we should have expected him to succeed best in irregular or romantic drama. The fact, therefore, that his tragi-comedies are greatly inferior to the three tragedies which he wrote under Corneille's influence is a strong testimony to the importance of Corneille's work. Though the tragedy of Racine conformed more strictly and more naturally to the rules than that of his predecessor, it did not fundamentally differ from it. Down to the romantic revolt of 1830 French tragedy in all essential points of construction remained as Corneille had made it.

This type of tragedy differs in so many respects from our own Shakespearian tragedy, that in order to judge of it fairly we must bear in mind what its aims and ideals really were. In the first place, in accordance with Aristotle's dictum that "drama is an imitation of action," it discards alike all epic and lyrical elements and confines itself to the representation of a single action. Moreover, it takes up that action so near to its *dénouement*, that, in the words of Goethe, it "is nothing but a crisis." To this result it is impelled—one may almost say compelled—by its strict adherence to the unities, which it regards as absolute laws. It pays special attention to the plot, which it works out as the logical solution of a problem. In the first act we have the "exposition" of the plot, or the statement of the problem[1]. The three middle acts deal with the complication, or the development of the plot, each scene leading up to the succeeding one by a strictly logical process. The incidents are determined solely by the characters of the actors and are linked together in a solid chain of causal sequence. The fifth act brings the solution of the problem, the untying of the knot, the *dénouement*. But the nature of French classical tragedy cannot be summed up better than in the words of its most finished artist: "A simple action," says Racine, in the preface to *Britannicus*, "charged with little incident, such as must be the nature of an action which happens in a single day, and which, gradually progressing towards its end, is sustained only by the interests, the sentiments, and the passions of the characters." Whether or not this type of drama is, as Lemaître says, well suited to the genius of the French nation, it was certainly well suited to the age of reason in which it was established. The *Discours de la méthode* is hardly more logical than a tragedy of Corneille.

[1] " Je voudrois donc que le premier acte contînt le fondement de toutes les actions" (Corneille, *Premier discours*).

But there is another point in which the *Discours de la méthode* may be illustrated by French classical tragedy. When Descartes says that he recognised that he "was a substance of which the whole essence or nature consisted in thought, and which, in order to exist, had no need of any place nor depended on any material thing," he reminds us of the characters of French classical tragedy. We are told nothing, not even by way of suggestion, about their outward appearance; we cannot picture to ourselves their habit as they lived. They are purely intellectual conceptions, appealing to the imagination, not through the senses, but through the intellect alone. Further, their temperament and character are only indicated in their general aspects; personal idiosyncrasies are left out of account. For this reason the plays of Corneille and Racine gain by representation on the stage, and even as we read them we call to our aid traditions of great actors and actresses—of Baron, Lekain, and Talma, of la Champmeslé, Adrienne Lecouvreur, and Rachel—who have in Matthew Arnold's words "filled out the parts with their own life and warmth."

But this method of portraying character, it must in fairness be remembered, is more or less inherent in the classical drama. It was the aim of French tragedy, as it was of Greek tragedy, to portray the universal rather than the particular in human nature—to idealise and to simplify character. Yet the greatest artists can create types which are, at the same time, individual, and even within the limits of the classical drama there is room for considerable difference of treatment. The characters of Euripides are more individual than those of Sophocles, and Racine's more than Corneille's. On the other hand, the characters of Corneille seem more alive than Racine's, when we read their plays for the first time. Chimène wins our love more easily than Andromache; Sévère and Pauline have more substance than Titus and Bérénice; we know Émilie better than Eriphile. The reason is that Racine's characters, with the exception of Phèdre and most of the characters in *Athalie*, make a less immediate appeal to our imagination than Corneille's—and this by reason of the difference in their methods. Racine creates by delicate psychological analysis, which requires careful attention on the part of the reader in order to have its full effect. Corneille's characters are more of a piece, simpler, and drawn with little light or shade. His style whips our imagination, and stimulates it into activity. We need long commune with Racine's characters to be really intimate with them; we know Corneille's almost at the first introduction.

In another way, too, the methods of classical tragedy limit the creative power. The compression of the action within twenty-four hours makes it almost impossible to represent the growth and development of character. French tragedy is practically confined to the analysis of a single passion or sentiment, or at most to a single stage of development. It is true that in *Britannicus* Racine has represented with extraordinary skill the metamorphosis of Nero from a dissolute boy to an actual criminal, and that in *Cinna* Corneille has depicted with equal skill the conversion of Augustus to a sense of the divine quality of mercy. But this is very different from the gradual development of a Macbeth or a Lear.

French classical tragedy, then, differs in many essential points from English Elizabethan tragedy; so much so that a critic like Brunetière, who regarded literature as a hierarchy of families and genera, each with its peculiar properties and functions, has denied the name of tragedy to *Othello* and *Lear.* There have been, he says, only two forms of tragedy—the Greek and the French—and only two forms of drama—the English and the Spanish. And earlier in the same essay he explains that tragedy rises above every form of drama "by its tendency to realise under an aspect of eternity all the subjects which it takes for its material." It is difficult to see how this statement excludes Shakespeare, and, at any rate, a classification which labels Corneille's plays as tragedies, and not Shakespeare's, seems somehow wrong. For, however highly we may rate the merits of Corneille as a dramatist, to the English reader he appears the least tragic of writers of tragedy. It is not only that he is fond of a happy ending—an old-fashioned and perhaps crude method of distinguishing between tragedy and comedy for which there is much to be said—but that his whole system of making his heroes dominate the action of the play is fatal to a really tragic issue. It is the element of blind chance, or destiny, or Providence—call it what you will—which makes Shakespeare's tragedies so profoundly tragic. The chance delay of Friar Laurence's messenger causes the death of Romeo and Juliet. Edgar is only just too late to save Cordelia. An accidentally dropped handkerchief brings about the catastrophe of *Othello*. "Iago and Edmund," says Walter Raleigh, "alone among the persons of Shakespeare's great tragedies believe in the sufficiency of man to control his destinies." But the Cornelian hero is "master of his fate." He is sublime, but he is not really tragic.

CHAPTER VIII

COMEDY BEFORE MOLIÈRE

THE history of comedy from Corneille's first visit to Paris to Molière's return there after his long wanderings in the provinces, or, in other words, from the production of *Mélite* (1629 or 1630) to that of *Les Précieuses Ridicules* (1659), is, except for Corneille's *Le Menteur*, a blank to the general reader. Yet this period of preparation for the great work of Molière is not wholly undeserving of attention, for during these thirty years French comedy learned at least two important lessons. It learned to be literary, and it learned to be amusing without being indecent. And, though all the examples of the period belong to a type of comedy very different from that which Molière introduced, we can still trace in them here and there the rudimentary beginnings of social comedy. Moreover, the mere fact that it became possible for respectable people to be spectators of comedy at all established those relations between comedy and society without which social comedy cannot exist. Lastly, if Molière found little or nothing in the work of his immediate predecessors that was of service to him for the particular type of comedy which he created, he doubtless learned something in the matter of structure and dialogue, while he certainly borrowed a good many hints and ideas from particular scenes.

French comedy, as distinguished from farce, began, like tragedy, with a play by Jodelle. There was, however, this difference—that his comedy of *Eugène* (1552) owed considerably more to its medieval predecessor, the farce, than his tragedy of *Cléopâtre* did to the medieval Mystery. But Renaissance comedy failed like Renaissance tragedy, and for the same two reasons—want of stage experience and the pursuit of a false light. Only in the case of comedy the false light, instead of Seneca, was Ariosto. Now, Ariosto's comedies—and Ariosto stands for a crowd of Italian play-wrights who took him as their model and wrote with hardly less skill—are excellent specimens of their kind. They are gay and interesting, and the dialogue is genuinely comic. But the characters are wholly conventional, and there is no interest apart from the plot. Thus Ariosto and Italian comedy led their French imitators astray from the true path of social comedy upon which Jodelle, with however stumbling footsteps, had set out. Of this Renaissance comedy the best representative is *Les Contents* (1584), a posthumous play by Odet de Turnèbe, a son of the well-known Greek scholar. But this was his only play, and the best-known writer of comedies during this period is Pierre Larivey. The character of his work brings out clearly the two special defects of Renaissance comedy. Firstly, all his plays, of which he published six in 1595, are fairly close adaptations from Italian originals; and, secondly, not one of them is suitable for representation on the stage. Their great merit is that they are written in excellent prose, which is not only idiomatic and expressive but is the language of true comedy.

But comedy thus divorced from the stage naturally languished, and when Valleran Lecomte was manager of the Hôtel de Bourgogne the comic element was supplied by pure farce. It was probably part of the duty of Alexandre Hardy to adapt the old medieval farces to modern require-ments. Little or no attempt was made either to enlarge their scope, or to give them a literary character, or in any way to tone down their coarseness.

We have seen that when Corneille came to Paris in 1630 to witness the performance by the new company of his first play, the comedy of *Mélite*, the stage had just begun to in-crease in reputation, and several competitors had already made, or were on the point of making, their début. "The surprising success" of *Mélite* is attributed by him partly "to the novelty of that kind of comedy," and partly "to the natural style, which imitated the conversation of polite society (*qui faisait une peinture de la conversation des honnêtes gens*)." In spite of this success, he did not repeat the experiment at once. But from 1631 or 1632 to 1633 he produced in succession four comedies, *La Veuve*, *La Galerie du Palais*, *La Place Royale*, and *La Suivante*. The influence of *L'Astrée* on all of these is unmistakable. Their one and only theme is love; the plot is worked out by means of misunderstandings, jealousies, or intrigues between the various lovers, and the only psychology which is attempted is that of the tender passion. They are, in short, pastoral plays without the pastoral element—plays in which young men and women of good society carry on their love affairs in their own characters instead of in the guise of shepherds and shepherdesses. They remind one a little of Shakespeare's early comedy, the *Two Gentlemen of Verona*, but without its poetry and without its comic scenes. For in Corneille's comedies of this period the comic spirit is entirely absent. They never provoke laughter, seldom even a smile. Corneille is quite right in describing them as "a new kind of comedy"; alike in their merits, the chief of which is their easy, graceful, and pointed style, and in their defects, they differ totally from the gay and fantastic pieces, for the most part imitated from Spanish originals, with which his contemporaries competed for the public favour. They attempt, at any rate, to portray real life and contemporary society, a society somewhat inferior in social status, but not greatly dissimilar to that which had its centre in the Hôtel de Rambouillet—a society of men and women who model themselves on *L'Astrée*, and who treat love, or rather love-making, as the most serious business of life.

The scene of all the plays is Paris, and one notes with interest the occasional introduction of local colour. The characters live in the fashionable quarter of the Marais and the Place Royale, the latter giving its name to one of the plays. Another, *La Galerie du Palais* (1632), is called after the hall of the Palais de Justice, and among the *dramatis personae* are a bookseller, a mercer, and a lace-seller, who, as the custom was, have their stalls in the *Galerie*. In his *Examen* of this play, Corneille calls attention to the fact that he has introduced for the first time the character of the *suivante*, or companion, in place of that of the nurse, a traditional part always played by men and generally of a more or less coarse type. This was a change in the direction not only of refinement, but of realism, for the companion figured prominently in French society of that day, and we have a well-known example in Mme de Chalais, the companion of Mme de Sablé and the friend and correspondent of Voiture.

But, in spite of Corneille's efforts to portray society as it was in his day, his comedies hardly give one the impression of real life. Their world of irrational and often tiresome imbroglio, in which lovers quarrel for the sake of the plot and are reconciled for the sake of the *dénouement*, strikes one as unreal and fantastic. The lines,

> O pauvre comédie, objet de tant de veines !
> Si tu n'es qu'un portrait des actions humaines,
> On te tire souvent sur un original,
> A qui, pour dire vrai, tu ressembles fort mal,

are not too severe a criticism of the play—*La Galerie du Palais*—in which they occur. *La Place Royale* is equally fantastic in its construction, and its hero, Alidor, is a ridiculous example of the glorification of the will. The best of these comedies is *La Suivante* (1633), for in this the complication, though it is sustained by a misunderstanding, is at any rate set in motion by the companion's jealousy of her mistress. This jealousy, moreover, is well depicted, especially in one scene (ii. 4) of genuine comedy.

A feature of these plays which calls for special notice is their decency and decorum. It is true that in 1660 Corneille made certain alterations in *Mélite*, in order to remove anything of doubtful propriety, but no changes were required in his later comedies. Partly owing to his example, and partly owing to the orders of the King and Richelieu, decency in comedy became the fashion. Rotrou in his dedication to the King of *La Bague de l'Oubli* (printed in 1635) boasted that, if his Muse was not beautiful, she was at least virtuous. In the *Gazette* of January 5, 1635, there appeared an official statement to the effect that "His Majesty, knowing that comedy, since the time when everything that could offend the most delicate ears was banished from the stage, is one of the most innocent and agreeable diversions of his good town of Paris, intends to support three companies of actors—the first at the Hôtel de Bourgogne; the second at the Marais, where Mondory opened the theatre last Sunday; and the third at the Faubourg Saint-Germain[1]." The last of these theatres had only a brief existence, but the other two flourished exceedingly. "Plays are all the fashion at present," says the bookseller in *La Galerie du Palais* (1632), and in the *Illusion comique*, a sort of extravaganza, produced by Corneille in 1635 or 1636, one of the scenes of which represents a scene on the stage, there is a long and interesting panegyric of the drama, beginning—

> A present le théâtre
> Est en un point si haut que chacun l'idolâtre
> Et ce que votre temps voyait avec mépris
> Est aujourd'hui l'amour de tous les bons esprits.

We have seen that the success of Mairet's *Sophonisbe* in 1634 gave a great impulse to tragedy. But the years from 1634 to 1637, judging from the plays which have come down to us, seem to have been equally favourable to comedy. Besides Corneille and Rotrou, Du Ryer, Benserade, Desmarests, and other more obscure writers, produced comedies during these years. It was in accordance with the orderly and law-abiding spirit of the age that comedy should be definitely separated from tragedy, and that the hybrid species of tragi-comedy should be gradually abandoned.

The substitution of comedy for farce brought with it a new and more refined type of actor, and the old favourites of the Hôtel de Bourgogne—Gros Guillaume, Gaultier-Garguille, and Turlupin—who all died about this time, were replaced in the public estimation by Bellerose (Pierre Le Messier), who, though he sometimes played in farce, was

[1] Quoted by L. Petit de Julleville, *Le Théâtre en France*, p. 138.

essentially a serious comedian. In April, 1641, Louis XIII
issued an edict forbidding all actors to use any words or
gestures which might offend public morality, and declaring
that the exercise of their profession, provided that it was
kept within proper bounds, "should not be imputed to
them for blame or prejudice their reputation."

Of all the comedies, however, which preceded *Le Menteur*,
only two besides Corneille's need be mentioned here—
Rotrou's *Les Sosies*, which was produced at the Hôtel de
Bourgogne at the end of 1636 and rivalled the popularity
of the *Cid* at the Marais, and Desmarests's *Les Visionnaires*,
which appeared in 1637. The chief interest of both to the
modern reader is that they gave hints to Molière, *Les Sosies*
for his own version of Plautus's *Amphitryon*, and *Les
Visionnaires* for *Les Femmes savantes. Les Sosies*[1] is a gay
and lively play, written in an easy, if incorrect, style; but
it lacks Molière's humour. A comparison between the two
plays is instructive, for it helps one to realise Molière's
extraordinary power of seizing the humorous side of a
situation and of bringing it out by means of soliloquy and
dialogue.

Les Visionnaires[2] had an even greater popularity, and it
is one of the few comedies of this period which is known by
name to the general reader. It may be regarded as an
attempt at social comedy, for nearly all the characters are
supposed to represent social types. But some of these types
are taken from literature rather than from real life, and all
are enormously exaggerated. Of the three sisters, the first,
who imagines herself to be in love with Alexander the
Great, is possibly meant for a caricature of Julie d'Angennes,
whose cult for Gustavus Adolphus has been mentioned in a
former chapter; the second, who imagines that every man
is in love with her, is the prototype of Molière's Bélise; and
the third, who is stage-struck (*amoureuse de la comédie*),
testifies to the great popularity of the drama in this famous
year of the *Cid*. The four men who are received by the
ladies' father as possible husbands are equally extravagant;

[1] Rotrou, *Théâtre choisi.*   [2] *Théâtre français*, vol. VII.

and the whole play is written in such a spirit of gross caricature that, in spite of its brilliant versification, it is tiresome to read. It, however, helps us to realise the genius of Molière, who, in satirising temporary social absurdities, has done it in such a way as to render them a perennial source of laughter.

We now come to *Le Menteur*, which was produced on the stage of the Marais in the winter of 1643–44, with Bellerose in the part of Dorante and Jodelet in that of the valet Cliton. It is founded on a play of Alarcon's, *The Suspicious Truth*, and for the first three acts follows it pretty closely. Corneille, always alive to the trend of public taste, had now evidently realised that if comedy was to compete successfully with farce it must employ the element of laughter. Consequently he abandons the serious and sentimental manner of his earlier comedies, and gives us a play which, except for a single scene—that in which Dorante is reprimanded by his father for his mendacity—is comic throughout. In the original play Dorante is forced to marry Lucrèce as a punishment; but Corneille explains in his *Examen* that he had to abandon the moral intention of his Spanish model in conformity to the French idea that a comedy should be entirely comic. In this he has entirely succeeded; indeed, some of the scenes, such as that between Dorante, his valet, and the two girls (i. 3), that between Dorante and his valet in the same act (scene 6), and the scene in which Alcippe appears immediately after Dorante's account of how he has killed him in a duel (iv. 2), are masterpieces of genuine comedy.

But Corneille, whose defect is that he is apt to construct his plays rather in accordance with some preconceived dramatic theory than on the surer basis of an unbiassed observation of life, has, as Brunetière truly points out, made his play too comic, and by so doing has missed reality. Dorante himself is a caricature, and the whole working out of the plot depends on improbabilities. Thus, in spite of the introduction of local colour, of the references to the Place Royale and the Palais Cardinal, and of the description of Parisian manners and customs in the first scene, we feel we are still in the fantastic and unreal world of his earlier comedies. An additional source of improbability is introduced by the more or less strict adherence to the rules. The scene is laid first in the Tuileries and afterwards in the Place Royale; and thus we have Géronte proposing for his son to Clarice (an act in itself quite contrary to French customs), and the final *dénouement*, which includes the betrothal of Dorante to Lucrèce, taking place in a public square.

Corneille himself was quite aware that this practice, which French comedy had taken over from the Italian stage, was an indefensible one, and in *La Place Royale*, as he points out in his *Examen*, he had departed from it. But the charm and gaiety of Corneille's masterpiece in comedy are so attractive that we forget its unreality and give ourselves up to the spell of its imaginary world. We are held captive, too, by its style, by the sparkling and vivacious dialogue, the brilliant, easy, and dramatic language. "It is our earliest literary comedy," says Brunetière; and though, mindful of *Les Contents* and *Les Esprits*, we may demur to this judgment as it stands, *Le Menteur* is beyond question the first literary comedy produced in France that was suited to the requirements of the stage. Corneille had at any rate successfully accomplished what Molière calls "the strange enterprise of making well-bred people laugh."

There is another feature in the play to which attention must be called, and that perhaps the most important, for it is the one by virtue of which, more than by any other, it stands far above the other plays produced during this period. We have seen that in the *Cid* Corneille had discovered the secret of true drama—namely, the art of developing the plot by and through the characters. Now, in *Le Menteur* the portrayal of character can hardly be said to exist. We have instead the representation of a mere "humour," which has not, apparently, any effect on the general character of the hero. But in the development of the play, which has no particular plot, this humour takes the place of character. Dorante's actions are determined by it, while they in their turn determine the course of the play. The intrigue, as in all the comedies of this period, is extremely complicated, but it does not depend solely on the arbitrary introduction of misunderstandings, disguises, changes at birth, and the rest of the well-worn machinery of the ordinary comic dramatist.

A play of this latter type is Rotrou's *La Sœur*[1], a gay and lively comedy with an intricate plot, which was produced in 1645. It is closely imitated from an Italian play of the same name by Giambattista della Porta, the distinguished physicist. Molière, whose company played it for five nights in 1662, borrowed either from it or from the Italian original hints for no less than five of his own plays. The valet of the piece, Ergaste, is a typical valet of comedy, full of resource and bravery, a true forerunner of Mascarille and Scapin.

In Jodelet, the valet of Scarron's first comedy, *Jodelet, ou le Maître Valet*, produced in the same year as *La Sœur*, we have a somewhat different type, determined partly by the play being taken from the Spanish, so that Jodelet represents the *gracioso* of Spanish comedy, and partly by the fact that the part was written for a favourite actor of low comedy, whose name on the stage was Jodelet and in real life Julien Bedeau. We know him best as the Marquis de Jodelet of *Les Précieuses Ridicules*.

In the following year (1646) Scarron wrote another play for the same actor, *Jodelet souffleté*, or, as he called it later, *Jodelet duelliste*. Doubtless, also, the parts of Filipin in *L'Héritière ridicule* (1649), of Don Japhet in *Don Japhet d'Arménie* (1652), and of Don Blaize in *Le Marquis ridicule* (1656), were all played by Jodelet, whose large nose, powdered face, and nasal accent were admirably suited to broad and boisterous farce. *Don Japhet d'Arménie* is a poor play, but it contains several scenes which would be highly amusing on the stage. It is therefore not surprising that it kept its place in the comic *répertoire* longer than any

[1] *Théâtre choisi.*

other of Scarron's pieces. Don Japhet himself is, as M. Morillot says, a true hero of burlesque, and, indeed, all Scarron's comedies testify strongly to that craze for burlesque which prevailed in France from about 1644 to 1654, and to which he so successfully ministered in his poems of *Typhon* and *Virgile travesti*. The difference between his comedies and the Spanish originals from which they are all borrowed is that, while in the Spanish plays the burlesque spirit is confined to the part of the *gracioso*, who serves as a foil to the idealism of the hero, just as Sancho Panza does to that of Don Quixote, in Scarron it gives the tone to the whole piece. As a playwright Scarron is unequal and incomplete. He can write effective scenes, but he cannot construct a whole play; he can sketch the rough outline of a character, but he cannot draw a complete portrait; he has considerable facility for language and rhyme, but his style is careless; he has some gift for comic expression, but he is often trivial and sometimes coarse. His most remarkable characteristic is his unfailing gaiety, and this is all the more remarkable when we remember that from his twenty-ninth year to his death, twenty-one years later (1660), he was never free from pain, and never even had a good night's rest.

> Passants, ne faites pas de bruit,
>   Et gardez-vous qu'il ne s'éveille,
> Car voici la première nuit
>   Que le pauvre Scarron sommeille[1].

Cyrano de Bergerac's *Le Pedant joué* (1654), which has the peculiarity of being written in prose, shares the two conspicuous faults of Scarron's comedies—loose and careless construction, and tasteless exaggeration of the comic element[2]. But Cyrano, like Scarron, has a good eye for comic situations, and he owes it to this that Molière has borrowed from him a whole scene for *Les Fourberies de Scapin*, including the famous words, "*Que diable allait-il*

---

[1] For Scarron's plays, see *Scarron, Théâtre complet*, ed. E. Fournier, 1879; see also P. Morillot, *Scarron et le genre burlesque*, 1888.

[2] *Œuvres*, ed. P. Lacroix, 1858.

faire dans cette galère?" and various hints for some of his other plays. Like Scarron, Cyrano was a student of Spanish literature, and he had a great admiration for Quevedo[1].

Another successful writer of comedy at this time who borrowed freely from the rich Spanish *répertoire* and provided parts for Jodelet was Thomas Corneille, the brother of the great Corneille, and his junior by nineteen years. He made his début in 1647, and his first two pieces were colourless imitations of Calderón; but in *Don Bertrand de Cigarral* (1650), imitated from Francisco de Rojas, and *Le Geôlier de soi-même*, a rendering of Calderón's *El Alcaide de si mismo* (1655), he successfully hit the public taste by introducing into a romantic and sentimental plot a strong element of burlesque. In both cases the burlesque part is written for the ever popular Jodelet, to whose peculiarities there are several allusions.

L'Amour à la mode[2] (1651 or 1652) is a comedy of a different type. Though Thomas Corneille follows, as usual, his model (which in this case is *El Amor al uso*, by Antonio de Solis, the historian of Mexico) pretty closely both in plot and dialogue, he has succeeded in giving something of a French air to Oronte, the hero of the play, and his valet Cliton. Moreover, the scene is laid, not in Spain, as in the majority of his comedies, but at Paris. The play, in fact, reminds one of *Le Menteur*, not only in the name of the valet, but in the characters of both the valet and his master, the latter of whom is nearly as good a liar as Dorante. It is, however, far inferior to it in wit and vivacity, and in the charm of the female characters, while the development of the plot bears no relation, as it does in *Le Menteur*, to the character of the protagonist. But in one respect the younger brother has the advantage over the elder. In the parts of Oronte and Cliton there are signs of observation

---

[1] On the other hand, Tristan L'Hermite's *Le Parasite* (1654)—V. Fournel, *Les Contemporains de Molière*, III.—with its conventional plot and its stock-characters of the parasite and the braggart captain, points to Italian models.

[2] For this and the other two comedies of T. Corneille, see *Théâtre français*, vol. VIII.; also G. Reynier, *Thomas Corneille, sa vie et son théâtre*, 1892.

and sympathetic study of character, which are not altogether due to the Spanish original. Hence, if there is less
wit, there is more humour than in *Le Menteur*.

There is also observation, though of a somewhat different
kind, in *La belle Plaideuse*[1] (1654) of Boisrobert, a play
from which Molière has borrowed a whole scene for his
Avare. The action during part of the play takes place in
the famous fair of Saint-Germain, and the first two acts
lead us to believe that here, at last, is true social comedy.
But the later acts degenerate into a network of trivial
intrigue, and once more we find ourselves in a world which
is none the less fantastic because it is peopled with
scoundrels.

There are not only observation and the elements of a
comedy of manners in Gillet de la Tessonerie's *Le Cam-
pagnard* (1657)[2], but there is a real attempt to create
character. The provincial *hobereau* in Paris, with his
blundering stupidity, his boasting, and his touch of *préciosité*, and his valet, the indispensable Jodelet, who is a
species of Sancho Panza, are crudely drawn, but they
are something more than mere types. Two years later
Molière appeared with his *Précieuses Ridicules* and showed
the way to better things. After the performance of
Les Fâcheux, at the fête given by Fouquet at Vaux in
August, 1661, La Fontaine sent to his friend Maucroix the
often quoted lines:

> Nous avons changé de méthode:
> Jodelet n'est plus à la mode,
> Et maintenant il ne faut pas
> Quitter la nature d'un pas.

[1] *Le Théâtre français au XVI*[e] *et au XVII*[e] *Siècle*, ed. E. Fournier, vol. ii.
[2] Fournel, *op. cit.*, iii. (with the omission of a few scenes).

CHAPTER IX

THE REIGN OF BAD TASTE

On December 4, 1642, the great Cardinal died, to be followed to the grave five months later by his submissive pupil, Louis XIII. It was not only in the political world that the change was felt; it affected the whole social atmosphere. The French nobles as a whole, including those who frequented the Hôtel de Rambouillet, behaved like schoolboys suddenly emancipated from the control of a stern and tyrannical schoolmaster.

This feeling of relief is well expressed by Saint-Évremond in a poem which he addressed to Ninon de Lenclos thirty years later, when he and his fellow-nobles were again suffering from the pressure of an autocrat's heavy hand. He recalls with regret *la bonne régence* of Anne of Austria, when "an indulgent policy favoured all our desires"; when "there was no constraint, nor too much liberty"; when "people were sociable, and conversation was natural and agreeable"; when "women were well informed without being blue-stockings" (*savaient sans faire les savantes*); when "a young duke, who held victory like a slave bound to his chariot, by his valour and the splendour of his glory made us forget Alexander and Caesar."

It is a strange period from many points of view, these eighteen years during which the rulers of France were the proud Spanish princess, Anne of Austria, and the Italian adventurer, Giulio Mazarini. Abroad, the policy of Richelieu, no longer hampered by that statesman's jealousy of too successful generals, was carried to a triumphant issue. At home, events shaped themselves into a drama of shifting fortunes—a drama in three acts, which might be appropriately labelled Anne, Retz, Mazarin.

The bonfires which hailed the death of Richelieu were a signal for the factious and discontented nobles to weave

new intrigues. The political exiles were recalled, and with
Mme de Chevreuse, the queen of conspirators, at their head,
began to plot afresh. Their first production was the "Cabal
of the Importants" (as they were wittily christened by
Mme Cornuel), under the nominal leadership of the empty-
headed grandson of Henry IV, the Duc de Beaufort[1].
Conspiracy became the ordinary diversion of nobles and
courtiers during the idle winter months, when the operations of war were suspended. They conspired to please their
mistresses, just as Cinna and Maxime conspired to please
Émilie.

Meanwhile, under this "good regency," as it seemed to
Saint-Évremond and his fellow-nobles, the misery and
suffering of the country increased. Richelieu had left the
finances in a deplorable state, and the revenues were
pledged for four years in advance. But money had to be
provided for the operations of war and the subsidies of
allies. Taxes were steadily increased; the State was driven
to desperate expedients, and before long it was on the verge
of bankruptcy.

Then came the second act of the drama, the tragi-
comedy of the Fronde—a comedy if you regard it as a
political revolution, a tragedy from the point of view of
the suffering people. Lastly, we have, as the third act, the
triumph of Mazarin—the seven years during which he ruled
France with absolute power, not only in reality, but even
in outward semblance, keeping Louis XIV, who had attained his legal majority of thirteen in 1651, entirely in the
background, treating Anne of Austria with the harshness
and want of courtesy which he habitually showed to the
women of his family, yet possessed of the entire confidence
of both mother and son; amassing an unheard-of fortune,
mainly from the revenues of his government and his abbeys
—he held twenty-seven, though it is a question whether he
was in Orders—partly by dishonest manipulation of the
public funds, and partly by avaricious practices worthy of

[1] See Retz's *Memoirs* for admirable portraits of Mme de Chevreuse and
the Duc de Beaufort.

a Harpagon, yet lavishing money freely on Court festivities and theatrical representations, and even on a free lottery, in which the prizes were worth over a million livres.

A hardly less conspicuous figure in this act of the drama is Nicolas Fouquet, the famous Superintendent of the finances. Preserving the State from bankruptcy by virtue of his own credit, and at the same time availing himself of the inextricable confusion between his private and public accounts to fill his own pockets, he lived from hand to mouth in almost regal splendour. His two country seats— at Saint-Mandé and at Vaux-le-Vicomte near Melun—were adorned by the chief living French artists, and were filled with superb collections of every sort and kind. He was a munificent patron of men of letters, and to follow the career of his patronage, a task rendered easy by the researches of M. Châtelain[1], is an instructive lesson in the literary taste of his time.

Since the retirement of Corneille, after the failure of *Pertharite* in 1653, his place had been taken by two younger dramatists. In 1656, the year in which Fouquet signed the contract with his architect for his new palace at Vaux, and Chapelain published the *Pucelle* and Pascal the *Lettres Provinciales*, both dramatists produced a romantic tragedy founded on one of the fashionable heroic romances— Quinault, *La Mort de Cyrus*, taken from *Le Grand Cyrus*, and Thomas Corneille, *Timocrate*, taken from *Cléopâtre*. Both were highly successful, especially *Timocrate*, which, with its extraordinary subject, its complicated plot, and its super-refined sentiment, exactly hit the public taste. It was played to a crowded house three days a week for six months. In the same year, 1656, Scarron dedicated to Fouquet his *Léandre et Héro*, a burlesque poem in which the burlesque character is considerably mitigated. In the following year Pellisson became Fouquet's confidential man of business and his adviser in matters of literary patronage, and Pellisson's taste in literature was as wide and as undiscriminating as his patron's.

[1] *Le Surintendant Nicolas Fouquet*, 1905.

It was in this year, too, that La Fontaine was introduced to Fouquet and presented him with the manuscript of his poem of *Adonis*. It was a great improvement on the ponderous epics which had preceded it, for it was not only very much shorter, but it was the work of a poet—of a poet, indeed, who had not found his true line, but still of a poet. The poems which La Fontaine produced, according to agreement, every quarter, by way of receipt for the pension granted him by Fouquet, are good examples of the poetical taste of the period. They are all occasional pieces— elegies, odes, epistles, *ballades*, *rondeaux*, madrigals, and other trivialities—all written to order, and consequently all devoid of inspiration. In 1658 he began, by order of his patron, a more ambitious work, the *Songe de Vaux*, a strange mixture of burlesque and epic and *préciosité*, which, though he worked at it at intervals for three years, was never completed.

In 1657 Thomas Corneille produced another tragedy, *La Mort de Commode*, which was eventually dedicated to Fouquet; and in 1658 Quinault's comedy of *Le feint Alcibiade* was played before him, and having met with his approbation, was also dedicated to him. Then in the same year, 1658, Fouquet encouraged the great Corneille to return to the stage, and suggested to him two or three subjects. Corneille chose that of Œdipus, and his tragedy of *Œdipe*, written in two months, was produced in January, 1659, with brilliant success, at the Hôtel de Bourgogne. Nothing, perhaps, gives us a better idea of the prevailing taste in literature than the fact that Corneille, in order to show that his hand had not lost its cunning and that he could produce as successful a play as his brother or Quinault, should have turned Sophocles's great and terrible tragedy into a romantic melodrama strongly tinged with *préciosité*. If Sévère has frequented the Hôtel de Rambouillet, Thésée is an *habitué* of Mlle de Scudéry's Saturdays. It was time, indeed, for Molière to appear with his *Précieuses Ridicules*.

Such was the condition of French literature when Boileau began to write his satires, the first of which was published in 1660. Let us see who were the writers—most of them in high repute—against whom his shafts were directed. They were Saint-Amant, Quinault, Desmarests de Saint-Sorlin, the Abbé de Pure, Georges de Scudéry and his sister Madeleine, La Calprenède, Cotin, Scarron, and, above all, Chapelain. Now, of these, Desmarests, Scudéry, and Chapelain had written prosaic and uninspired epics; Scarron was the inventor of burlesque; and Saint-Amant, besides writing an epic, excelled in a somewhat similar art—that of trivial description; while Quinault, Mlle de Scudéry, La Calprenède, the Abbé de Pure, and Cotin, all more or less represent *préciosité*. Thus, it may be said that Boileau made war on three forms of bad taste—on dull epics or pedantry, on burlesque or vulgarity, and on *préciosité* or affectation. Burlesque, indeed, has sometimes been regarded as a reaction against *préciosité*; but M. Lanson well points out that this view is negatived by the absence of any critical intention from the writings of Scarron and his school, and the same view for somewhat different reasons is taken by Brunetière[1].

Of the epic epidemic, it is sufficient to note that it began in 1651 with the *Saint-Louis* of Père Le Moyne (completed in 1653), and that it continued with the *Moïse sauvé* of Saint-Amant (1653), the *Alaric* of Georges de Scudéry (1654), the *Pucelle* of Chapelain (1656), and the *Clovis* of Desmarests de Saint-Sorlin (1657). All except *Moïse sauvé*, which its author does not call an epic, but a heroic idyll, were modelled on Tasso's *Jerusalem Delivered*, and were preceded by a treatise on epic poetry. That of Desmarests is noteworthy as the beginning of his controversy with Boileau on the use of the *merveilleux chrétien* in epic poems.

The origin of the trivial and tiresome kind of poetry which was called burlesque is not absolutely clear. It was foreshadowed, no doubt, by the heroi-comic poetry of Saint-Amant, modelled on Tassoni's *La secchia rapita*, which he inaugurated with the *Passage de Gibraltar*, written in 1636, but not printed till 1640. Saint-Amant, indeed, is

---

[1] See *La Maladie du Burlesque* in *Études critiques*, 8ᵐᵉ série, 1907.

sometimes regarded as the founder of French burlesque, but there are marked differences between his poetry and that of the true burlesque-writers. The transition from one to the other seems to have been brought about by one of those strange freaks of fashion to which "smart sets" in all ages are subject, and which, in this case, took the form of imitating the language of street porters and fishwives. It was specially patronised by the Duc de Beaufort, who was nicknamed *Le roi des Halles*[1]. From society it spread to literature, where the language of the fishmarket was reinforced by the addition of archaic words and phrases, mostly borrowed from Clément Marot. With the appearance of Scarron's *Typhon* in 1644 burlesque became a recognised literary form with a special metre of its own, the octosyllabic couplet. In 1648 Scarron produced the first three cantos of *Virgile travesti*, and in the same year François d'Assoucy, who, next to Scarron, was the chief practitioner of the art, burlesqued Ovid in his *Jugement de Paris*. The travesty of heroic poems, especially of classical poems, was henceforth regarded as the special province of burlesque. "The rage for burlesque," says the worthy Pellisson, "reached such a pitch that the booksellers would take nothing which did not bear that name." But by 1653, when he wrote his *History of the Academy*, the fashion, he tells us, had begun to decline. The lines in which Boileau has pilloried the art of Scarron and D'Assoucy are well known. An interesting commentary on them is furnished by a letter of Nicolas Poussin, who, writing from Rome, says: "I have received a ridiculous book by M. Scarron"— it was *Typhon*—"I have skimmed it once, and that is enough. You will allow me to refrain from expressing all the disgust I feel for works of this kind." Such was the attitude towards burlesque of the first French classicist, the great painter who, a generation before Boileau, devoted himself with stern and unbending fidelity to the pursuit of the classical ideal.

[1] "Il parloit, il pensoit comme le peuple, dont il fut l'idole quelque temps" (Retz).

Burlesque as a literary form owes something both to Italy and Spain. An Italian travesty of the *Æneid* by Giambattista Lalli had preceded Scarron's by fifteen years, and he was evidently acquainted with it. The name itself is said to have been imported from Italy by Sarasin, but Scarron's work differs considerably in treatment from the Italian burlesque of Berni and his followers. Notably it lacks the satiric intention which is hardly ever absent from the latter. Scarron also owes something to the Spaniard, Góngora.

The question of the influence of Spain and Italy on French literature during the first half of the seventeenth century is a difficult one, and though some important and useful contributions have been made to the subject, it has never yet been treated satisfactorily as a whole. The old idea that the bad taste which more or less tainted French literature throughout the whole period, and which, under the rule of Anne of Austria and Mazarin, became a serious evil, was entirely due to the contamination of Spain and Italy—of Spain through Góngora, and of Italy through Marini—must now be abandoned. As regards Góngora, M. Lanson has shown pretty conclusively that his famous *Soledades* (Solitary Musings), in which *culteranismo* reaches its obscurest point, were little known and less appreciated in France, and that his influence was practically confined to the domain of burlesque.

With Marini the case is somewhat different. As we have seen, he came to France in person, lived for eight years in Paris, frequenting the Hôtel de Rambouillet, and finally published there his epic poem of *Adone*, which, with its far-fetched metaphors and constant striving after novelty, was received as a masterpiece by his French admirers. But it did not introduce what the Italians call *secentismo* into France. For, as Signor Belloni, the latest historian of Italian seventeenth-century literature, has pointed out—and, indeed, the fact is beyond dispute—the elaboration of metaphor and antithesis, the abuse of emphasis and refinement, of ornaments and conceits—in a word, of all the artifices which serve to mask essential poverty of thought, sentiment, and inspiration—though it is specially character-istic of the seventeenth century, had existed in germ long before this period, and had already manifested itself in the "pyrotechnic displays" of Cariteo and Tebaldeo and Serafino dell' Aquila towards the close of the fifteenth century, and in the "cold elegances" of Bembo and the other Petrarchists in the first half of the sixteenth. And all these poets had been imitated in France from the time of Saint-Gelais onwards; by Scève, by the poets of the Pleiad, by Desportes, and lastly by D'Urfé, whose verses in *L'Astrée* show the influence alike of Desportes and of the Italian poets whom they both imitated. Marini, then, who, be it noted, freely plagiarised his predecessors, merely continued, or at most increased, the infiltration of Italian ingenuity and conceit into French literature.

The nationality of Marie de' Medici doubtless helped to strengthen the current of Italian influence, and a similar impulse was given by the Italian Mazarin. The epics of this period were, as we have seen, inspired by Tasso's *Jerusalem Delivered*. But Tasso's influence had begun long before this. We find it in Bertaut's poetry as far back as 1585, and in the pastoral dramas which flourished from about the same year to 1610. Throughout the first half of the seventeenth century the leading French men of letters were thoroughly familiar with Italian literature, and Chapelain, indeed, piqued himself on knowing it as well as any Italian. Voiture was exceptional in preferring Spanish literature to Italian.

Apart from *Amadis de Gaula* and Jorge de Montemôr's *Diana*, Spain exercised no real influence on French litera-ture during the sixteenth century. It was not till about the year 1620, says M. Lanson in his careful investigation of the subject[1], that the knowledge of Spanish, to which a stimulus had been given by the marriage of Louis XIII with Anne of Austria (1615), became general in French society. But from the very beginning of the century

[1] *Rev. d'hist. litt.*, 1896, 1897 and 1901.

Spanish literature had begun to make its way in France. It had come first in the form of theological and devotional treatises, such as the writings of the great mystics, St Teresa and St Juan de la Cruz, the famous *Guide to Sinners* of Luis de Granada, which was one of the favourite books of Regnier's Macette, and the works of the celebrated Jesuit, Ribadeneira. A complete contrast to these devotional treatises was furnished by the picaresque novels, *Guzmán de Alfarache*, *Marcos de Obregón*, *Il Gran Tacaño* (The Great Rogue), all of which were translated into French, and which produced a French offspring in Sorel's *Francion* (1623) and Scarron's *Le roman comique* (1651). Quevedo's *Sueños* (Visions), his next most characteristic work to *Il Gran Tacaño*, was also popular, and, as well as Gracián's *El Héroe*, found a French translator. The *Exemplary Novels* of Cervantes appeared in French in 1615, two years after their publication in Spain. *Don Quixote* followed in 1618.

Finally, the rich Spanish drama was freely exploited by French authors. Rotrou seems to have led the way with his comedy of *La bague de l'oubli* (produced in 1628), which he borrowed from Lope, as he did some of his later plays. But he by no means confined himself to Spain; Italy and the ancient drama had their share in his patronage. Corneille's debt to Spain is well known, and has already been mentioned. It was not till the time of Scarron and the younger Corneille that the Spanish drama threatened to overwhelm the French stage. They no longer went to Lope, but to their contemporaries, Calderón and Francisco de Rojas. Their scenes were laid in Madrid, and there was no attempt to disguise the Spanish origin of their pieces. Their work as adapters was, in fact, chiefly confined to the task of "reducing" their romantic originals to the rules of the French classical drama.

On the whole, unless we accept the unconvincing view of M. Martinenche[1] that it was from the Spanish stage that Corneille learnt the importance of action in drama, it can-

---

[1] *La comédie espagnole en France de Hardy à Racine*, 1900.

not be said that Spanish literature left any deep or permanent traces. It was little more than a passing fashion. It coloured and animated some of the side-channels and backwaters of French literature; it even muddied for a time the main current; but it neither diverted its course nor in any way permanently affected it.

The question of Spanish and Italian influence has a special importance in connexion with the third part of our present subject, for that form of bad taste which is known as *préciosité* has been ascribed to the influence of both Góngora and Marini. But we have seen that the influence of Góngora was confined to his burlesque poems, while that of Marini, though of somewhat greater importance, had been preceded by the similar influence of earlier Italian writers. The real origin of *préciosité* and the time of its first appearance have been the subject of considerable discussion. It is agreed, indeed, to accept the statement of the Abbé de Pure in his *La Précieuse*, published in 1656, that the word *Précieuse* had at that date only recently come into vogue; but it is said that the spirit which the word denoted existed at the very beginning of the century, and it is generally added that it was in the Hôtel de Rambouillet that this spirit was fostered. But we must be on our guard against confusing that special form of affectation in speech and literature which is known as *préciosité* with earlier manifestations of the same disease. In order to avoid this confusion we must first ascertain what the special characteristics of *préciosité* really are, and then consider when these began to make their appearance. "The chief requisite of a *Précieuse*," says Somaize in his *Grand Dictionnaire des Pretieuses*, published in 1661[1], "is *esprit*; to qualify for the title it is absolutely necessary for a woman either to have *esprit*, or to appear to have it, or at least to be persuaded that she has it." But he goes on to say that all women of *esprit* are not *Précieuses*; "only those who write or criticise the writings of others, or whose reading consists chiefly of romances, or especially those who invent new and strange

[1] Ed. Ch.-L. Livet, 2 vols., 1856 (Bibliothèque Elzévirienne).

modes of speech." Under the heading "*Morale*" we learn
that the *Précieuses* have ten general maxims, of which the
fourth is to value imagination more than truth in matters
of pleasure; the fifth is to give their opinions only in the
presence of those they esteem, and never to speak of a
person's defects without adding some praise; the eighth is
to use a different language from that of ordinary folk, in
order that their ideas may only be understood by those
whose intelligence is above the common; and the ninth is
never to remain silent in conversation without expressing
their sentiments by signs and gestures. Finally, at the end
of each letter of the alphabet Somaize adds a short list of
précieux phrases culled from the works of such writers as
Balzac, Voiture, the two Corneilles, Chapelain, Mlle de
Scudéry, and Saint-Amant.

From these scattered remarks of this not over-intelligent
observer we can, with the help of our knowledge from
other sources, fairly well construct the *précieux* ideal as it
existed in 1661. We see the importance attached to *esprit*,
and especially to the display of it in conversation; the
desire to be distinguished, and to avoid, above all things,
the commonplace; the love of select coteries and mutual
admiration; the partiality for new and strange modes of
speech; the aspiration to authorship, or at least to criticism; and lastly, the preference for imagination rather than
for truth in literature. It is to be noted that Somaize uses
the term *Précieuses* only, and that there is no corresponding
term for men, who are variously described as *hommes
d'esprit*, or *hommes de qualité*, or *hommes galants*. The fact
is significant of the glorification of woman which marks the
whole movement. "That fair half of the world," says
Voiture's nephew, Martin de Pinchesne, in the preface to his
edition of his uncle's works, "is as capable of criticism as we
are, and is at the present day mistress of man's glory." It
is to be noted, further, that Somaize, in his preface, following the example of Molière, distinguishes between the
second-rate or ridiculous *Précieuses*, the object of Molière's
satire, who, in their endeavour to be something out of the

common (*se tirer hors du commun*), read every romance and work of gallantry that is published, and the true *Précieuses*, "who, having all their lives cultivated the *esprit* with which Nature has endowed them,…have become as learned as the greatest authors of the age, and are versed in several languages, as well as in the art of writing in verse and prose."

Somaize dates the beginning of the empire of the *Pré cieuses* from the time of Voiture, whom he calls its "founder and great minister," and accordingly he includes in his Dictionary all the frequenters of the Hôtel de Rambouillet during the period of its greatest splendour. But as his acknowledged aim is to prove the antiquity of the *Précieuses*, we are justified in declining to accept without examination the noble ancestry which he has provided for them. We must consider for ourselves to what extent the characteristics of a *Précieuse* of the year 1661 are to be found in the society which met in Mme de Rambouillet's salon. As I said at the conclusion of the chapter devoted to that institution, most of those characteristics undoubtedly existed there, at least in germ. We find the same devotion to *esprit* and conversation, the same aspiration towards refinement and distinction, the same exaggerated deference to the self-esteem of others, the same tone of florid but respectful gallantry, modelled on *L'Astrée* and the other popular romances of the day. On the other hand, Mme de Rambouillet and her friends made no claim to superior learning; nor, as far as the ladies were concerned, did they aspire to authorship. They were simply a circle of friends who met together for refined social intercourse. Chapelain, writing to Balzac in 1638, says of the Blue Chamber that "there is no place in the world where there is more good sense and less pedantry," and he contrasts it with the salon of a certain Mme d'Auchy or d'Ochy, which she called an "Academy," and on which Arnauld de Corbeville, the *poète-carabin*, wrote an unpublished satire.

It may be said that these distinctions are unsubstantial, and that Chapelain was too much of a pedant himself for his testimony to be of much value. But if we turn to the

letters of Voiture, whom Somaize regards as "the founder
of the empire of the *Précieuses*," and whom Brunetière
terms "the living incarnation of *préciosité*," or to those of
Balzac, of whom Somaize says that *parler précieux* and
parler Balzac are the same thing—and, after all, it is the
influence of the *Précieuses* on language and literature that
concerns us most—we do not find in them, to any marked
extent, the search after grotesque metaphors, the avoidance at all hazards of the *mot propre*, and the other affectations of language which Molière ridicules in his comedy, and
Somaize registers with solemn pains in his Dictionary. In
the letter, for instance, which Voiture wrote to Julie from
Avignon (1642), and which M. Bourciez calls "an inflated
and 'precious' description of the Rhone," there is only one
passage of which the language can be fairly described as
"precious." Voiture's letters abound in exaggerated com-
pliment and exaggerated sentiment, but you have to search
them long and carefully for examples of extravagant metaphor and pretentious periphrasis. The one mark of affectation which may be justly laid to his charge is an occasional
abuse of antithesis.

Balzac's case is somewhat different. With his natural
tendency to emphasis, and with less tact than Voiture, he
falls more often into the abuse of metaphor and periphrasis. But if you test him fairly—if, instead of separating
his metaphors from their context after the manner of
Somaize, or taking them from the mouth of Hortensius, the
pedant of Sorel's *Francion*, who in some respects is a caricature of Balzac, you examine his own writings, it will be
found that his offences against good taste are far from
frequent and seldom glaring. It is true that he begins one
of his letters with, "I have been almost drowned in a flood
of phlegm, and am not yet dry after my shipwreck," and
continues throughout the letter in a strain of grandiloquent
metaphor. But such examples are rare. While Sorel says
of Hortensius that "he always talked *Phébus*" (the current
term for affected and grandiloquent language), Balzac himself refers with disapproval to a certain provincial town

where "*Phébus* passed for the height of eloquence, and a temperate style was derided."

After Voiture, who reflects the tone of conversation of the Hôtel de Rambouillet, and Balzac, who was regarded as its oracle, let us consult Corneille, who, as was pointed out in the chapter on Comedy, says of his first comedy, *Mélite* (1629 or 1630), that one of the reasons for its surprising success was that its style represented the conversation of polite society (*des honnêtes gens*). But when *Mélite* was written, Corneille was an obscure provincial who had never visited Paris, and its style must be regarded rather as a reflection of *L'Astrée* than as a rendering at first hand of the conversation of a Paris salon. Let us, rather, take his third play, *La Veuve*, which was produced in 1631 or 1632. He tells us in the preface that "he has endeavoured to put in the mouths of his actors the words which the characters that they represent would probably utter, and to make them talk like gentlefolk (*en honnêtes gens*), and not like authors." And in his *Examen* he says of the style of *La Veuve*, that it is "more free from conceits than *Mélite*" (*plus dégagé des pointes dont l'autre est semée*). In fact, a perusal of the play leads to the conclusion that what may be fairly called *préciosité* of language is confined to the lovers' speeches.

Corneille's greatest tragedies, from *Le Cid* to *Polyeucte*, though they faithfully reproduce some of the types of contemporary society—the political woman, the soldier hero, the *honnêtes gens* who conversed in Mme de Rambouillet's salon—are, for the most part, free from *préciosité* even in their love-making. There is a touch of it, however, in *Polyeucte*, the play which, it will be recollected, was read in the Blue Chamber before its production. But in *Le Menteur* and *Pompée*, both played in the winter of 1643–44, Corneille returns in his lovers' speeches to the style of his early comedies. This is how Julius Caesar makes love to Cleopatra:

Je l'ai vaincu, princesse; et le dieu des combats
M'y favorisait moins que vos divins appas;
Ils conduisaient ma main, ils enflaient mon courage;
Cette pleine victoire est leur dernier ouvrage:

C'est l'effet des ardeurs qu'ils daignaient m'inspirer;
Et, vos beaux yeux enfin m'ayant fait soupirer,
Pour faire que votre âme avec gloire y réponde,
M'ont rendu le premier et de Rome et du monde.

La déclaration est tout à fait galante, as Elmire says to Tartuffe. And Tartuffe himself, when he declares his abominable passion for Elmire, uses the same figurative style. His speeches are studded with *attraits, appas, feux, flammes, soupirs, transports, bontés, douceurs,* and all the conventional terms of the *galant* of his day. For in the twenty years or more which had elapsed since the production of *Pompée,* the language of lovers had become even more affected, and had degenerated into a regular jargon. Philinte, the *honnête homme* of *Le Misanthrope,* proposes to Éliante in the following terms:

Et moi, de mon côté je ne m'oppose pas,
Madame, à ces bontés qu'ont pour lui vos appas;
Et lui-même, s'il veut, il peut bien vous instruire
De ce que là-dessus j'ai pris soin de lui dire.
Mais si, pas un hymen qui les joindrait eux deu▼,
Vous étiez hors d'état de recevoir ses vœux,
Tous les miens tenteraient la faveur éclatante
Qu'avec tant de bonté votre âme lui présente,
Heureux si, quand son cœur s'y pourra dérober,
Elle pouvait sur moi, madame, retomber!

A modern reader is probably disturbed by what seems to him the affectation of these lines, but they are rather to be regarded as a faithful reproduction of the language in which an *honnête homme* of Molière's day would have made a proposal of marriage to a woman whom he esteemed but did not love. If we still have any doubt on this point, we may turn to *L'Avare,* and read in plain prose the opening lines:

Hé quoi! charmante Élise, vous devenez mélancolique, après les obligeantes assurances que vous avez eu la bonté de me donner de votre foi....Vous repentez-vous de cet engagement où mes feux ont pu vous contraindre?

So, too, in Racine's *Andromaque,* produced four months

before *L'Avare*, Pyrrhus declares his passion for Andromaque in much the same strain:

> Je souffre tous les maux que j'ai faits devant Troie:
> Vaincu, chargé de fers, de regrets consumé,
> Brûlé de plus de feux que je n'en allumai.

Orestes is equally *galant* in his language to Hermione.
When Boileau, referring to an earlier period, wrote,

> Et sans pointe un amant n'osa plus soupirer,

did he realise that Molière and Racine, the great protago-
nists of the Natural school, were open to the same charge?

It appears, then, that French society of the seventeenth
century prescribed the use of a certain conventional
language for those declarations of love which a *galant
homme* considered himself bound to make to the ladies of
his acquaintance, and which in most cases were only half
serious. Both the figurative language and the attitude of
respectful adoration were largely due to the influence of
L'Astrée, which in its turn traces back to the Petrarchism
and Neo-Platonism of the sixteenth century. It is a mistake, however, to suppose that this *style figuré, dont on fait
vanité*, as Alceste calls it, indispensable though it was for
sonnets and madrigals and the other compliments of
gallantry, is in any sense a measure of the ordinary conversation of the Blue Chamber, or the salons of Mme de
Sablé and the Princesse de Condé. Further, it must be
borne in mind that it did not originate either in the Hôtel
de Rambouillet or in *L'Astrée*. In the *Trésor des douze
livres d'Amadis*, published in 1560, the declarations of love
are couched in the same precious style. In Estienne
Pasquier's *Colloques d'Amour* (1567) love problems are discussed much as they were in Mme de Rambouillet's salon.
There is, in fact, little difference between the *Colloques
d'Amour* of the sixteenth century and the *Questions
galantes* of the seventeenth.

In Mme de Rambouillet's circle and in the general
society of her day the conventional and high-flown language

of gallantry was doubtless stimulated by the excessive desire to please which formed part of the social creed. From this defect of a social virtue sprang also the exaggerated compliments which formed part of the ordinary social currency. Almost the only criticism which Tallemant passes on Mme de Rambouillet is that she was *un peu trop complimenteuse.* "Voiture and Conrart," says the same observant chronicler, "mounted on stilts to praise Balzac." Balzac writes to Godeau: "Everything that you write has such a charm for me that I cannot judge of it calmly, unless passion and transport admit of calm judgment." Voiture's compliments to him are equally emphatic and more ingenious. "When I crossed the borders of the ancient world in order to find something rare, I saw nothing so rare as your works. Africa had nothing to show me more novel or more extraordinary." Chapelain was a past master in the art of log-rolling. The fashion of paying insincere compliments still continued in Molière's day. It is this, more than anything else, which rouses Alceste to revolt against society.

In other respects, it cannot be said that the Hôtel de Rambouillet was visibly affected by *préciosité* during its palmy period. It is not, at any rate, until just before the close of the reign of Louis XIII that we begin to detect symptoms of positive disease. The *Guirlande de Julie*; the touch of gallantry in *Polyeucte*, and the larger dose of it in *Pompée*; the publication of the first volume of La Calprenède's heroic romance of *Cassandre* (1642), which, according to Somaize, "taught the *Précieuses* and their admirers *(leurs alcôvistes)* the true way to make love," may perhaps be regarded as such symptoms, but they all relate to the particular department of gallantry. A further stage is possibly marked by the advent of Mme de Rambouillet's youngest daughter, Angélique, who, on Julie's marriage in 1645, left her convent to take her sister's place. For the first Mme de Grignan—she married M. de Grignan in 1658 —with her exaggerated purism and her exaggerated prudery, was decidedly something of a *précieuse,* just as the third Mme de Grignan was something of a *femme savante* But when all is said, it is not in the Blue Chamber that we must look for the rapid development of *préciosité*, but in the salon of Mme de Scudéry.

It was in the year 1639, at the latest, that Madeleine de Scudéry joined her brother Georges in Paris, she being in that year thirty-one[1], and he seven years older. They were the children of a Provençal gentleman of good family, who held the appointment of captain of the Havre ports. Georges de Scudéry has already appeared in these pages, not altogether to his advantage. He was a bit of a swash-buckler, vain and presumptuous; but there was a generous vein both in his heart and in his Muse, for he was loyal to his friends and in occasional lines a poet of some merit. His sister, on the other hand, was remarkable for her modesty, her tact, and her sweetness of temper. Throughout her long life—she died in 1701, in her ninety-second year—she never made an enemy, and she was universally respected even by those who were most opposed to her literary ideals. Boileau, who composed his *Héros de Roman* in 1665, did not print it till after her death, because he "did not wish to give annoyance to a lady who, after all, had great merit, and whose integrity and honourable con-duct, if all those who knew her are to be believed, even surpassed her intelligence." She was introduced by her brother to the Hôtel de Rambouillet soon after her arrival in Paris, but we hear little of her during its flourishing period. Her first novel, *Ibrahim ou l'Illustre Bassa*, ap-peared in 1641 under her brother's name, and from 1644 to 1647 she was living with him at Marseilles. It was in 1653, when the Fronde had been finally put down in Paris, that she began her celebrated Saturdays in the Rue Vieille du Temple in the quarter of the Marais. They were attended by some of the former *habitués* of the Blue Chamber, by Mme de Sablé, Mme de Maure, M. and Mme de Montausier; but the general tone was *bourgeois* and literary rather than aristocratic. Prominent among the lady visitors were the

[1] She was baptised on December 1, 1608 (Rathery and Boutron, *Mlle de Scudéry*, 1873, p. 4).

witty Mme Cornuel, the wife of a government official, and her stepdaughters, Mlle Legendre and Mlle Cornuel; Mme Aragonais, the rich widow of another government official; and three spinsters, Mlle Robineau and the two Mlles Boquet. The men were chiefly authors—Chapelain, Ménage, Sarasin, Conrart (whose unpublished papers are a mine of information for the *précieux* society), and Pellisson, whose long attachment to Mlle Scudéry has been mentioned in a former chapter.

It has been said truly that this *bourgeois* and literary atmosphere in itself contributed to the increase of *préciosité*. The refinement and distinction which were the natural inheritance of Mme de Rambouillet and her aristocratic friends were only attained with a certain effort by the professional class which frequented the Rue Vieille du Temple. That interest in literature which gave an intellectual character to the Blue Chamber turned to pedantry in the hands of Ménage and Chapelain. There was all the difference between a hostess who was a woman of the world and a hostess who was an authoress. The very name of Sapho, by which Mlle de Scudéry was known to her admiring guests, carries with it a flavour of *préciosité*. The conversations, which in Mme de Rambouillet's salon pursued a natural course, assumed a formal character at the Saturdays. Subjects for discussion were selected beforehand, and even a report of the proceedings was sometimes drawn up.

It is from Mlle de Scudéry's two most famous and characteristic novels, *Le Grand Cyrus* and *Clélie*, that we can form the best idea of the difference between the tone of the *Samedis* and that which prevailed at the Hôtel de Rambouillet. For while *Le Grand Cyrus*, which appeared at intervals from January, 1649, to September, 1653, represents the society of the Blue Chamber in its latter days, as seen through Mlle de Scudéry's spectacles, *Clélie* (1654–60) depicts that of her own salon. In these novels Mlle de Scudéry, while keeping to the historical background and the complicated plot of *Cassandre* and *Cléopâtre*, returns virtually to the manner of *L'Astrée*, transferring the interest in a large measure from the narrative of adventure to the analysis of sentiment. Moreover, the historical background is little more than a pretence. Though the scene is laid in the one case in ancient Persia, and in the other in ancient Rome, the characters veiled under transparent disguises belong to Mlle de Scudéry's own day. The hero and the heroine of *Le Grand Cyrus*[1] are Condé and his sister, Mme de Longueville; and among the other characters are Mme de Rambouillet and her daughters, Mlle Paulet, Mme de Sablé, Montausier, Voiture, Godeau, Conrart, Chapelain, and Mlle de Scudéry herself. The formal conversations, which are a special feature of the book, begin in the fifth part (written in 1650). Many of these deal with *questions galantes*, such as the advantage of being loved by a man who has never loved before, avarice and prodigality in a lover, marriage, the *air galant*; but other subjects find a place, such as youth and old age, the fear of death, learned women, and conversation itself. It is in these conversations that Mlle de Scudéry is at her best, for they show much good sense and considerable power of analysis. Many years later (1680–92) they were published separately.

In the sixth part of *Le Grand Cyrus* there begins the elaborate series of "portraits," the fashion for which Mlle de Scudéry may be said to have set. During the next few years it increased to an absurd extent, and in 1659 a collection of "portraits," partly written by no less a person than Mlle de Montpensier, and partly contributed by her friends, was published by her secretary, Segrais. In *Clélie* the pretence of a historical setting is transparent, and Brutus, Tarquinius, Horatius Cocles, Lucretia, Clelia, and the rest, amuse themselves in exactly the same way as the guests at the Saturdays—making portraits of their friends and taking part in formal conversations on questions of gallantry. The portraits—which include Scarron and his wife, Fouquet, Arnauld d'Andilly, Sarasin, and Pellisson— and the conversations are more numerous than in *Le Grand*

---

[1] For a long but lively analysis of *Le Grand Cyrus* see Saintsbury, *op. cit.* I. 176–217.

Cyrus, and the general tone of the book is more affected
and sentimental. It is in *Clélie* that we are introduced to
the famous *Carte de Tendre,* with its three towns of *Tendre*
on the three rivers of *Inclination, Reconnaissance,* and
Estime, and its minor towns of *Petits soins* and *Empresse-
ment* and *Billet galant* and *Billet doux,* all of which Molière
laughs at in *Les Précieuses Ridicules.*

In the preface to *Les Héros de Roman,* Boileau says that
he attacked in the romances "their precious affectation of
language, their vague and frivolous conversations, the
flattering portraits of persons who had either very ordinary
good looks or were even exceedingly ugly, and all the end-
less jargon of love." As we might expect, the love-making
in Mlle de Scudéry's novels is carried on with an even
greater affectation of language than we find in the tragedies
and comedies of the period. But, apart from this, traces of
jargon similar to that which Molière puts in the mouths of
his *Précieuses* are extremely rare. Mlle de Scudéry's ordinary
style is loose, incorrect, and diffuse, but it can hardly be
called "precious." As regards the flattering character of
the "portraits," Boileau's remarks are perfectly just. They
dwell so entirely on the excellences of the individual, and
they magnify these to such an extent, that they are true
neither to Nature nor to Art. There is no better example
than the portrait of Mlle de Scudéry herself, who was an
ugly woman with a singularly swarthy complexion.
"Sapho," she says, "is not one of those great beauties in
whom envy can find no defect, but she is capable of inspiring grander passions than the greatest beauties in the
world....As for her complexion, it is not of the purest white-
ness, but it is so brilliant that you may call it beautiful."
Then follows a long description of the beauty of her eyes,
and lastly we are told of her admirable hands: "hands to
catch hearts...hands worthy to cull the fairest flowers of
Parnassus." Her moral and intellectual virtues are painted
in even greater detail, and with an even more generous
brush. Yet Mlle de Scudéry in private life was, we are told,
an exceedingly modest person.

The grand passion which Sapho is said to be capable of inspiring refers to Pellisson's faithful attachment. He would gladly have become her husband—it will be recollected that he was even more ugly than the lady—but she had a pronounced aversion to marriage. Not that, like Molière's Cathos, she thought it *une chose tout à fait choquante*, but she loved independence. "I regard marriage," says Sapho in one of the conversations in *Le Grand Cyrus*, "as a long slavery."

The celebrated *Samedis* soon found imitators, and produced a large number of *cercles*, or *ruelles*, as they were now generally called, in which the *précieux* spirit, stimulated by *Le Grand Cyrus* and *Clélie*, developed with ever-increasing rapidity. From Paris the fashion spread to the provinces. At Poitiers, Bordeaux, Aix, Arles, Montpellier, and especially at Lyons, where Molière's company had for a time its headquarters, there were salons of some repute. Here *préciosité* ran riot; delicacy became absurd prudery, and language a mere jargon. From these second-rate imitators Mlle de Scudéry and the true *Précieuses* were careful to distinguish themselves. In the concluding part of *Le Grand Cyrus* we hear a great deal of a certain Damophile who "set herself up to be the Sapho of her quarter," and whose inferiority to the real Sapho is insisted on at great length, the chief difference being that, while Sapho made no pretence of learning but knew everything, Damophile, who knew nothing, posed as a tenth Muse. Similarly, the Abbé de Pure, in *La Précieuse ou le Mystère des Ruelles* (1656), speaks of the hatred of the *Précieuses* for pedantry and provincialism. And Saint-Évremond appends to his poem *Le Cercle*, also of the year 1656, a note, in which, after repeating Ninon de Lenclos's celebrated definition of the *Précieuses* as "the Jansenists of love," he says that they are a small society, "in which some who are really delicate have led others to affect a ridiculous delicacy."

The foregoing investigation would seem to show that, if we use the term *préciosité* in its wider and more general sense of a striving after novelty and conceit in language,

we must go much further back than the Hôtel de Rambouillet for its origin. On the other hand, the manifestation
of that special form of affectation practised by the *Précieuses* and attacked by Molière and Boileau was confined
to the period of Mazarin's ministry. Moreover, though we
can detect its first appearance as a visible disease in the
salon of Mme de Rambouillet during the last five years of
her sway, it is not till after the Fronde that it breaks forth
into patent absurdity. Even then we must distinguish between the *véritables Précieuses* who frequented the Saturdays of Mlle de Scudéry and their second-rate imitators,
whether at Paris or in the provinces, whom Molière ridi
culed in his immortal farce. But though Molière's satire
was directed primarily against the inferior *Précieuses*, he,
like Boileau, recognised in Mlle de Scudéry and her novels
the source and origin of the evil. The two *Précieuses* in his
play were doubtless called Madelon and Cathos because
their parts were played by Madeleine Béjart and Catherine
de Brie; but we may guess that he regarded it as a happy
coincidence that Mlle de Scudéry also bore the name of
Madeleine.

In parting, however, from Mlle de Scudéry, we must do
her the justice to remember that in her analysis of the
human heart she was contributing to the pure and direct
stream of French literature. Correct her psychology by a
study of Descartes's *Traité des Passions* and by a more
sincere observation of life at first hand, purge her long
romances of their improbable elements and reduce them to
the limits of a short story, as had already been done by
Segrais in *Les Divertissements de la Princesse Aurélie* (1657),
and you have *La Princesse de Clèves*, the parent of the
modern novel.

In periods of transition, when the literature of a nation
is slowly feeling its way towards new ideals, it is almost
inevitable that it should sometimes stray in wrong directions, especially when there is no standard of national taste
to regulate its footsteps. Such a standard Richelieu,
whether wisely or not, had attempted to set up; but just

as the strong central government which he had built up with such pitiless determination seemed after his death to be in danger of crumbling away before the forces of licence and disorder, so a like outburst of unreason and false sentiment threatened to overwhelm literature. The bad taste and affectation which displayed themselves in burlesque and *préciosité* were a reflection of the false sentiment, the romanticism, the craving after adventure and personal glory which mark the period of the rule of Mazarin. Mlle de Montpensier was stuffed with romance and sentimentality. Henri, Duc de Guise, whose mysterious adventures with Anne di Gonzaga, the future Princesse Palatine, were begun when he was still Archbishop of Reims, and who is best known for his madcap attempt to seize the crown of Naples, was, in the words of Mme de Motteville, "the true picture of a paladin." The egoism which lay at the bottom of these and similar manifestations reached its height when the great nobles, in order to satisfy their petty vanities and vague ambitions, plunged their country into the miseries of civil war, or even allied themselves openly with her foes.

In the year 1656 one of these nobles, who without any real capacity for political conspiracy had been led by the influence of women and by an exaggerated sense of his own importance to take a part in all these purposeless intrigues and seditions, returned to Paris disillusioned and morose. Just as one woman, Mme de Longueville, had drawn him into the web of conspiracy, so another woman, Mme de Sablé, soothed his wounded vanity, and turned him to his true bent, society and literature. It was in her salon in the Place Royale that La Rochefoucauld learnt from the lips of the Chevalier de Méré the *credo* of the perfect *honnête homme*. It was in her hôtel adjoining Port-Royal, whither she moved in 1659, that he chiselled and shaped with the precision of a medallist his maxims on society and conversation and the corruption of human nature. Mme de Sablé was now in her sixtieth year. With all her oddities and inconsistencies, her morbid dread of illness, her Jansenism, and her love of good living, she was a woman of sound judgment, cultivated understanding, and sure literary taste. It was she, and not Mlle de Scudéry, who was the true successor of Mme de Rambouillet. It was in her salon and with her help that the *Maximes* were purged of *préciosité*.

CHAPTER X

DESCARTES—PORT-ROYAL—PASCAL

I

In the last chapter we saw that the critical spirit inaugurated by Malherbe and fostered by the Académie Française, had led to the belief that a knowledge of literary rules can supply the place of inspiration and genius; that the spirit of refinement created by the Hôtel de Rambouillet had degenerated into *préciosité*; that the spirit of Comedy, after being purified by Corneille of its coarser elements, had been contaminated afresh by contact with burlesque; and that even Tragedy, which in the *Cid* and *Polyeucte* had produced the two greatest achievements of French literature during the first half of the seventeenth century, had sunk to the level of *Œdipe* and *Timocrate*. It seemed as if the gradual advance towards the classical ideal which had been made during the reigns of Henry IV and Louis XIII was in danger of being driven back by the forces of bad taste. But amidst the general disorder we can discern three strongholds, which served first as rallying-places, and then as vantage-posts for fresh conquests. The very year (1656) which saw the successful production of *Timocrate* and *La Pucelle* and *Le Marquis ridicule* was also the year in which *Les Lettres Provinciales* were read with ever-increasing interest and applause. It was during this reign of bad taste that the teachers and writers of Port-Royal were instilling into French thought and style a spirit of earnestness and sincerity, and that the Cartesian philosophy, with its serried logic and steadfast pursuit of truth, was gradually exerting its influence over the leaders of the younger generation. It is these three influences—that of Descartes, that of Port-Royal, and that of Pascal—that I propose to consider in the present chapter.

As regards the period and extent of Descartes's influence, there is a wide difference of opinion among French historians of philosophy and literature, ranging from those who see in nearly every literary phenomenon of the seventeenth century the direct result of the Cartesian philosophy to those who, like Brunetière, deny that it exercised any influence at all outside science and philosophy until the last decade of the century. The truth of the matter seems to lie between these extreme views. From the time of the publication of the *Discours de la méthode* (1637) Descartes's reputation, not so much by the sale of his books, of which his publishers were continually complaining, as by the oral transmission of his doctrines, was steadily increasing throughout the learned world, and at his death, in 1650, his philosophy had made a deep mark not only on metaphysics, but on nearly every branch of positive science. It is inconceivable that intelligent men of letters who were still young enough, between 1640 and 1660, to receive the impression of new ideas should not have been deeply interested in the main features of the new philosophy.

Perhaps the best way of approaching the subject is to consider what were the features in Descartes's philosophy which are most likely to have impressed the more thoughtful laymen of his day. They would have seen that by completing the emancipation of the human reason from the authority of the Church, and by inventing a purely mechanical theory of Nature, he had given the death-blow to medieval scholastic philosophy. They would have realised that he had re-established order and unity in the world of thought, rescuing it from the anarchy and confusion into which it had fallen during the Renaissance, and setting up the human reason as the sole and absolute criterion of truth. They would have learnt from him that thought is the only reality which we can apprehend immediately, and that it is only through thought that we can attain to a sure knowledge of the material world. But this feeling for order, this glorification of reason, this elevation of man over Nature, were no novelties; they proceed from the same spirit that inspired the doctrines of Malherbe, the work of the Académie, and the plays of Corneille. In many respects Descartes is only the representative of his age, working out its principles in the regions of philosophy and science. But, granting this, we may agree with M. Lanson that his philosophy had the effect of intensifying these principles in the domain of literature. The reason of Boileau which he sets up as the true criterion of literary taste is substantially identical with the reason of Descartes. It may be said, indeed, that Boileau's distrust of the imagination is a common characteristic of the seventeenth century, already found in a marked degree in Malherbe. But when it is remembered that one of the maxims of the *Précieuses*, as recorded by Somaize, was " to value imagination more than truth in matters of pleasure," we shall be disposed to conjecture that Boileau, whom we know from his *Arrêt burlesque* to have been favourable to the Cartesian philosophy, welcomed it as a valuable ally in his campaign on behalf of truth in literature.

So, too, Pascal and Bossuet were, up to a certain point, followers of the Cartesian philosophy; and to these we must, of course, add Malebranche. It is otherwise with La Fontaine and Molière, who were too imaginative, too great lovers of the concrete, to have much sympathy for the idealising rationalism of Descartes. La Fontaine, though he pays a graceful tribute to the great philosopher,

> Ce mortel dont on eût fait un dieu
> Chez les païens, et qui tient le milieu
> Entre l'homme et l'esprit[1],

protests in the same fable, and in others, against the doctrine that animals are automata.

Finally, we must not lose sight of the fundamental antagonism, so well pointed out by M. Lanson, between Cartesianism and the classical ideal. For Cartesianism is the triumph of the geometrical spirit, and as such is in complete opposition to the spirit of poetry and art. More-

---

[1] *Fables*, x. 1.

over, in the quarrel between the ancients and the moderns, which marks the beginning of the decline of the Classical Age, the whole authority of Cartesianism, with its belief in the law of human progress, was cast on the side of the moderns, and thus, as M. Lanson says, helped to deal a mortal blow to the classical ideal[1].

There is one treatise of Descartes's which must have specially appealed to his lay contemporaries, and that is the *Traité des passions de l'âme*, published in 1649, the year before his death. By its orderly arrangement, its careful analysis, and its observation of physiological and psychological data, it must have helped to stimulate and methodise the growing interest in psychological analysis. The advance from the psychology of *Le Grand Cyrus* and *Clélie* to that of Molière and La Rochefoucauld, of Bossuet and Bourdaloue, though mainly the result of personal observation and experience, was in some measure due to the influence of the *Traité des passions* and kindred works[2].

In this treatise Descartes does not confine himself to an analysis of the passions and an investigation of their causes. He writes as a moralist as well as a psychologist. He says that "all the passions are good in their nature, and that we have only to avoid the bad or immoderate use of them." The remedy against this misuse lies in the exercise of the will. But the difficulty is to set our will-power in motion, to fortify it and brace it to action. This, says Descartes, is the work of the reason[3]; we must have right opinions and sound judgment. We must learn first to distinguish good from evil, and then we shall know which

[1] In *Revue de Métaphysique et de Morale* for July, 1896.

[2] Boileau, in his satire on human nature, does not refer to Descartes's work, but to those of Coëffetau (*Tableau des passions humaines*, 1615), Cureau de La Chambre (*Les caractères des passions*, 5 vols., 1640–62), and Senault (*L'usage des passions*, 1641).

[3] Cf. Corneille, *Rodogune*, act i. scene 5:

> Et ma raison sur moi gardera tant d'empire
> Que je desavoûrai mon cœur, s'il en soupire;

and *Polyeucte*, act ii. scene 2:

> Et sur mes passions ma raison souveraine
> Eût blâmé mes soupirs, et dissipé ma haine.

passions to encourage and which to keep in check. There is no word of prayer or grace as means to virtue; and though it would not be true to say that the treatise shows no traces of Christian influence, for the purely Christian virtues of humility and repentance are commended, its ethical tone is essentially non-religious.

Yet Descartes's influence, not only on religion but on orthodox theology in France, was not insignificant. His own attitude to the Church was that of a professing Catholic, obedient even to timidity. Nor, like his rival Gassendi, priest and Epicurean philosopher, did he wholly dissociate faith from reason, marking them off into separate provinces, which, though conterminous, had no intercourse with each other. His conception of God as an infinite, eternal, omniscient, all-powerful, and all-creative Substance, is thoroughly, if not distinctively, Christian. His recognition that the mysteries of religion cannot be apprehended by the human reason and his absolute submission to the Church in all matters of faith are more intimate proofs of the sincerity of his Christianity. It needed the penetration of Pascal to see that Cartesianism would never bring unbelievers to Christ, and of Bossuet to recognise that the exaltation of the human reason to be the one criterion of truth must lead to free-thought as its logical conclusion.

Meanwhile the philosophy of Descartes was welcomed by the majority of Catholic theologians in France as a buttress against scepticism, more especially by the Oratory and Port-Royal. The *Discours de la méthode* was, it is said, the fulfilment of a promise made by Descartes to Cardinal de Bérulle, and it was the Oratorian Malebranche who based on Cartesianism a Christian philosophy. If it met with less uniform favour from the Solitaries as a whole, it found an enthusiastic adherent in their most active theologian, Antoine Arnauld. His theses for the doctorate of Divinity (1638–41) made a deep impression by their entire freedom from scholasticism, and by the strong Cartesian influence which they displayed. The same method inspired the treatise on logic entitled *L'art de penser*, but generally known as *The Logic of Port-Royal*, which Arnauld wrote in conjunction with Pierre Nicole (1662), and which is based on common sense instead of on the subtleties and refinements of medieval logic. The same method, with its rigid dialectic, its absence of ornament, its preoccupation with the bare truth—in a word, its geometrical spirit—is conspicuous in *La Fréquente Communion*, the work by which Arnauld, in 1643, revealed Jansenism to the world and inaugurated the long struggle between Jansenism and Jesuitism. But before I discuss this episode I must say something of the community which became so closely identified with Jansenism—namely, Port-Royal.

II

In 1602 Jacqueline Arnauld, one of the ten children—four sons and six daughters—of Antoine Arnauld, a celebrated advocate, was appointed Abbess of the Cistercian monastery of Port-Royal, about eighteen miles to the west of Paris. The new Abbess, whose name in religion was Angélique, was in her eleventh year. The condition of the monastery was typical of that of many religious houses in France at this time. There were only thirteen nuns, of whom the eldest was thirty-three, and though Angélique's predecessor had administered the convent with decency, the discipline was anything but strict. "There was no pretence of monastic seclusion....Every sister had her own private property....In dress they conformed as nearly as might be to the fashions of the day, wearing starched linen, displaying their hair, and using gloves and masks to preserve the complexion. The grossest religious ignorance prevailed; the offices of the Church were negligently performed; the hour of matins was postponed from 2 to 4 a.m.; and when the services of the choir were at an end, a game of cards or a walk filled up the day[1]."

But in 1608 the young Abbess, having been awakened

---

[1] C. Beard, *Port-Royal*, I. 30.

to a new conception of the religious life, or, as the phrase was, having been converted to religion, determined to reform her convent and to enforce the observance of its primitive discipline. It was not an easy task, but the victory was assured on September 25, 1609, when she observed the vow of seclusion against even her father, and, in spite of his threats and objurgations, refused to speak to him except through the grating. It took some years to carry out the work of reform, and when it was completed Angélique was sent to another Cistercian convent, that of Maubuisson, where she had received her religious education, and where the need for reform was far more urgent than it had been at Port-Royal.

In 1623 she returned to Port-Royal, which had been governed in her absence by her sister Agnès, and which now numbered eighty nuns. The site was unhealthy and the buildings were in an unsanitary condition. Fifteen deaths occurred in two years. Accordingly Mme Arnauld, who now had five daughters in the convent, persuaded Angélique to transfer the whole community to Paris (1625).

We may now pass on to the year 1636, when the Mère Angélique returned after another absence of a few years, and the Abbé de Saint-Cyran became spiritual director to the sisterhood. As Sainte-Beuve says, this is the decisive year in the history of Port-Royal, for it was through its new director that it became identified with Jansenism.

Jean Du Vergier de Hauranne, born at Bayonne in 1581, had devoted several years to the study of the works of St Augustine in company with his friend Cornelius Jansen. In 1620 he was made Abbot of Saint-Cyran, a monastery in Poitou, and a year later he made the acquaintance of Arnauld d'Andilly, Angélique's eldest brother, and through him of other members of the Arnauld family. In the same year he went to live at Paris, where he acquired great reputation and influence. Among his friends were Cardinal de Bérulle and Vincent de Paul. Richelieu had a high opinion of him, mingled with some jealousy, and he offered him several bishoprics, all of which he refused. During this period of his career he was engaged in two controversies with the Jesuits, the first of which arose from a refutation, which he had published anonymously, of the *Somme Théologique* of the Jesuit Père Garasse. "Garasse," says Bayle wittily, "was the Helen of the war between the Jesuits and the Jansenists." It was owing to the influence of Saint-Cyran that Antoine Le Maître, the son of Angélique's eldest sister, renounced a splendid career at the Bar for a religious life (1637), and, with his brother, M. de Séricourt, was provided with a temporary lodging in the courtyard of Port-Royal. In the following year (1638) Saint-Cyran, who had dared to oppose Richelieu both on a political and a theological question, was imprisoned by his orders, and Les MM. de Port-Royal, or the Solitaries, as Le Maître and his friends were called, were ordered to leave Paris and go to Port-Royal des Champs. Ten years later (1648) the nuns returned to their original home, and the Solitaries retired to Les Granges, a farm on the hill just above the monastery.

It is with the Solitaries that the student of French literature is more particularly concerned. They were bound by no vows and wore no distinguishing dress. They were simply recluses who had retired from the world in order to devote themselves to learning, education, and religion. Among their number were Antoine Singlin, Saint-Cyran's successor as spiritual director; Claude Lancelot, his biographer; Nicolas Fontaine, the future chronicler of the community; and Isaac Le Maître, Antoine's youngest brother, commonly known as Le Maître de Sacy, who in 1650 succeeded Singlin as director, and who is best known at the present day by his translation of the Bible.

Another resident at Les Granges, though not a regular member of the community, was Arnauld d'Andilly, who joined them in 1646. An experienced courtier and politician, this hale man of fifty-seven brought with him a somewhat novel element. He was an expert and enthusiastic gardener, cultivating monster pears, and making flowers blossom in the wilderness. Retaining a lively interest in public affairs, he formed a link between the Solitaries and the outside world. Mme de Sévigné records a visit which she paid to him in 1674, when he was in his eighty-fifth year. He was an active writer, and by his elegant translations of Josephus and other authors did good service to the cause of French prose.

The year in which he joined the Solitaries (1646) is marked by the organisation of the "Little Schools[1]." They had originated in the active brain of Saint-Cyran, who was devoted to children and had a deep-rooted belief in the importance of education. But his imprisonment prevented him from carrying his ideas into effect himself, and he had to entrust their execution to his Solitaries. Among the earliest pupils were the two sons of Jérôme Bignon, the distinguished man of learning whom his contemporaries surnamed the French Varro, and the first of that dynasty which presided for nearly a century and a half over the fortunes of the Royal Library. The elder of the two boys, Jérôme II, besides holding several important legal offices, succeeded his father as Royal Librarian. In 1646 the number of scholars was only twenty-four, and at no time, thinks Sainte-Beuve, did it exceed fifty. In most years it must have been considerably less. But the importance of Port-Royal education is not to be measured by the number of its scholars. "The spirit of the Jansenist method," says M. Compayré, "survived the ruin of their schools." Its dominating feature, like that of the Oratory, was the use of French instead of Latin as the basis of instruction. But there were certain differences between the Port-Royal schools and those of the Oratory. Less attention was paid to history and geography, to mathematics and natural science, though none of these studies was neglected. On the other hand, the French language and literature were studied with greater thoroughness and for their own sakes, the pupils being taught to write French partly by translation from Latin and partly by reading French authors. At

[1] See H. C. Barnard, *The Little Schools of Port-Royal*, Cambridge, 1913, and *Port-Royal*, Cambridge, 1918.

the same time, the importance of Latin was fully recognised. A wide range of authors was read, and their subject-matter was regarded as of more importance than the style. In the first stage of Latin the teaching was by oral translation, and not, as in the Jesuit schools, by written composition. In the higher forms "themes" or Latin essays were preferred to Latin versions of French passages, and—admirable provision—the writing of Latin verse was confined to those boys who showed a taste for it.

The chief teacher of Port-Royal was Claude Lancelot. It was he who wrote the various *New Methods* for learning Greek, Latin, Italian, and Spanish. It was he who in conjunction with Arnauld was the author of the Port-Royal Logic, which embodies, as we have seen, the Cartesian method, and of the *Grammaire générale et raisonnée*, the first philosophical grammar. Another of the Port-Royal teachers was Pierre Nicole, the author of the *Essais de morale*, the devoted friend of Antoine Arnauld, who helped him in his numerous writings and "shared for five-and-twenty years his fatigues, his combats, and his dangers." If the greatest of the Port-Royal pupils was Racine, who owed to Lancelot his admirable knowledge of Greek literature, the one who best reflects the spirit of its education is Sébastien Le Nain de Tillemont, the modest and profoundly learned historian of the Roman Empire and the early Christian Church.

We may now return to Antoine Arnauld and *La Fréquente Communion*. It was published, as we have seen, in the year 1643, two months before the death of Saint-Cyran, who thus had the satisfaction of reading before he died the "first manifesto," to use Sainte-Beuve's expression, of the school of religious thought which he had created, written by his most illustrious convert and disciple. Since the *Introduction to the Devout Life*, published thirty-five years before, no book of devotion, says Sainte-Beuve, produced so great a sensation or had such important consequences. Written in a clear and correct, if cold and austere, style, free from the scholastic pedantry and the affectation which marked the ordinary theological treatise of the day, it made the Jansenist doctrines known to a circle far wider than that reached by the unpolished and somewhat obscure writings of Saint-Cyran. From the time of its publication Jansenism began to make a deep impression on society. It even became fashionable, and fine ladies neglected their romances for the writings of the Solitaries.

Among those present at the impressive funeral service that was held for M. de Saint-Cyran in the church of Saint-Jacques-du-Haut-Pas was Marie di Gonzaga, the future Queen of Poland, whose thoughts had been recently turned to religion, possibly under the sombre impression made on her by the death of Cinq-Mars, who had aspired to her hand. From this time she and the Princesse de Guéméné and Mme de Sablé made a habit of passing several days under the roof of Port-Royal, causing thereby considerable anxiety to the Mère Angélique.

A far more sincere convert than any of these three ladies was Marie di Gonzaga's god-daughter, the Duchesse de Luynes, who about the year 1650 contemplated retiring from the world with her husband, the only son of the favourite of Louis XIII and his intriguing wife, Mme de Chevreuse. With that intention they began to build a château at Vaumurier, a hundred paces from Port-Royal-des-Champs. But the duchess died in child-birth in 1651, and her husband, inconsolable for a time, retired to Port-Royal itself, pending the completion of his own house. He was an eager Cartesian and had translated the *Meditationes* into French (1647).

It was in a measure owing to the Princesse de Guéméné and Mme de Sablé that *La Fréquente Communion* was written. For Mme de Guéméné, who was under the spiritual direction of M. de Saint-Cyran, having refused to go to a ball on a day on which she had received the Sacrament, Mme de Sablé, who had had permission to attend the ball, reported Saint-Cyran's views to her Jesuit confessor. He at once proceeded to refute them in a pamphlet. To this

Arnauld, urged by Saint-Cyran, prepared a reply, which took the form of an attack on the whole Jesuit position with regard to penitence and absolution and the duty of Communion. The world was now able to judge of the profound difference between the Jesuit and the Jansenist conception of religion. The Jesuits stood for compromise and indulgence, the Jansenists for strictness and austerity. The Jesuits wished to accommodate religion to the needs of men and women of the world; the Jansenists wished to raise the standard of human conduct to the level of the primitive Christian pattern. The Jesuits laid stress on conformity to outward rules and forms; the Jansenists looked chiefly to the inward conversion of the heart. In Saint-Évremond's witty *Conversation of Maréchal d'Hocquincourt with Père Canaye* he makes the Jesuit Father declare with great frankness that the animosity between the Jesuits and the Jansenists had nothing to do with the controversy about Grace or the five propositions, but that it arose entirely from their rivalry in the government of consciences. Add to this the suspicion with which the Jesuits regarded the "Little Schools," as an interference with their monopoly of education, and their hereditary quarrel with the Arnauld family—for Antoine Arnauld, the elder, was counsel for the University of Paris in their second action against the Jesuits—and you have all the elements of a bitter and prolonged contest.

Moreover, three years before the publication of *La Fréquente Communion* there had appeared Jansen's *Augustinus* (1640), in which, in the name of St Augustine, he had attacked the Pelagian and semi-Pelagian doctrines of Grace. Thereupon the controversy between the strict Augustinian theory and the semi-Pelagian view held by the Jesuits, which had slumbered since 1607, broke out afresh. In 1649 Nicolas Cornet, Syndic of the Faculty of Theology at Paris, drew up seven theological propositions, which he submitted to the Faculty for a decision as to their orthodoxy. He made no reference to Jansen's book, but it was understood that he was acting in concert with the Jesuits, and that his aim was to procure the condemnation of the *Augustinus*. Finally, after much wordy warfare, five of the propositions were submitted to the Pope, and in 1653 a Bull condemning them was issued. It was accepted and published in France, and both sides agreed to an armistice. But two years later (1655), when the Duc de Liancourt, a friend of Arnauld's, was condemned for Jansenist tendencies, Arnauld renewed the contest. He published two letters, in the second of which, addressed to the Duc de Luynes, he declared that the five propositions were not in the *Augustinus*, and on his own account quoted St Augustine to the effect that Grace had failed St Peter, when he denied his Lord. The Jesuits brought the letter to the notice of the Theological Faculty, and after long deliberation Arnauld was condemned by a large majority, first on the question of fact, as to whether the five propositions were or were not in Jansen's book (January 14, 1656), and then on the question of law, as to whether his pamphlet contained heretical matter or not (January 29). But before the second voting took place a greater than Arnauld had intervened in the dispute, and there had appeared the first Provincial Letter (January 23).

III

The author, Blaise Pascal, now in his thirty-third year, was a man of high distinction, both as a physicist and as a mathematician. More than eight years before this he had won the admiration of learned Europe by his account of the experiments on the nature of a vacuum which he had been led to make by Torricelli's great discovery[1], and a year later he had completed his work of verification by the crowning experiment of the Puy-de-Dôme[2]. He was even more distinguished as a mathematician. At the age of sixteen he had written a work on conic sections, which comprised the well-known Pascal's Theorem, and fourteen

[1] *Nouvelles expériences touchant le vide* (published October 4, 1647).
[2] September 19, 1648.

years later (1654) he presented to one of the scientific Academies at Paris several important mathematical treatises, including one on the properties of the arithmetical triangle, and another on the theory of Probability. The year 1654 had also been for him one of deep religious struggle. He had always been a conforming and believing member of the Catholic Church, but without the intense conviction which alone could satisfy his scientific mind. At last, on November 23, after much bodily and mental suffering, the crisis had terminated in a species of trance or ecstasy, which brought him certainty and peace. He was confirmed in his desire to separate himself from the world, and on January 7, 1655, by the orders of his Jansenist director, M. Singlin, he left Paris for Port-Royal in the company of the Duc de Luynes. There he resided with the Solitaries, but, like M. de Luynes, he was not a member of their community.

It was on the suggestion of Antoine Arnauld, whose own pamphlet in his defence had not satisfied his friends, that he wrote the first Provincial Letter. It was published on January 23, 1656, forming a small pamphlet of eight quarto pages. The other seventeen letters appeared at intervals until March 24, 1657. In May of that year the complete collection was bound up together and issued by a French publisher, with the following title of his own composition: *Les Provinciales, ou Les Lettres écrites par Louis de Montalte à un provincial de ses amis et aux R.R. P.P. Jesuites sur le sujet de la morale et de la politique de ces Pères*, and with a preface by Nicole giving a history of the controversy[1].

It will be seen that in the above title nothing is said about the controversy between Arnauld and the Jesuits; but the first four letters and the last two are concerned with this question. It is only in the fourth letter that Pascal passes to the more general question of Jesuit casuistry and direction. Further, it should be noticed that the last eight letters are no longer addressed to a supposed provincial friend, but to the Jesuits themselves.

---

[1] The latest edition is that by H. F. Stewart, Manchester, 1920; the introduction and notes are sound and scholarly.

In forming an opinion as to the merits of Pascal's case, it must be remembered, in the first place, that he is writing, not as a judge, but as an advocate, even as a passionate advocate, and that, therefore, after the manner of advocates, he presents only the bad side of his opponent's case. He also resembles an advocate in this, that he is writing from a brief. He was not himself a theologian, and much of his material was supplied to him by his Port-Royal friends, especially by Nicole, who revised several of the letters. But ten years before he had read many of the Jansenist writings, and for the purpose of his present work he had read Escobar, the celebrated Jesuit casuist, through twice. Moreover, he had verified all his references. All the efforts of his opponents have only convicted him of two or three inaccuracies, and of a few cases in which, by an unfair presentation of his authorities, he has misrepresented their meaning. It may be added that he sometimes wilfully ignores those shades of distinction which are so important in casuistry. But when all has been said, when all exceptions have been taken to the fairness of his attack, when all the pleas that may be fairly urged on behalf of his opponents have been admitted, the fact remains that his indictment against the confessional methods of the Jesuits is unanswerable[1].

The Jesuits aimed at being the exclusive spiritual directors of society. Consequently casuistry, which originally and in its proper sense dealt only with cases in which one duty clashed with another, had now to decide cases in which a religious duty clashed, not with another duty, but with the code of the fashionable world. It was not for nothing that the first work on casuistry, which was merely a manual for the use of confessors, was written by a Spanish Dominican, and that it was in Spain that casuistry in the hands of Loyola's successors reached its fullest development. For Spain was at once the country where religion on its formal side had its strongest influence, and where the "point of honour" exercised a sway even more

[1] See H. F. Stewart, *The Holiness of Pascal*, Cambridge, 1915, pp. 40–43.

potent than that of religion. Moreover, the rise of the
director, or permanent keeper of the conscience, as opposed
to the temporary confessor, and the increase in the habit
of frequent Communion, coupled with the unpleasant and
sometimes serious consequences which the refusal of absolution entailed, made it more and more necessary for directors
to effect some compromise between the code of Christ and
the code of honour, if they were to retain their hold on
fashionable society.

Pascal's attack was directed against the whole edifice of
Jesuit dominion, on the ground that it rested on an insecure
foundation, that of relaxed morality. His chief justification
lies in his success—not in the popularity which the "Little
Letters" achieved by their wit and irony, their lucidity and
passion, their dazzling brilliance of style, but in the fact
that they accomplished their purpose. The attack was
directed, not against individuals, but against a system;
and the Jesuits acknowledged their defeat by reforming
their system. Though the Jesuits never forgave the *Provincial Letters*, they changed their methods of confession.
It has been said that Bourdaloue, who, alike in the pulpit
and the confessional, was the sternest and most candid of
moralists, is the best refutation of Jansenism. It may be
said with greater truth that this "most Jansenist of
Jesuits" is the best tribute to the strength of Pascal's case.

Finally, it must be remembered that, supposing Pascal
to be right in his main argument, it does not follow that he
is equally right on the question of the original controversy.
Opinions differ as to whether the five propositions are to
be found virtually, if not textually, in Jansen's book; but
as regards the difficult theological question of Grace, the
majority of plain Christians, whether Protestants or
Catholics, will be more inclined to agree with the Jesuit
than with the Jansenist doctrine. Moreover, even on the
question of spiritual direction, a belief that the Jesuits
were wrong does not necessarily imply a belief that the
Jansenists were right. "The Jansenists, wishing to make
all men saints, do not find ten persons in a whole kingdom

fit to be Christians as they would have them. Christianity
is Divine, but those who receive it are men; and, do what
we may, we must accommodate ourselves to humanity.
A too austere philosophy makes few wise men; a too
vigorous policy makes few good citizens; a too severe
religion makes few religious for long....It is certain that
confessors who are too rigid make themselves rather than
sin the object of aversion. The repentance which they
preach makes men prefer the easy course of continuing in
vice to the difficulties of abandoning it. But the other
extreme seems to me equally bad. If I hate those morose
spirits who say everything is a sin, I hate equally those
easy and indulgent confessors who say nothing is a sin,
who favour moral disorder and become secret partisans of
vice. In their hands the Gospel is more indulgent than
morality; religion as interpreted by them offers to crime
a more feeble opposition than reason." These words are
reported by Saint-Évremond, a pupil of the Jesuits, from
the lips of his Scottish friend, Ludovic Stewart, Lord
d'Aubigny, who was connected with Port-Royal[1]. The criticisms are very just, and we may add to them the saying of
Cardinal de Bérulle, that "the guidance of a single soul is
more difficult than the government of a kingdom."

The "Little Letters" came to an abrupt termination.
Pascal had begun a nineteenth letter, and had planned a
twentieth, when all of a sudden he abandoned the attack.
One reason seems to have been the disapprobation of the
Mère Angélique, who thought that the Jesuits should be
opposed by more charitable methods. Another possible
motive was the exhortation of a Jesuit pamphleteer "to
turn his pen against the remains of heresy, the free-thinking
and impious tongues, and the other corruptions of the age."
Whether this weighed with him or not, it is certain that five

[1] Fourth son of the Duke of Lennox. He became a Canon of Notre-Dame
at Paris, and Grand Almoner to Catharine of Braganza, the wife of
Charles II. He died at Paris in 1665, a few days after receiving the news
that he had been nominated a Cardinal. It is often stated that he was
educated at Port-Royal, but he was twenty-seven when the "Little Schools"
were first opened.

years before his death—that is to say, in 1657—he began
to put into execution his design of writing a work to confute
the free-thinkers, and that for a whole year he spent all his
leisure in putting down his ideas on paper (*recueillir les
différentes pensées qui lui venaient là-dessus*). Meanwhile his
plan had taken definite shape, and in June, 1658, he expounded it to some of his friends in a discourse which lasted
two or three hours. The work, he often said, would require
ten years of health for its completion; but this was denied
him. In the middle of 1658 his health, which had long been
bad, became much worse, and, though he was not confined
to his bed, or even to his room, he was rendered "almost
incapable of any application." During the last four years
of his life, however, he used to write down or dictate any
ideas or expressions that he thought might be serviceable
to his design, using for that purpose "any scrap of paper
that came to his hand." Thus, when he died, on August 19,
1662, all that was found of his intended work was a
number of fragments erased and altered, and often barely
legible.

Yet it is a consoling thought that these scratched and
scored remains, with all their repetitions, obscurities, and
inconsistencies—these scattered blocks, some, indeed, ready
to be fitted into their places, but for the most part only
rough-hewn, or even fresh from the quarry—appeal to us
with a more convincing accent than possibly the finished
edifice might have done. For it was an essential feature of
Pascal's design that his *Apologia* should be based on human
experience; and here we behold the foundations laid bare
before us, here we have faithfully sensitised the workings
of a suffering human soul—its passionate cry for help, its
torturing perplexities in face of the enigma of human life,
and finally its confident assertion that in Christianity, and
in Christianity alone, is to be found at once a solution of
the problem and an answer to the cry.

Though all attempts to piece together these fragments
into an intelligible whole have hitherto failed, we are not
without indications as to Pascal's design, as, at any rate,

he provisionally conceived it[1]. For the substance of that exposition which he gave to his friends in the summer of 1658 was reported by one of his listeners eight years afterwards, and is preserved in the preface of Étienne Périer prefixed to the Port-Royal edition of the *Pensées*, and more fully in the *Discours* of Filleau de La Chaise, which was intended to form that preface, but which was rejected as too long. We know also from other trustworthy sources that Pascal's argument was mainly directed against the free-thinkers of his day.

From about 1615 to 1625 free-thought was represented at Paris chiefly by a group of young men who were at once free-thinkers and free-livers. These *libertins*, as they were called, had come under the spell of the Italian Vanini, who from 1615 to 1617 carried on an active propaganda in Paris, and was burnt for heresy at Toulouse in 1619. His principal doctrine, "Live according to Nature"—meaning by Nature, not the universal Nature of the Stoics, but the individual nature of each man—was found very attractive by his disciples. The most eminent of these, the poet Théophile de Viau, thus expressed it in verse:

> J'approuve qu'un chacun suive en tout la nature,
> Son empire est plaisant, et sa loi n'est pas dure.

After the death of Théophile in 1626, his younger friend, Jacques Des Barreaux, whose brilliant parts and easy-going character made him a most attractive companion, became the leading spirit among the *libertins*[2].

Before long free-thought spread to more fashionable circles. La Rochefoucauld and Saint-Évremond, both of whom attained their majority in 1634, were deeply affected by it. So were the Princess Palatine (Anne di Gonzaga) and the great Condé, though in later years their conversion inspired Bossuet with eloquent passages in two of his finest funeral orations. The free-thought, however, of these il-

[1] See H. F. Stewart in *The French Quarterly*, III. 132 ff.
[2] M. Lachèvre, than whom there can be no more competent judge, says that "the rôle of the *libertins* in the 17th century with the exception of Théophile has been greatly exaggerated."

lustrious personages was of a more or less dilettante
character. It claimed no philosophical foundation, and
made no attempt at propagandism. Its breviary was
Montaigne's *Essays*, from which it culled the sceptical
passages and ignored the rest. A more solid basis presented
itself in the teaching of the distinguished physicist, Pierre
Gassendi, who lectured at Paris from 1641 to his death in
1655. Professing the atomic theory of Epicurus, he had
considerable influence on his hearers, among whom were
Chapelle, Bernier, and Molière. But he himself was in
priest's Orders and a devout Churchman, shutting off his
philosophy and his religion in water-tight compartments.
Among his more intimate friends were the English philosopher Hobbes, Gabriel Naudé, the librarian of the
Bibliothèque Mazarine, who was a decided free-thinker,
and Guy Patin, the physician, who, though a *frondeur* in
religion, hated atheists as much as he did Jesuits.

But on the whole, when Pascal began to plan his Apology,
free-thought in France was on the decline. Des Barreaux
had besotted himself with drink, and, in Pascal's words,
had become "a brute beast." Though he scoffed at religion
when he was in health, in sickness he became devout, and
in 1666, seven years before his death, he was definitely
converted. This was the case, indeed, with many of the
esprits forts of the day. In ordinary times they might shock
honest citizens by noisy displays of blasphemy, but under
fear of death they hastened to reconcile themselves with
the Church.

Pascal, however, like Molière a few years later, fore-
saw with the prescience of genius the conflict between
incredulity and religion which must inevitably arise. During his residence in Paris in 1652 and 1653 he had been
intimate with two free-thinkers of considerable interest
and intelligence—the Chevalier de Méré, whom we have
already encountered, and another follower of the gospel
of *honnêteté*, named Mitton. We know little of the latter,
except that he was a finished man of the world, and a
noted gambler, affecting to care for nothing but play

and society, and, in Pascal's opinion, concealing a fund
of egoism beneath his outward urbanity. "Le moi est
haïssable; vous, Mitton, le couvrez, vous ne l'ôtez pas
pour cela."

In the remarkable and more or less connected fragments
which form the first section of the Port-Royal edition of
the *Pensées*, Pascal divides unbelievers into those "who
seek God with all their heart because they do not know
Him," and those "who live without knowing Him and
without seeking Him." "Let the latter give to the
reading of these pages some of the hours which they
spend so uselessly in other pursuits, and, whatever re-
luctance they bring to the task, they may perhaps find
something of interest, and at any rate they will not lose
much. But for those who come with perfect sincerity
and a real desire to find the truth, I hope that they
will get satisfaction, and that they will be convinced of
the proofs which I have brought together of so divine
a religion[1]."

We have seen that Descartes was hailed by the majority
of Churchmen as a welcome ally against the free-thinkers.
But Pascal was too clear-sighted not to detect the weakness
of Cartesianism as a demonstration of the truth of the
Christian religion. While he follows Descartes in distinguishing between intuitive ideas and knowledge which is
the result of demonstration, he assigns the former, unlike
Descartes, to a distinct faculty. This faculty he calls sometimes the heart and sometimes the judgment. "We know
truth," he says in a fragment which Vinet considers to be
the keynote of the *Pensées*, "not only by the reason, but
also by the heart[2]," and he goes on to explain that it is
by this faculty that we apprehend instinctively or in-
tuitively all first principles. In another fragment he says,
"The heart has its reasons, of which the reason is ignorant.
...It is the heart which feels God, and not the reason.
This is faith: God sensible to the heart, not to the reason[3]."

[1] Ed. Brunschvicg, 194.
[2] *Ib.*, 282.   [3] *Ib.*, 277, 278.

Similarly, in the fragmentary treatise *On the Geometrical Spirit* he says that God alone can put the Divine truths into the mind, and that He has willed that they should enter the intellect through the heart, and not the heart through the intelligence. Thus he deposes what he calls "that superb power of the reasoning faculty" from the throne to which Descartes had exalted it.

Further, he saw that Descartes's celebrated proof of the existence of God from the idea of perfection would not convince the free-thinkers. They wanted a scientific, and not a metaphysical, proof. Their watchword was Nature. To Nature they should go. But Pascal had no confidence in the ordinary appeal to the works of Nature, which Grotius, for instance, had made with such eloquence in his *De veritate religionis Christianae* (1627). The proof must come from the nature of Man himself. So Pascal paints his celebrated picture of man without God, of man in his misery and inconstancy, in his ignorance and presumption. "But though he is merely a reed—the feeblest thing in creation—he is a thinking reed," and therefore superior to all the rest of creation. "He knows that he is miserable,... but he is great because he knows it." "In spite of the sight of all our miseries, which touch us, which hold us by the throat, we have an instinct which we cannot repress, which exalts us." (This instinct, it may be noted, is practically the same as Descartes's idea of Perfection or Infinity.) The Sceptics and the Dogmatists are therefore both wrong—the former in ignoring the greatness of man, the latter in ignoring his misery.

This line had already been taken by Pascal in a conversation which he had with M. de Sacy at Port-Royal in 1654 on the subject of Epictetus and Montaigne. A full report of it has been preserved, and it is of the greatest importance for the understanding of the *Pensées*. For Epictetus may be taken as representing not only ancient Stoicism, but the Christianised Stoicism of Pascal's own day, as seen in Balzac and Corneille and Descartes; while Montaigne, who is here considered solely on his sceptical side, stands for the free-thinkers who professed themselves to be his disciples.

As a man of the world, then, Pascal recognised the fact of our dual nature, and as a man of science, he refused to accept any solution which did not explain this fact. But in the Christian religion, with its doctrines of Original Sin and Grace, of the Fall of Man and his Redemption, he believed that he had found the true solution, the only solution which reconciled the contradictions of human nature.

CHAPTER XI

PASCAL AND FRENCH PROSE

In the preceding chapter I have endeavoured briefly to indicate Pascal's relation to the thought of his time under the aspect of his threefold opposition to the Jesuits, to Descartes, and to the free-thinkers. I must now discuss at somewhat greater length his position as a writer of French prose. "Pascal," says M. Faguet, "is the true creator of classical French prose, as Corneille is the true creator of classical French verse." And again: "The language, as one may speak it, and as one ought to write it after the lapse of two and a half centuries, is that which originated with the *Cid* in poetry, and with the *Provincial Letters* in prose." No competent judge has ever contested the claim that is thus put forward on Pascal's behalf; but in order clearly to realise its validity, we must know something about the condition of French prose before Pascal began to write.

Among the prose-writers of the sixteenth century, four stand out as pre-eminent—Rabelais and Calvin in the first half, Amyot and Montaigne in the second. Of Rabelais and Montaigne it may be said, without exaggeration, that no prose-writer in any age or in any country has shown greater genius in the treatment of language. But though from both may be learnt lessons of style which are of the very highest importance, neither can be taken as a model. The language of their day was still fluctuating and uncertain. The exact meaning of words was not fixed; the syntax had not disentangled itself from Latin; the power of constructing a well-balanced period was in its infancy. And neither Rabelais nor Montaigne was the man to reduce this anarchy to order. Both were a law unto themselves, and both aimed at expressiveness rather than correctness. Rabelais uses a dozen words to express the same idea, rather than select the most appropriate one. Montaigne hides the lack of precision in his thought by flitting from metaphor to metaphor.

Calvin, with far less genius, far less colour and distinction than Rabelais, is a much better model. Writing, not to give pleasure, but to convince, he aimed, above all things, at lucidity. This made him more progressive than Rabelais, for in the pursuit of clearness he abandoned many picturesque archaisms of vocabulary and grammar, while his syntax, originally modelled on a close study of Latin, became in time less Latin and more French.

But Calvin was little read in France except by Protestants and had little influence on other than Protestant writers. The writer of the sixteenth century who did most to improve the general standard of French prose was Amyot. Like his disciple Montaigne[1], he was a thorough artist, but in a different way. He regarded his art, not like Montaigne, as an expression of the individual artist, but rather as a craft of which the secrets were to be acquired by continual study and practice. Thus he was always improving, till in the end he achieved a perfect balance and harmony in the construction of his phrases. But he never abandoned the redundancy of the sixteenth century, and often used three words where one would have sufficed.

The chief representative of French prose during the main part of the reign of Henry IV was Cardinal Du Perron. Though he retains the long sentences and the redundancy of his predecessors, his style is clear and unembarrassed, while in its greater logical precision and its absence of metaphor it points decidedly forwards. Largely owing to Du Perron's example, the *style figuré*, or highly metaphorical style, which was in fashion during the greater part of the reign of Henry IV, was replaced by one of greater plainness and simplicity.

Du Perron was in high repute as an orator, and it is chiefly in the oratorical period that he excels. The task that still awaited accomplishment was to fit French prose for

---

[1] Amyot's first important work, the translation of Plutarch's *Lives*, was published twenty-one years before the *Essays*.

the expression of every kind of idea and sentiment, and to set up a general standard of style which might serve as a model to the ordinary writer. The man who prepared the way for this achievement was Malherbe. The purity, the clearness, and the precision which he prescribed for poetry he also practised in prose; and when his friends asked him why he did not write a grammar, he referred them to his translation of the thirty-third book of Livy. But the younger generation found something defective in this model, as may be seen from the following remarks of one of his most respectful disciples. "One of the most celebrated authors of our time," says Vaugelas, "who was consulted as an oracle on the question of the purity of language, and who, beyond a doubt, greatly contributed to it, for all that lacked *netteté* of style, alike in the position of his words and in the form and measure of his periods. He sinned generally in all these matters, and could not even understand what was meant by a finished style (*style formé*), which, in fact, is nothing but the art of putting one's words in their right order, and of properly constructing and co-ordinating one's periods." It will be seen that I have not attempted to translate *netteté*, for which there is no exact equivalent. Perhaps the nearest word is "finish," and, in fact, Vaugelas uses the phrase *style formé* to denote the same quality.

The two writers whose authority had the greatest weight with Vaugelas were Du Perron and Nicolas Coëffeteau, the Dominican Bishop of Marseilles. The latter's earliest writings date from 1603. His best-known ones are his *Tableau des Passions* (1615) and his *Histoire Romaine*. Though his style is wanting in distinction and originality, it is pure, clear, and free from affectation. But it is also diffuse, and the periods are not only too long, but they have ragged ends, due to the common fault of tacking on relative clauses without regard for balance and harmony. French rhetoric had still to await its professor.

He appeared in the year following Coëffeteau's death (1624), and his name was Jean Guez de Balzac; we have

already met him as the distant oracle of the Hôtel de
Rambouillet. It was in this year that he published the first
instalment of his Letters, and he was at once recognised as
the reformer of French prose. "This young man," said
Malherbe in a spirit of generous prophecy, "will go further
in prose than anyone has yet done in France."

We are concerned here with the style of Balzac's writings,
and not with their substance; but it may be well to point
out in passing that it is a mistake to suppose that he was
utterly devoid of ideas, or was merely an empty phrase-
monger. His literary criticisms are marked by good sense
and good taste, as may be seen by his appreciations of
Montaigne and Malherbe, and by his remarks on the famous
controversy of the *Cid*. "Since Corneille has succeeded
while violating the rules of art, it shows that he has a
secret which succeeds better than the rules." And again:
"To know the art of pleasing is not so valuable as to know
how to please without art." The intellectual weakness of
Balzac's style lies in its abuse of commonplace and vague
generalities, and in the elaborate art with which he develops
the most ordinary ideas as if they were novel and profound
truths. But as a master of rhetoric and of the formal
qualities of style Balzac is admirable. The opening and the
close of the much-admired letter of consolation which he
wrote to the Cardinal de La Valette will serve as examples:

MONSEIGNEUR,
    Quoique je suis le plus inutile serviteur que vous ayez, et que
de vous le dire, ce ne soit pas une nouvelle qui mérite de passer les
Alpes; néantmoins puisque le zèle donne du courage à l'impuissance,
et de la valeur aux choses viles, je me hazarde encore de parler à vous,
et de vous faire souvenir d'une vieille passion que je conserve toujours
en mon âme, et qui vous a toujours pour objet.
    Autant qu'il y a d'hommes dans le monde, autant à présent, ou
peu s'en faut, il y a des spectateurs qui vous considèrent. Au moins,
monseigneur, vous êtes regardé de tous les yeux du monde chrétien.
Et si c'est apparemment en Italie, où le commun ennemi va faire
ses grands et ses extrêmes efforts, vous ne doutez pas que vous
n'ayez entre vos mains les esperances de plusieurs princes, et le destin
d'une infinité de peuples.

       *   *   *   *   *

Je parle hardiment d'une âme, dont je connais il y a longtemps la solidité. L'obstination de cette violente Fortune, qui ébranlerait la constance d'un vieux Romain, se brisera sans doute contre la vôtre. Mille malices de sa façon ne seront pas capables d'élever en votre esprit un mouvement d'impatience, ou un commencement de murmure. Qu'a-t-elle gagné jusques à présent? Elle ne saurait vous reprocher, monseigneur, le moindre péché d'omission, soit contre la patrie, soit contre la parenté. Et quelque dangereux choix qu'elle semble vous présenter en vous montrant, d'un côté un père qui vous envoie des soupirs, et de l'autre un roi qui vous fait des commandements, je la défie de me dire ce que vous oubliez en cette rencontre, pour vous acquitter de l'une et de l'autre obligation; pour satisfaire à la première et à la seconde piété, que la Nature exige de vous.

Vous serez donc tous deux, si elle ne cesse, un continuel spectacle à toute la terre, et l'on ne vous regardera pas moins sur le théâtre, Vous et la Fortune, que Vous et les Espagnols. Elle suivra sa coutume, monseigneur, et vous la vôtre: ella fera ses désordres ordinaires, et vous ferez votre devoir comme auparavant.

The monstrous hyperbolas of the first passage, and the empty commonplaces of the second, are highly characteristic of the writer; but, leaving these out of account, we see that the architecture of the sentences is admirable. They are perfect in balance and harmony, qualities which not only have a pleasing effect upon the ear, but which, combined with the propriety and precision of the language, help to make the meaning (such as it is) transparently clear and lucid. Here for the first time in periodic French prose we have complete *netteté*.

Balzac's reputation as a master of style continued till his death in 1654, and during that period French prose was largely modelled on his pattern. Even of Voiture, who was his senior by seven years, it can be said that "he had studied rhetoric under Balzac." But Voiture imported an element of wit and urbanity into his letters, which, in spite of some strained and affected passages, show greater ease than his master's. Saint-Évremond, an excellent judge, says of them that "they have an indefinable charm, and are so ingenious and so polished, so delicate and so agreeable, that they destroy one's taste for Attic wit and Roman urbanity." So far, indeed, as substance goes, they are, for the most part, little but agreeable nonsense; but with their short and crisp sentences, and their general lightness of touch, they are surprisingly modern in form.

On the other hand, Descartes's excellence as a writer comes from the clearness, the orderly sequence, and the vigour of his thought. He cared nothing for the rhetorician's art; he eschewed all graces and ornaments of style; his sole aim was to express himself simply and clearly. Yet in the older histories of French literature a conspicuous place was assigned to him as a prose-writer, and the *Discours de la Méthode* was said to mark the beginning of classical French prose. Nowadays a somewhat lower and, as it seems to me, a juster estimate is usually taken of his merits as a writer. "He is not a pioneer," say MM. Hannequin and Thamin; "his phrase is precisely that of his time." "The reproach that can be brought against his style," says M. Fouillée, "is that it is too much encumbered by Latin constructions....His phrase, which often drags, and which lacks flexibility, is not free from awkwardness; its movement is too measured and too calm; it lacks colour and relief." "Descartes as a writer," says M. Lanson, "has perhaps been overpraised. His phrase is long, hampered with accessory and subordinate clauses, heavy with relatives and conjunctions, redolent of Latin and the schools....He has neither the well-turned phrase of Voiture, nor the ample period of Balzac."

I have fortified myself with these authorities, because Professor Saintsbury, a most competent judge of style, takes a different view, and in his *Short History of French Literature* has maintained it with great vigour and confidence. Referring to a famous passage of the *Discours de la Méthode*, he says that "all is simple, straightforward, admirably clear; but at the same time the prose is fluent, modulated, harmonious, and possesses, if not the grace of superadded ornament, those of perfect proportion and unerring choice of words." Professor Saintsbury admits that Descartes's sentences are sometimes very long—in one of his letters there is a sentence which contains about four hundred words—but he qualifies this by saying that "the length is more apparent than real, the writer having chosen to link by conjunctions clauses which are independently finished, and which by different punctuation, even without the omission of the conjunction, might stand alone." But it is just this "linking by conjunctions" which destroys the balance and harmony of Descartes's sentences, and effectually deprives them of that *netteté* upon which Vaugelas insists. But I will give part of the passage to which Professor Saintsbury refers, so that my readers may judge for themselves. It forms the opening of the Second Part of the *Discours de la Méthode*.

J'etais alors en Allemagne, où l'occasion des guerres qui n'y sont pas encore finies m'avait appelé; et, comme je retournais du couronnement de l'empereur vers l'armée, le commencement de l'hiver m'arrêta en un quartier où, ne trouvant aucune conversation qui me divertit, et n'ayant d'ailleurs, par bonheur, aucuns soins ni passions qui me troublassent, je demeurais tout le jour enfermé seul dans un poêle où j'avais tout le loisir de m'entretenir de mes pensées; entre lesquelles l'une des premières fut que je m'avisai de considérer que souvent il n'y a pas tant de perfection dans les ouvrages composés de plusieurs pièces, et faits de la main de divers maîtres, qu'en ceux auxquels un seul a travaillé. Ainsi voit-on que les bâtiments qu'un seul architecte a entrepris et achevés ont coutume d'être plus beau et mieux ordonnés que ceux que plusieurs ont tâché de racommoder en faisant servir de vieilles murailles qui avaient été bâties à d'autres fins. Ainsi ces anciennes cités qui, n'ayant été au commencement que des bourgades, sont devenues par succession de temps de grandes villes, sont ordinairement si mal compassées, au prix de ces places régulières qu'un ingénieur trace à sa fantaisie dans une plaine, qu'encore que, considérant leurs édifices chacun à part, on y trouve souvent autant ou plus d'art qu'en ceux des autres, toutefois, à voir comme ils sont arrangés, ici un grand, là un petit, et comme ils rendent les rues courbées et inégales, on dirait plutôt que c'est la fortune que la volonté de quelques hommes usant de raison qui les a ainsi disposés.

It is easy to see the faults of this passage, especially of the last sentence. Its length is no mere matter of punctuation, for it forms only one complete period, the clauses of which are inextricably linked together. But there are so many *que*s, so many incidental and relative clauses, that though the meaning is clear, it requires something of an effort to disentangle it. It is true that somewhat similar sentences may be found in Pascal; but in him they are the exception, whereas in Descartes they are almost the rule. His phrase, in short, "is the phrase of his time."

Brunetière says of Descartes's style that it is but little superior to that of Antoine Arnauld, the author of *La Fréquente Communion* (1643). Indeed, in the formal qualities of style it is decidedly inferior to it. Even the enemies of Port-Royal admitted that the Solitaries had greatly contributed to the perfection of the language, and of their writers the most illustrious was Antoine Arnauld. But the forty-four stately volumes of his works repose untouched on the shelves of public libraries, and no one now reads even *La Fréquente Communion*. Yet Arnauld is admirable in argument; he is clear, lucid, and cogent; and his sentences, unlike Descartes's, are well balanced and harmonious. But when he wishes to be impressive he becomes wooden, laboured, and monotonous. As Bossuet says of the whole school of Port-Royal, his style lacks variety and charm. There is no individuality about it, and it is individuality even more than formal grace and perfection that is the great antiseptic of literature.

Having now got some notion as to the respective styles of Balzac, Descartes, and Antoine Arnauld, who may be regarded as the three most conspicuous writers of French prose during the second quarter of the seventeenth century, we are in a better position to appreciate what were the elements introduced by Pascal, and why it is that he is called the first writer of French classical prose. For as Brunetière has justly pointed out, it is not sufficient to say with Voltaire that he is the first writer of genius—a statement which is not even correct, for Rabelais and Montaigne are certainly writers of genius—but we must try and discover in what way his genius acted, and how it affected the whole character of French prose, so that even at the present day, after the lapse of two hundred and fifty years, his writings are the foundation of a good prose style.

Pascal was a man of few books, but, as might be expected from the ardour and intensity of his temperament, the books which he read affected him deeply. In the year 1646, at the time of his first conversion, as it is called, he became familiar with the chief Jansenist works, with Arnauld's *La Fréquente Communion*, and especially with Saint-Cyran's *Lettres spirituelles*. It was doubtless his friends, the Duc de Roannez and the Chevalier de Méré, who introduced him to the writings of Balzac, and he may well have been thinking of the *Grand Épistolier* when he says that *l'éloquence continue ennuie*, or when, in a well-known *pensée*, he contrasts an author with a man.

It was, beyond a doubt, in the society of the same friends that he became acquainted with Montaigne. As I have said, Montaigne was the breviary of men of the world and free-thinkers like Méré and Mitton; and it has been recently shown that Pascal's references to the *Essays* are to the edition which was published in 1652, the year of Pascal's first visit to Paris[1]. How profound was the impression which Montaigne made upon Pascal we know not only from the *Pensées*, but from the *Conversation with M. de Sacy*. And Pascal must have been impressed not only by the substance, but also by the style of Montaigne's book. Here was no mere author, but a man—an artist in style, it is true, but an artist whose guiding principle was to make his language a faithful mirror of his thought.

And this, too, is the dominant quality of Pascal's style. But while Montaigne's restless and proteiform speech corresponds to the vagrant fancies of his ever-changing thought, Pascal's is the expression of a deeply-pondered conviction. The one plays on the surface, the other penetrates to the depths. Montaigne's dissipates his thought as through a prism into a rainbow of many colours; Pascal's concentrates it in a focus of white light. Montaigne glances from metaphor to metaphor; Pascal's metaphors are rare, but they are illuminating. Yet in his marvellous lucidity and

[1] He was at Paris from February to October, 1652, and again from May to December, 1653.

precision he only differs in degree from Balzac and Descartes and Arnauld. As Brunetière has well pointed out, it is rather by its variety that Pascal's phrase differs from that of his predecessors. "While theirs is illumined by a uniformly white and cold light, the air circulates and plays through that of Pascal, filling it with heat, movement, and life." Heat, movement, life—these in very truth are the crowning qualities of Pascal's style; the qualities which distinguish it from the cold and lifeless monotony of a rhetorician like Balzac, or of a real thinker like Antoine Arnauld, who, though he could reason with force and lucidity, could not breathe into his style the emotion and the fire which he undoubtedly felt. Thus the apology which he proposed to publish in his own defence failed to satisfy his friends of Port-Royal. They listened to it "in respectful silence." So, turning to Pascal, he said: "You who are young—you ought to do something"; and Pascal, accepting the suggestion, produced the first Provincial Letter.

The secret of Pascal's success in making his style a true and living reflection of his genius lies mainly in his freedom from any sort of trick or mannerism. You can no more parody him than you can parody Plato, or Boccaccio, or Cardinal Newman. For a mannered style becomes stiff instead of flexible. Instead of moulding itself to the thoughts and emotions of the writer, it stamps them with its own impress. It imprisons them instead of sharing their freedom. It becomes a mask instead of a mirror. Pascal's style, on the contrary, is as free as air, and as supple as a glove. Whereas Du Vair has only one period, the oratorical; whereas Balzac is always the rhetorician; whereas Descartes and Arnauld can only reason; Pascal has as many notes to his instrument as Rabelais. He is by turns eloquent, ironical, dramatic; he can narrate with absolute simplicity, or reason with the close logic of Descartes. All this is true of the *Provinciales*, with which alone we are at present concerned. But in the *Pensées* he rises even to a higher note. "Pascal," says Sainte-Beuve finely, "is an admirable writer in his finished work; but he is, perhaps, even superior in the one in which he was interrupted." And he adds the reason: "The style of the *Pensées* appears even more transparently sincere because it has been caught so near to its source, at the very point where it springs from the mind."

With Pascal our survey fitly closes. He not only stands on the threshold of the new era, but he is almost of it. The men of 1660 might have said of him, as the men of 1830 said of Chateaubriand, "Nous sommes tous partis de lui." Boileau, in the words of Sainte-Beuve, "is the literary offspring of the *Provincial Letters*." Ardent partisan of the ancients though he was, he declared that Pascal surpassed them all[1]. Mme de Sévigné's enthusiasm for the "little Letters" is expressed in rapturous terms: "Can you have a more perfect style, a more natural, a more delicate irony, a more worthy descendant of Plato's dialogues? And then when, after the first ten Letters, he addresses the reverend Fathers, what seriousness! what solidity! what force! what eloquence! what love for God and the truth!" Both La Rochefoucauld and La Bruyère are Pascal's pupils in the study of human nature, and the dramatic touches with which La Bruyère enlivens his *Characters* recall those of the *Letters*. The Jesuit Bourdaloue protested from the pulpit against the unfairness of Pascal's attack, but the pure and lofty standard of morality which he upheld during his long career as a preacher and spiritual director was that for which Pascal had contended. Molière's morality was of a less austere type, but in *Tartuffe* he borrows more than one shaft from Pascal's armoury. Racine, the pupil of Port-Royal, after attacking his former teachers in "a masterpiece of malice and wit," renounced the stage under the influence of his Jansenist bringing up. And as for his "delicious" prose, the lightest, the easiest, the most modern prose of the seventeenth century[2], the prose of the two malicious

---

[1] Boileau expressed this opinion at a dinner-party at which his friend Bourdaloue and another Jesuit were present (see a letter of Mme de Sévigné dated January 15, 1690).

[2] "Cette prose du Racine est un délice. C'est, de toutes les proses du xviie siècle, la plus légère, la plus dégagée, et celle aussi qui contient le moins d'expressions vieillies" (J. Lemaître, *Jean Racine*).

letters, and of the abridged history of Port-Royal, does it not proceed, as M. Gazier says, directly from Pascal?

Exactly nineteen months after the publication of the last *Provincial Letters*, Molière, who had just returned to Paris from the provinces, played for the first time before the King. A little more than a year later he produced *Les Précieuses Ridicules*. In March, 1661, Mazarin died. Before Michaelmas, Fouquet, who had aspired to be Mazarin's successor, was arrested at Nantes, and Louis XIV became in fact as well as in name the absolute monarch of France. Nineteen days before this Molière's *Les Fâcheux* had called forth from La Fontaine the lines quoted on a former page:

> Et maintenant il ne faut pas
> Quitter la nature d'un pas.

The Classical Age was established.

Here it may be pertinently asked; why, if Pascal's prose shows, as it certainly does, all the qualities of the Classical Age, the beginning of that age is dated from *Les Précieuses Ridicules*, and not from *Les Lettres Provinciales*? The answer is that, widely though the Letters were read, and deeply though they impressed the best intellects of the day, they did not inaugurate a literary revolution. Popular though they were, they were not so popular as the *Timocrate* of Thomas Corneille; for more than three and a half years after the publication of the first Letter, *préciosité* and other forms of bad taste continued to flourish under the munificent patronage of Fouquet. But Pascal's prose admirably enables us to measure the distance that we have travelled in the course of these pages. Put it by the side of the prose of Montaigne, and we see the full extent of the change from imagination to reason, and from disorder to form. This change, which we find pervading the whole of French literature, was due primarily to a corresponding change in the temper of the nation. The religious wars had made people weary of that individualistic spirit by which imagination is fostered. The unreason of the League had well-nigh reduced France to a Spanish Province. The whole nation craved for rest and order and sobriety. Malherbe's influence was largely due to the fact that he embodied this new spirit, and it was in true conformity with the same spirit that he insisted on the value of form in literature, that he taught writers to criticise their own work—in a word, to reason about it.

At the same time France began to rebuild her social fabric. Religion was once more established as a controlling and beneficent force, and by her side arose a new power, Society; while, on the initiative of Richelieu, the work of organisation was extended to language and literature.

But the old forces, good and evil, still struggled for mastery, and the first man of genius who illustrated the new era testifies to the conflict of its aims. Corneille is at once a romanticist and a classicist. His heroes and heroines reflect his own strongly individualistic temperament, but at the same time he recognises the influence of society and official criticism in the domain of taste. He submits his plays to the *habitués* of Mme de Rambouillet's salon, though he ignores their judgment. He receives with respect the views of the Academy, though he defends his own with the subtlety of a Norman. He had three masters to conciliate: the critics, the public, and his own genius. Sometimes he followed one, sometimes the other; more often he compromised with wonderful adroitness between the three. It was to please the public, and to prove that his hand had not lost its cunning, that he wrote *Œdipe*. Its success was a clear sign that the public was not yet converted to the true faith. With *Les Précieuses Ridicules*, produced later in the same year (1659), the school of Nature may be said to have launched their assault, but it required the concerted attack of Molière, Boileau, La Fontaine, and Racine before the final victory was won.

The victory was not achieved without loss. In the Classical Age we miss some qualities which were not to return for many a long year. Imagination and emotion were, of course, not absent, for literature cannot exist without them; but reason held them in severe check. Especially do we miss that primary function of the imagination which consists in seeing images, in calling up at will the outward appearance of things. In a word, literature becomes more abstract and less concrete. This is especially noticeable in the language. It is more logical, but less picturesque. It appeals to the intellect directly instead of through the imagination. "En nostre langage," says Montaigne, "je trouve assez d'estoffe, mais un peu faute de façon." The "fashioning" was now perfect, but there was some loss of "stuff." But whatever the loss, the victory was complete. At last French writers had surprised the secret, not only of classical literature, but of all abiding literature and all abiding art; that it is founded upon two principles, truth to Nature, and truth to the ideal of the individual artist.

APPENDIX A

CHRONOLOGICAL TABLE

1601 *La Sagesse*.
1602 St François de Sales at Paris.
1605 Malherbe comes to Paris.
1606 Death of Desportes.
1607 *L'Astrée* (completed 1627).
1608 Regnier's *Satires*.
 Introduction à la Vie dévote.
1609 Jesuit College of Clermont re-opened.
1610 Death of Henry IV.
1611 Death of Bertaut.
 Oratoire founded.
1615 Coëffeteau's *Tableau des Passions*.
1617? *Pyrame et Thisbé*.
1618 Alterations to the Hôtel de Rambouillet completed.
1624 Richelieu first Minister.
1625 Death of Théophile de Viau.
 ,, ,, D'Urfé.
 Balzac's first volume of Letters.
 Les Bergeries.
 Nuns of Port-Royal move to Paris.
1626 *Sylvie*.
1628 Death of Malherbe.
 Ogier's preface to *Tyr et Sidon*.
1629 (or 1630) *Mélite*.
1630 Malherbe's collected poems.
 Silvanire.
 Compagnie du Saint-Sacrement founded.
1631 *Le Prince*.
1633 Tristan L'Hermite's *Plaintes d'Acante*.
1634 Théâtre du Marais opened.
 Sophonisbe.
1636 War declared against Spain.
 Mariane.

1636 *Les Sosies.*
    The *Cid* (winter of 1636–7).
    Saint-Cyran becomes director to Port-Royal.
1637 Académie Française legally constituted.
    Discours de la Méthode.
    Les Visionnaires.
1638 MM. de Port-Royal move to Port-Royal des Champs.
1640 *Horace.*
    Cinna.
    Augustinus.
1641 Gassendi begins to lecture at Paris.
    Nicolas Poussin at Paris (1641–2).
1642 Death of Richelieu (December).
    Polyeucte (winter of 1642–3).
1643 Death of Louis XIII.
    Rocroi.
    La Fréquente Communion.
    Le Menteur.
    La Mort de Pompée (winter of 1643–4).
1644 *Scévole.*
    Typhon.
    Rodogune (winter of 1644–5).
1645 *Saint-Genest.*
    La Sœur.
    Jodelet, ou le Maître Valet.
    Le Sueur's paintings of the life of St Bruno (1645–8).
1646 Organisation of the "Little Schools."
    Héraclius (winter of 1646–7).
1647 *Venceslas.*
    Virgile travesti.
    Les Remarques.
1648 Outbreak of the Fronde.
    Death of Voiture.
    Cosroès.
1649 *Traité des Passions.*
    Voiture's *Œuvres diverses.*
    Le Grand Cyrus (completed 1653).
1650 Death of Descartes.
    ,,   ,, Rotrou.
1651 *Nicomède.*
    Saint-Louis.

1651 *Moïse sauvé.*
      Le roman comique.
      L'amour à la mode (or 1652).
1652 End of the Fronde.
      Pertharite.
      Socrate Chrestien.
1653 *Histoire de l'Académie Française.*
1654 Death of Balzac.
      Clélie (completed 1660).
      Alaric.
      Le Parasite.
      Le Pedant joué.
      La belle Plaideuse.
1656 *La Pucelle.*
      Les Provinciales.
      Timocrate.
      La Précieuse.
1657 *Clovis.*
      Le Campagnard.
1659 *Œdipe.*
      Les Précieuses ridicules.
1660 Death of Mazarin.

APPENDIX B

ENGLISH TRANSLATIONS[1]

The first important work of our period to appear in an English dress was L'ASTRÉE, of which the First Part (1607) was translated by John Pyper in 1620. But before this, *i.e.* not later than 1614, Fletcher had made use of the Second Part (1610) for his tragedy of *Valentinian.* The same source provided him in part with material for his comedy of *Monsieur Thomas* (date uncertain)[2].

[1] My chief source of information is A. H. Upham, *The French influence in English Literature, from the accession of Elizabeth to the Restoration.*
[2] Upham, *op. cit.*, pp. 365–368.

The marriage of Charles I with Henrietta Maria of France (1625) gave a direct impulse to intellectual intercourse between the two nations. In that year James Howell returned to his friend Sir John Smith a copy of BALZAC's *Letters* (published in 1624), with the remark that he found some of them "flat," and others "puffed with profane Hyperboles, and larded up and down with gross Flatteries[1]." A translation of the Letters appeared in 1634, followed by translations of the succeeding volumes in 1638 and 1639. The *Prince* appeared in 1648.

It was at the Queen's command, or, at any rate, under her auspices that an English translation by Joseph Rutter of CORNEILLE's *Cid* was staged in 1638. But within twenty months of the publication of *Horace* and before that of *Cinna* the theatres were closed and all plays were suppressed by ordinance (September 2, 1642), and it was not till fourteen years later that stage plays began to put in a timid appearance in private houses. It was therefore only in 1655 and 1656 that translations of *Polyeucte* and *Horace* followed that of the *Cid*, and they were of very poor quality. The translator was Sir William Laver, who held a post in the household of the Prince of Orange at the Hague. After the Restoration Corneille found a more worthy translator in Mrs Katherine Philips, the "Matchless Orinda," whose rhymed version of *Pompée* was acted in Dublin and London in 1663. She also translated four acts of *Horace*, but she died before completing the work (1664), and the fifth act was supplied by Denham. Versions of *Héraclius* and *Nicomède* were also acted, the former in London in 1664, the latter at Dublin in 1670. In 1671 Charles Cotton made a new translation of *Horace*[2]. Pepys, who thought *Horace* a "silly tragedy," witnessed this performance of *Héraclius* "to his extraordinary content."

The French ROMANCES found great favour in this country during the Commonwealth. *Polexandre* appeared in an English dress in 1647, and from 1652 to 1661 translations of La Calprenède and Mlle de Scudéry were published in continuous

[1] *Epist. Ho-Elianae*, 11th ed., 1724, Howell has put this letter, which contains general remarks on Letters, at the head of his collection. He says that a letter should be "short-coated and closely couched," which Balzac's certainly are not.
[2] See A. T. Bartholomew in *The Cambridge History of English Literature*, VIII. 180.

succession—*Cléopâtre* in 1654–59, *Cassandre* in two translations from 1652, *Ibrahim* in the same year, *Le Grand Cyrus* in 1653–55, *Clélie* in 1656–61.

SCARRON was also popular; two of his comedies were translated in 1657, three of his *Nouvelles tragi-comiques* in the same year, four more in 1662, and the complete collection in 1667. His *Roman comique* was not translated till 1676. But it was his burlesques which, partly in translations, but chiefly in exaggerated imitations, had the greatest vogue in this country[1]. His *Virgile travesti* was to a great extent the model for style of Butler's *Hudibras* (1663).

Turning to more sober fare, DESCARTES's *Traité des Passions* was Englished in 1650, VOITURE's *Letters* in 1655, and PASCAL's *Lettres Provinciales* under the title *The Mysterie of Jesuitism* in 1657, the year in which the last letter was written.

---

[1] See Upham, *op. cit.*, pp. 426 f.

INDEX

For EU product safety concerns, contact us at Calle de José Abascal, 56–1°, 28003 Madrid, Spain or eugpsr@cambridge.org.

www.ingramcontent.com/pod-product-compliance
Ingram Content Group UK Ltd.
Pitfield, Milton Keynes, MK11 3LW, UK
UKHW012331130625
459647UK00009B/203